JOHANN WOLFGANG VON GOETHE: ONE HUNDRED AND FIFTY YEARS OF CONTINUING VITALITY

Edited by
Ulrich Goebel
Wolodymyr T. Zyla

Texas Tech Press
Lubbock, Texas
1984

Johann Wolfgang von Goethe: One Hundred and Fifty Years of Continuing Vitality constitutes the proceedings of the Fifteenth Annual Comparative Literature Symposium, organized by Texas Tech University's Interdepartmental Committee on Comparative Literature, and held on 27 through 29 January 1982. The Comparative Literature Symposium was founded by Wolodymyr T. Zyla, Professor of Germanic and Slavic Languages, Texas Tech University. Copies of these and other proceedings may be purchased from Texas Tech Press, Sales Office, Texas Tech University Library, Lubbock, Texas 79409, U.S.A. Recommended citation for this title as a single work is: Goebel, Ulrich, and Wolodymyr T. Zyla, eds. *Johann Wolfgang von Goethe: One Hundred and Fifty Years of Continuing Vitality.* Lubbock: Texas Tech Press, 1984.

ISSN: 0084-9103
ISBN: 0-89672-117-5
Library of Congress Catalog Card Number: 84-50028
Texas Tech Press
Texas Tech University, Lubbock, Texas 79409
Printed in the United States of America

Contents

Preface

One of the first scholarly meetings in America commemorating the one hundred and fiftieth anniversary of the death of the great German author Johann Wolfgang von Goethe (1749-1832) was held at Texas Tech University on the 27th through the 29th of January, 1982. The conference theme of Goethe's continuing vitality in world literature placed emphasis on the complex relationship between the influence which aroused and inspired him and the influence which, in turn, he exerted on others in literature and music. In various ways, all of the speakers at the Symposium contributed to the development of the general theme, and their essays make up this volume.

For the first time in the long history of the Comparative Literature Symposium at Texas Tech University all of the major activities of the Symposium were recorded on video tape. These tapes are stored in the Southwest Collection on the Texas Tech campus and represent, along with this volume, the permanent record of the Fifteenth Annual Comparative Literature Symposium.

Prior to the presentation of the first paper on the evening of the 27th, the Symposium was dedicated to Carl Hammer, Jr., Horn Professor Emeritus of German at Texas Tech. In his address, "Recollections of the Past—Fifty Years with Goethe," Carl Hammer reminisced about his experiences as a Goethe scholar, referred to past celebrations and centennials honoring the poet, and recalled a number of delightful anecdotes about colleagues and their scholarly contributions over the past five decades. The principal address of this evening session came from Hans-Jürgen Schings, Professor at the University of Heidelberg in West Germany. In "Symbolik des Glücks. Zu Wilhelm Meisters Bildergeschichte," Schings presented a unique interpretation of the novel, inviting the audience to consider *Wilhelm Meisters Lehrjahre* as "Anti-Werther und symbolischen (nicht psychologischen) Roman des Glücks."

The next four papers were presented on the following day. In the presentation "Heroic Egotism: Goethe and the Fortunes of *Bildung* in Victorian England," David DeLaura, Professor of English at the University of Pennsylvania, brought up the question of Goethe's theory of self-cultivation, explained how it was received in nineteenth-century England, and traced the development of Goethe criticism up through the 60s and 70s of that century. Victor Lange, Professor of Modern Languages, Emeritus, at Princeton University, gave a lecture on "Goethe's Theory of Literature," in which he discussed Goethe's place within the tradition of eighteenth-century aesthetic theory and the criteria which are critical in defining the character of Goethe's notion of literary judgment. Stuart Atkins, Professor of German at the University of California, Santa Barbara, considered the problem of moving from one language to another—specifically from German to English—in his lecture "On Translating *Faust*." His observations about translation and the translator illustrated the truth that, in recreating a literary masterpiece like Goethe's *Faust*, translation becomes an art. In the final lecture of the day, "Ivan Franko: Goethe's Translator and Interpreter," Wolodymyr Zyla, Professor of Germanic and Slavic Languages, Texas Tech University, considered the contributions of Ivan Franko, translator of many of Goethe's works into the Ukrainian language. Zyla observed that Franko, who was a writer of consequence in his own right, was influenced by Goethe and drew from his understanding of Goethe's work.

Henry H. H. Remak, Professor of German at Indiana University, presented the first of four lectures during the course of the next day. In his paper "Goethe and the Novella," Remak gave "a historical and critical assessment of Goethe's role in the evolution of the novella," examining and analyzing a number of Goethe's novellas, para-novellas, and stories. Meredith Lee, Associate Professor of German at the University of California, Irvine, discussed how one artist's work affects the creation of another in her paper entitled "Goethe, Klopstock and the Problem of Literary Influence: A Reading of the Darmstadt Poems." Lee argued that, despite the tenacious notions within Goethe scholarship about his "original genius," Goethe was influenced by his literary past; specifically by Klopstock. She examined three of Goethe's early poems to support her observation that, in fact, Goethe sought recognition as Klopstock's equal. In "Absolute and Affective Music: Rameau, Diderot, and Goethe," John Neubauer, Professor of German at the University of Pittsburgh, discussed Goethe's theory of music, pointing out that Goethe's theory focused on two main issues: "the fundamentals of harmony in nature and the problem of musical representation." Neubauer examined the eighteenth-century debate on music and compared Goethe's position to Rameau's and Diderot's. He stated that Goethe's notion is similar to the theory of Rousseau and the encyclopedists who saw music "as an expression of mood and a vehicle to communicate affects." The final symposium lecture was given by Alexander Gelley, Associate Professor of English at the

University of California, Irvine, who spoke about "Frame, Instance, Dialogue: Narrative Structures in the *Wanderjahre.*" Gelley pointed out that the *Wanderjahre* did not fit the mold of the traditional *Bildungsroman* since the interrelationship between the minor episodes and the main strand of the novel is by no means clear.

The luncheon speaker, Meredith McClain, Associate Professor of German at Texas Tech University, in her presentation "Goethe and Music: 'Nur wer die Sehnsucht kennt . . . ,'" reviewed the musicians on whom Goethe exerted the greatest influence. Her presentation centered on the musical settings of the poem referred to in the title of her lecture, and several of these settings were performed at the luncheon by William Hartwell and Lora Deahl, Professors of music at Texas Tech University.

The symposium papers were followed by lively panel discussions and comments from the audience. It is unfortunate that some of these discussions cannot be reproduced in this volume verbatim, since they often clarified thoughts expressed by the speakers and, on occasion, focused on interesting interconnections between symposium lectures. Discussants included the guest speakers as well as A. Leslie Willson, The University of Texas at Austin, Luanne T. Frank, Denes Monostory, The University of Texas at Arlington, Theodore G. Gish, Gertrud B. Pickar, University of Houston, Otto W. Tetzlaff, Angelo State University, Thomas Di Napoli, Louisiana State University, guest panelists; Norwood Henry Andrews, Jr., Thomas I. Bacon, Ulrich Goebel, Thomas A. Langford, Meredith McClain, Janet W. Perez, Joel Weinsheimer, James S. Whitlark, Julia C. Whitsitt, and Greg Geis, Texas Tech University.

The lectures, discussions, and luncheon address were complimented by a television program and theatrical and musical performances. Moderated by Meredith McClain, the television program entitled "Johann Wolfgang von Goethe: One Hundred and Fifty Years of Continuing Vitality" was aired twice during the course of the Symposium by the Texas Tech Educational Television Station (KTXT-TV). The program featured Professors Victor Lange, Meredith Lee, and Henry H. H. Remak—all speakers at the Symposium. At the final session, a scene from *Faust*, directed by Professor Ronald Schulz, was presented by actors of the University Theater. The theatrical performance was followed by a *Goethe Liederabend*, which the Symposium cosponsored and which featured Emilia Simone, Sue Arnold, and John Gillas, faculty members of the Department of Music. Emilia Simone sang *Die Trommel gerühret, Freudvoll und leidvoll* (Ludwig van Beethoven), *Die Spröde, Die*

Bekehrte (Hugo Wolf), *Liebe schwärmt auf allen Wegen*, and *Gretchen am Spinnrade* (Franz Schubert). John Gillas performed *Wer sich der Einsamkeit, Wer nie sein Brot, An die Türen, Liebhaber in allen Gestalten, Prometheus* and *Der Rattenfänger* (Franz Schubert). Sue Arnold sang *Der Fischer, Erster Verlust, Der Musensohn* (Franz Schubert), *Heiß mich nicht reden, Nur wer die Sehnsucht kennt, So laßt mich scheinen*, and *Kennst du das Land* (Hugo Wolf). Emilia Simone and John Gillas also sang *Ich denke dein* (Robert Schumann). The singers were accompanied on the piano by William Westney.

Finally, on behalf of the Interdepartmental Committee on Comparative Literature at Texas Tech University, we wish to express our thanks to all speakers and guests who participated in the symposium. We thank the departments of Classical and Romance Languages, English, Germanic and Slavic Languages, Music, and Speech and Theater Arts for their helpful cooperation and the University library for displaying the two exhibits entitled "Goethe—A Man for all Seasons" and "Visiting Lecturer's Works." We are especially grateful to the Texas Tech Press, without whose support this publication would have been impossible. Our sincerest thanks go to those who served as chairmen of the symposium sessions: John R. Darling, Kenneth W. Davis, Ulrich Goebel, J. Knox Jones, Jr., Lawrence L. Graves, Thomas A. Langford, Theodor W. Alexander, Harley D. Oberhelman, Lorum H. Stratton, Harold T. Luce, Thomas I. Bacon, and Richard Crider. We are especially grateful to Lawrence L. Graves, Dean of the College of Arts and Sciences; J. Knox Jones, Jr., Vice President for Research and Graduate Studies; John R. Darling, Vice President for Academic Affairs; and Lauro F. Cavazos, President of Texas Tech University, for their continuing generous support of the comparative literature symposia. We would also like to thank Furr's, Inc. and Dr. Richard Thoma, Director of the Goethe Institute, Houston (German Cultural Center), for providing additional financial support to this Symposium.

The Editors

Dedication

The proceedings of the Fifteenth Annual Comparative Literature Symposium are dedicated to Carl Hammer, Jr., in acknowledgment of his outstanding contributions to the study of Goethe in America. As an inspiring teacher and a distinguished scholar and writer, Carl Hammer has had a lasting impact upon Goethe scholarship.

"Das widerfährt auch dem Menschen von seinem Lehrer": Dedicatory Remarks for Carl Hammer, Jr.

Ulrich Goebel

Johann Wolfgang von Goethe's creative genius spans the centuries, bridging one generation with the next and one culture with another. It seems most appropriate on this, his anniversary, to commemorate the genius of this poet by devoting the Fifteenth Annual Comparative Literature Symposium at Texas Tech University to this purpose.

It is particularly fitting that such a commemoration take place at this university where Goethe's memory lives on and is given focus through the research and scholarship of a dedicated faculty. To recognize the achievements of one of the truly distinguished Goethe scholars in America, it is my distinct pleasure to dedicate this Symposium and its proceedings herewith to Carl Hammer, Jr., Horn Professor Emeritus of German at Texas Tech University. The official dedication in the Symposium Brochure acknowledges his outstanding contributions to the study of Goethe in America. The statement proceeds: "As an inspiring teacher and a distinguished scholar and writer, Carl Hammer has had a lasting impact upon Goethe scholarship." This recognition is most appropriate, for in dedicating this Symposium to Carl Hammer, we honor a man who has lived a lifetime with Goethe and of whom we may truly say that he has wrought and taught in the finest tradition of our profession.

Carl Hammer was born in 1910, near Salisbury, North Carolina, in a section settled by Pennsylvania Germans, from whom he is descended on his mother's side, being partly of North German provenience through his father.

After earning his Bachelor of Arts degree (magna cum laude) at Catawba College in 1934, Carl Hammer pursued graduate study at North Carolina, Vanderbilt (from whence he received his Master of Arts degree in 1936), Jena, and Illinois, where he earned the Ph.D. and was elected to Phi Beta Kappa in 1939. During that year, however, both of these honors were overshadowed by an event which was much dearer to young Carl Hammer's heart: namely, his marriage to Mae Armes of Wilkes County, North Carolina—a lady who has accompanied this wandering scholar on his travels for the many years since their marriage.

Subsequently Carl Hammer taught at Vanderbilt and Louisiana State University. As a post-doctoral Ford Fellow in 1953-54, he studied comparative literature at Columbia, Princeton, and in Tübingen. He came to Texas Tech University in 1964, holding, from 1967 on, a Paul Whitfield Horn Professorship. He also served as the first Chairman of the Department of Germanic and Slavic Languages from 1967 to 1977. During his tenure as Chairman, Carl Hammer watched the growth of undergraduate and graduate programs rooted in the traditional values of sound oral proficiency coupled with the rigorous study of German Literature and Culture. He continued to be as deeply committed to his subject as he was determined to uphold critical standards during the decade of his chairmanship at Texas Tech University.

In Carl Hammer's case, the numerous honors, recognitions, and accolades, which have been bestowed upon him, are but dim reflections of his many truly outstanding accomplishments over the years. It seems appropriate, however, to point to one recognition which appears to characterize most accurately Carl Hammer's concerns during his four decades of service. In 1956 he received a Schiller Sesquicentennial Medal from the Federal Republic of Germany in recognition of "efforts on behalf of promoting cultural relations between the United States and Germany."

He has published some 37 articles and essays, over half of them dealing with Goethe. He has made numerous presentations, read countless papers at professional meetings and symposia, edited a number of periodicals and monographs, published many book reviews and abstracts, and served in various capacities in regional and national organizations. His prominence is well documented in *Who's Who in America, Directory of American Scholars,* and *Personalities of the South.*

Most importantly, Carl Hammer has also written several books, among them the following which may be of particular interest to the readers of this volume: *Goethes "Dichtung and Wahrheit," 7. Buch — Literaturgeschichte oder Bildungserlebnis?* (1945); *Longfellow's "Golden Legend" and Goethe's "Faust"* (1952); and *Goethe and Rousseau: Resonances of the Mind* (Winner of the 1972 Kentucky Foreign Language Conference Award). He has also edited the volume *Goethe After Two Centuries* (1952) for the Goethe bicentennial observance in 1949.

The following select list of Carl Hammer's published writings may best exemplify his scholarly vision and provide an overview of his scholarly interests.

Books and Monographs:

Coeditor with John G. Frank: *Deutsch für Mediziner* (New York: Harper, 1941)

Rhinelanders on the Yadkin (The Story of the Pennsylvania Germans in Rowan and Cabarrus Counties, North Carolina; Salisbury, N.C., 1943). Second Edition, Revised (Salisbury, 1965)

(In collaboration with John G. Frank and C. M. Lancaster): *Two Moods of Minnesong* (Nashville: Vanderbilt University Press, 1944)

Goethes "Dichtung and Wahrheit," 7. Buch-Literaturgeschichte oder Bildungserlebnis? ("Illinois Studies in Language and Literature," XXX, No. 1, Urbana, 1945)

Editor: *Goethe After Two Centuries* ("Louisiana State University Studies, Humanities Series," No. 1. Baton Rouge, 1952)

Longfellow's "Golden Legend" and Goethe's "Faust" (Louisiana State University Studies, Humanities Series," No. 2, Baton Rouge, 1952)

Editor: *Studies in German Literature* (in Honor of John T. Krumpelmann) ("Louisiana State University Studies, Humanities Series," No. 13, Baton Rouge, 1963)

Goethe and Rousseau: Resonances of the Mind (Lexington: University Press of Kentucky, 1973)

Bygone Days in Rural Rowan (Salisbury, N.C.: The Salisbury Post, 1974, published serially)

Articles and Essays:

"Goethe's Estimate of Oliver Goldsmith," *Journal of English and Germanic Philology*, XLIV (1945), 131-138

"Enlivening the Scientific German Class," *The German Quarterly*, XVII (1945), 109-115. "Enlivening the Scientific German Class," *The Teaching of German/ Problems and Methods*, Anthology, ed. Eberhard Reichmann (Philadelphia, National Carl Schurz Association, Inc. 1970; actually, 1971). 402-403. (Abridgment of an article earlier published in *The German Quarterly*)

"Outside Reading for *Faust*," *The German Quarterly*, XIX (1946), 139-142

"Organ Church and the Broken Key," *American-German Review*, XIII (1947), 33-36

"*Simplicissimus* and the Literary Historians," *Monatshefte*, XL (1948), 457-468

"*Wilhelm Meisters Wanderjahre* and Rousseau," in *Southwest Goethe Festival: A Collection of Nine Papers*, ed. Gilbert J. Jordan ("Southern Methodist University Studies," No. 5, University Press in Dallas, 1949), pp. 34-50

"German Classical Texts for the Second Half of the Twentieth Century," *The German Quarterly*, XXIII (1950), 226-234

"Faust Legends before Goethe," in *Southern Illinois Goethe Celebration: A Collection of Nine Papers*, ed. H. A. Hartwig (Southern Illinois University, Carbondale, 1950), pp. 9-14

"The Import of Goethe's *Faust* for Twentieth Century Living," ibid., pp. 37-48

"The Perennial Lure of Goethe's Life and Poetry," ibid., pp. 49-55

"Late German Documents from Organ Church," *American-German Review*, XVII (1951), 14-16

"Louisiana State University's Participation in the Goethe Bicentennial," *Foreword* to *Goethe After Two Centuries*, ed. Carl Hammer ("Louisiana State University Studies, Humanities Series," No. 1, Baton Rouge, 1952). ix-xii

"Re-examining Goethe's Views of Corneille," *The Germanic Review*, XXIX (1954), 260-268

"Goethe, Prévost, and Louisiana," *Modern Language Quarterly*, XVI (1955), 332-338

"Nineteenth Century German Drama in English," *The German Quarterly*, XXX (1957), 32-36

"Stress the German-English Cognates!," *The Modern Language Journal*, XLI (1957), 177-182

"Holbach According to Goethe," *Romance Notes*, I (Nov. 1959), 18-21

"Poetic Translations for the German Class," *The German Quarterly*, XXXIII (1960), 14-21

"Goethe's Silence Concerning Ronsard," *Modern Language Notes*, LXXV (1960), 697-698

"Longfellow's Lyrics 'From the German'," in *Studies in Comparative Literature* ("Louisiana State University Studies, Humanities Series," No. 11, Baton Rouge, 1962), pp. 155-172, 296-299

"Faust's Taciturnity in Dialogue," *The South-Central Bulletin*, XXII, No. 4 (Winter, 1962), 42-46

"John T. Krumpelmann," in *Studies in German Literature* ("Louisiana State University Studies, Humanities Series," No. 13, Baton Rouge, (1963), xiii-xviii

"German Poetry (Before 1900) in Recent Translations," *The German Quarterly*, XXXVIII (1965), 200-211

"Jacobi's Memorial to Rousseau," *Die Neueren Sprachen*, Heft 6 (Jahrgang 1965), pp. 280-283

"The Current Re-Emergence of Gottsched," *The South Central Bulletin*, XXVI, No. 4 (Winter, 1966: *Studies By Members of SCMLA*), 35-42

"The 'Philosophers' Quarrel' as Seen by Goethe," *Romance Notes*, IX, No. 2 (Spring, 1968), 232-234

"The French Discovery of German Literature," *Proceedings of the Comparative Literature Symposium* (Texas Technological College, April 22-24, 1968), Vol. I, ICASALS Special Report, No. 8, ed. W. T. Zyla, Lubbock, 1968, pp. 45-67

"Goethe and Marianne—after the *Divan*," *The South Central Bulletin*, XXVIII, No. 4 (Winter, 1968: *Studies by Members of SCMLA*), 134-138

"Goethe's Astronomical Pursuits," *The South Central Bulletin*, XXX, No. 4 (Winter, 1970: *Studies by Members of SCMLA*), 220-224

"Caroline Herder's Critique of *Die natürliche Tochter*," *Far-Western Forum*, I, No. 2 (1974), 267-269

"Emigration From the Palatinate." (Chapter I of) *Michael Braun of The Old Stone House: His Influence and Descendants*. Ed. Roscoe Brown Fisher. Charlotte: Delmar, 1975, pp. 1-9

"Intimations of Molière in Goethe's Leipzig Comedies." *Molière and the Common-wealth of Letters.* Eds. Roger Johnson, Jr., Guy T. Trail, and Editha S. Neumann. Jackson: University Press of Mississippi, 1975, pp. 276-286

"Montaigne and Goethe Record Their Italian Journeys." *The South Central Bulletin,* XXXVI, No. 4 (Winter, 1976: *Studies by Members of SCMLA*), 147-149

"A Glance at Three Centuries of German-American Writing." *Ethnic Literatures Since 1776: The Many Voices of America,* ed. W. T. Zyla and W. M. Aycock. Proceedings of the Comparative Literature Symposium, Vol. IX, Part 1 (Lubbock: Texas Tech Press, 1978), 217-232

"Molière Tartuffe and Goethe's Großkophta," *Romance Notes,* XVIII, 3 (Spring, 1978), 368-374

"Goethe's Homage to Marot in *Egmont." The South Central Bulletin,* XXXVIII, No. 4 (Winter, 1978: Studies by Members of SCMLA), 145-148

Carl Hammer is a man of a kind that Texas Tech University, and indeed any university, is fortunate to have had on its faculty. His colleagues are particularly pleased about this dedication, for it is an honor well deserved and long overdue. His influence on his colleagues and students was exercised not only through his writings but also through his teaching. It is, after all, as a teacher that he is remembered by generations of students who have learned from him. It seems to me that Goethe, perhaps reflecting on his own experiences as a student, most aptly described this teacher when he wrote: "In der Schmiede erweicht man das Eisen, indem man das Feuer anbläßt und dem Stabe seine überflüssige Nahrung nimmt; ist er aber rein geworden, dann schlägt man ihn und zwingt ihn, und durch die Nahrung eines fremden Wassers wird er wieder stark. Das widerfährt auch dem Menschen von seinem Lehrer" ("Aus Makariens Archiv," No. 16).

Texas Tech University

Symposium Lectures

On Translating *Faust*

Stuart Atkins

Abstract

After agreeing in the fall of 1980 to edit a new translation of *Faust*, I soon discovered that, to meet the desired deadline of publication in 1982, I would have to do the translating myself. To see if this was feasible and whether what I might produce would be acceptable to the editors of the selection of Goethe's works in which it was to appear, I prepared over the next three months versions of shorter and longer sections of the text, illustrating my treatment of different levels of tone and diction. I determined that a verse translation could be completed in about nine months if made a full-time activity, and I was pleased when my fellow editors approved my sample translations in which rhyme was retained only for a few special contexts. Having already translated much of *Faust* into rhymed verse (for a book on *Faust*, then for my revision of Bayard Taylor's translation, and, still later, in manuscript for a more radical revision of that translation), I had finally decided that a version which simply reproduced much of the text's metrical variety could best provide an adequate impression of the formal virtuosity of the original. This would also entail the least sacrifice of other elements or of readable, idiomatic English. While completing my translation I regularly consulted the work of predecessors, reviewed the history of *Faust* translations, reflected on the principles as well as the practical techniques of translating, and discerned features of *Faust* that more leisurely readings of the text had not forced upon my attention. Some of the things to be learned from translating *Faust* are the subject of my lecture. (SA)

The first English translation from *Faust* was published in 1810 by a reviewer of Part One who warned that "the absurdities of this piece are so numerous, the obscenities so frequent, the profaneness so gross, and the beauties so exclusively adapted for German relish, that we cannot conscientiously recommend . . . the translation of it . . . to our English students of German literature."[1] Since then, at least 56 English translations of Part One have appeared, and 21 of

Part Two, representing more than 60 translators, to whom must be added Louis MacNeice as translator of two-thirds of Parts One and Two together.[2] All translations to date, except for seven of Part One and three of Part Two, are in English verse that, with some exceptions, relies more regularly on rhyme than on rhythm to persuade the reader that the original is a work of poetry. As an anonymous British reviewer of the Shawcross translation commented in 1959, "With every new version of *Faust* one cannot but marvel at the apparently inexhaustible ingenuity and invention with which, in particular, Goethe's highly idiomatic doggerel lines are turned into more or less idiomatic English doggerel. . . . the reader familiar with the original will enjoy comparing the especially difficult bits to see what the new translator has done with them. The reader who has no German may perhaps be content with the scores of translations already available."[3] The praise later lavished— perhaps by the same reviewer—on Barker Fairley's prose translation for offering "*spoken* English" in an age when "not only the dramatic poem but also the drama in verse have now ceased to be forms which working poets use," can surely be credited as much to the absence of doggerel as to the virtues of speakability and of "accurate . . . reproduction of the sense, spirit and tone of the original" that the reviewer thought to discern in it.[4]

Ever since Charles T. Brooks translated, with considerable skill, Part One (1856) in more or less exact English equivalents of Goethe's verse forms, a majority of translators of *Faust* have emulated his example, although it is an obvious truth, as B. Q. Morgan declared in the Preface to his prose translation, that "no translation can retain [even] the rhythm of an original work without some distortion of the sense."[5]

But since no translation of an extended text, even a prose translation of a work in prose, can preserve, or find equivalents for, all its rhythmic and other acoustic qualities, a translator is always deciding whether euphony—rhythm and sound effects that may include rhyme-like elements—determined features of the original that, for lack of a better term, might be termed "semantically incidental." As example, B. Q. Morgan offers use of *versöhnt*, (v. 43), to mean "satisfies (an audience)," because a rhyme with *gewöhnt*, "accustomed to," is wanted, and observes, "In such cases . . . it becomes necessary to correct Goethe, as it were, or to assume that his prose would have been somewhat different from his verse. That this assumption is not unfounded can easily be demonstrated by a comparison of the prison scene in the *Urfaust*, as written in prose, with its versified and partially rhymed form in the final version."[6] In rendering Faust's "Ins Freie!" (v. 4537)—his answer to Margarete's questioning "Dahinaus?"—one can, with Fairley be literal, and say "Into the open!" (with Jarrell, "Out into the open," and with MacNeice, "Into the air"). But "Ins Freie!" replaced a prose "Freiheit"—elliptical for "Out there is freedom"— to provide the beginning of an iambic line, and so the apparent mistranslation "To freedom" (Bayard Taylor before the *Urfaust* was known, and many others since then) is surely better than any variant of the first English prose translator's "Into the free air." What matters to Faust is that Margarete be liberated, not that she breathe fresher air than that "behind the dankness of this wall" (v. 4407—"hinter dieser feuchten Mauer").

To turn from a moment of tremendous pathos to one which, before Faust and Wagner appear, depicts life's comfortable banalities, the scene "Outside the City Gates." A student watching servant girls go by exclaims: "Blitz, wie die wackern Dirnen schreiten!" (v. 828). Hayward, whose prose translation of 1833 was the first complete English version of Part One, rendered the line, "The devil! how the brave wenches step out!", and in 1976 Randall Jarrell still has our student exclaim, "Lord, look at the way those girls step out!" In between, *Blitz!* has been "Blitz," "Donner and Blitz," "Gad," "Gads," "Zounds," "Damn," "Jove," "Christ," "My," "Deuce," "Wow," "Gee," "Jupiter," and "Hell," with only one or two translators omitting it. As for "the brave wenches" (alias "lasses," "girls," and—once—"women"), who have also been "buxom," "strapping," "sturdy," and "lusty," they variously "step," "stride along," "hit their stride," "sail," "go a lick," "step on," "foot it," "step along," "do their paces," "move," or "walk." *Blitz!* is here hardly more than an exclamation asking the listener or observer to pay attention to what is going to be said; if the way the girls walk is important, it is because they are acting more unself-consciously than their middle-class "betters"; and so I would translate the line: "See that stride! Those girls have some life in them!", although it may be that even "that stride" is superfluous, since *schreiten* possibly functions only as a rhyme with "Wir müssen sie begleiten," the speaker's proposal to join them.

I suppose that all translators of verse become aware in texts they are translating of what might be called language skewed for the sake of meter or rhyme, and that when they do so, they are careful to translate its sense and not its individual words. But with a text like *Faust*, in which such skewing occurs only erratically, it is easy to relax one's guard. To reassure Faust that the dog who has joined them on their Easter walk is simply an ordinary animal, Wagner says, "Verliere was, er wird es bringen" (v. 1170). Between Hayward—"Lose aught, and he will fetch it to you"—and Arndt—"Lose something, and he will retrieve it"—there have been a few translators who obviously paused to ask themselves whether ordinary dogs voluntarily undertake searches for lost articles; deciding in the negative, they have Wagner say "Drop something" or "Let something drop," which seems the natural English idiom. (At first sight, Fairley's "throw something away" or Prudhoe's "See if he'll fetch your walking-stick / From the water" seems even more natural; but if Goethe had wanted Wagner to imagine a dignified, professorial Faust playing with a strange dog, he could have let Wagner say, with no metrical difficulty, "Wirf etwas hin"; it is thus more probable that "Verliere was" is a substitute for what would not fit metrically, viz. "laß etwas fallen".)

All the passages I have instanced were written in the form they now have when Goethe was completing Part One in the later 1790s or early 1800s. In passages written in the 1770s, and not subsequently changed, versificatory skewing is less a problem for the translator, since Goethe had then allowed himself more metrical freedoms. In these older sections of the text there is, however, always the possibility that words have meanings not commonly attached to them three to four decades later. In "Urfaust" (*ca.* 1775), in *Faust. Ein Fragment* (1790), and in Part One (1808), at different points in their respective actions, but always before he kills Valentin and becomes a proscript, Faust speaks of himself reproachfully as "der Flüchtling . . . , der Unbehauste" (v.3348). Wayne's "the uprooted, the homeless jade," and my 1962 revision of Bayard Taylor, "a man inconstant, homeless roaming," are exceptions in a long tradition of translating "Flüchtling" as "fugitive." In *Die Leiden des jungen Werthers*, written at approximately the same time as this section of *Faust*, Werther refers contemptuously to "Flüchtlinge und üble Spaßvögel" (Erster Teil, Am 15. Mai), a context in which "Flüchtling" must be a person with no responsibilities, or with no sense of responsibility; the translators from Bayard Taylor to Fairley and Jarrell who make Faust a fugitive before the fact, only weaken his self-reproach.

In sections of *Faust* written half a century later, that is, in most of Part Two, Goethe seems to have enjoyed accepting the constraints imposed by strict versification, even more readily sacrificing idiomaticality to them than around 1800. All translators soon find ways to handle neologistic elements of vocabulary and syntax consequent upon this, but it is difficult to remain constantly alert to their presence. That "durch Schrift und Zug bestätigt" (v. 10,966) means "in a signed document" is clear, and so it makes little difference—since the phrase occurs in a wordy alexandrine verse— whether one says "ratified in writing" (as I do) or "confirmed in writing and duly signed" (Fairley), although completely unidiomatic formulations like "'stablished . . . by manual sign and deed" (Martin—accepted by Bruford) needlessly give the reader pause at a point when any extra ritardando may convert comic into real boredom.

When two words in *Faust* are connected as in "Schrift und Zug" by *und* (in Part Two often *wie* or *sowie*), the translator is regularly forced to decide whether two separate concepts need to be expressed. If the second duplicates the first (as in "house and home") or forms a compound with it to express a single concept (as in "Schrift and Zug," which means *Schriftzug*, "writing"), it will obviously often be more idiomatic (and, in a verse translation, more metrically advantageous) not to reproduce in English the doublet or hendiadys. Similarly, an epithet that is purely formulaic is often best omitted in English: when Get-Quick says "Da liegt das rote Gold zuhauf" after a chest has broken and its gold coins have spilled on the ground, to have him speak of "the red gold," of "ruddy gold," or even—as is at least natural in English—of "the yellow gold" (Arndt), is to stress the color of the coins more than the only important fact, that, scattered about, they cannot now be conveniently taken *en masse* as booty.

The *rot* of "rotes Gold" could be regarded as a "false friend"—as a German word with an English equivalent so obvious that no second thoughts are required of the translator. But a translator can even create a "false friend": when Fairley has Care say, of someone who is so prone to worry that he always postpones all immediate tasks to some later day, "he . . . never quite grows up"—"so wird er niemals fertig" (v. 11,466)—it is surely because, some 11,000 lines before, he had interpreted, with idiomatic correctness, *fertig* (v. 182) as "adult." Here, however, as all other translators have recognized, it means "finished" ("He gets nothing done at all").

False friends are thus of two kinds: (1) German words that evoke false English associations, and (2) English words or forms that the translator—usually, but not always, without being aware that he does so—as it were invents to provide the level of diction he seeks to establish, which may simply be that of "poetry" as opposed to that of "the prosaic." (Curious word-order and fillers often accompany the second class, and will be copiously illustrated *en passant* as I treat other topics. That they occur frequently in rhymed and unrhymed verse is to be expected, but they are also found in prose, as when Barker Fairley inserts "again" in the following passage [v. 11,882-87]: "These again are messengers of love, telling of the creative spirit that surrounds us. Would that it [*it*, referring apparently to *love*, is a Germanism, since it has no proper English antecedent] could kindle me, whose mind in cold confusion labours [a surprise verbal inversion!], with senses dulled and unremitting pain [a dangling modifier-phrase of *me*, and one in which the first noun is followed, the second preceded, by its modifier]." The most notorious example of my second class, however, is an unusual one: Bayard Taylor's translation of *herzen*, "to press to the heart"; Margarete fantasizes, as all other translators convey some way or other, "All night I have been holding [my baby] close to my heart" [v. 4444], but Taylor, who found that *Herz*, "feeling," could often be translated effectively as "rapture" or "bliss," lets her say, "I blissed it [i.e., my baby] all this livelong night"—which represents an associative leap of the same sort as is involved in Fairley's translation of *fertig werden* as "grow up.")

The normal false friend is a German word that looks like an English one different in meaning, that so closely resembles some other familiar German word that it is mistaken for it, or that has a secondary meaning easily forgotten. *Entzwei*, "apart, into (many) pieces," frequently becomes "in two" even when fragmentation is described. *Erst*, "just (now), recently," becomes "first" even when it refers to the last of a series of events. The correlative pair *Wie . . . wie*, "Even as . . . even so," is taken to be simply an emphatically repeated "how." *Schaffen*, which can be the strong verb "shape, create," is just as often the weak verb "put, set, place, get," but passages are often tortured to fit the inapposite meaning to both its senses, especially since Creativity is a major *Faust* theme. *Weil* or *dieweil* can mean "while, as long as," not just "because," but when it does so is usually not recognized, so well have English students of German been taught that "while" is always "indem" or "während (daß)." *Fördern*, "to advance (a project), take care of (a matter)," is read—even by B. Taylor—as if it were *fordern*, "to demand, require." *Schlange* is "snake," especially in Mephistophelo-Satanic contexts, but in at least two passages it is "dragon." *Entgegnen* suggests "to go against, or toward," but, despite various ingenious efforts to twist several passages so that it can be translated in them as "to meet," it usually means "to answer" (for example, v. 8750). *Bild* is "picture," but it may also be "person." *Sammeln* is "to gather," but "gesammelt" does not mean "(having) assembled" but "composed, with composure, reflecting." *Einher* may look like a form of "in, into," but it simply means "along." *Chor* is both "chorus" and, no less often, simply "group" (or "band") of people, something often overlooked because its first value occurs so frequently in stage directions. *Natur* is ordinarily "nature," but in v. 3511 ff. it means "physical constitution," so that when Faust gives Margarete the drug to put her mother to sleep he does not say "three drops . . . will make / All nature sleep at peace beneath their pall" but simply: "Put three drops in what she drinks and she'll sleep deep and happy" (Fairley). And an exclamatory *Nein!* is not a negation, but the equivalent of "But," "I say," or of an emphasis otherwise affirmatively expressed.

But let me turn from isolated words such as *springen* and *hüpfen* (translated "spring, leap, hop" even when the sense is "dance"), to less simple lexical matters. In translating *Faust* a lapse of time can divorce words from their total context and produce literally possible, apparently idiomatic, and yet still incorrect translations. To take an eleven-line passage first: one can only assume that the translators of Faust's first speech after he is blinded by Care (v. 11,499 ff.) have done it piecemeal if they translate "Laßt glücklich schauen, was ich kühn ersann" (v. 11,504) as "Let me see with my eyes what I so boldly planned" (Fairley). "Let all behold" (Swanwick) and "bring my bold conception to full view" (MacNeice) represent translations that take the immediate context into account without needlessly puzzling the attentive reader (as, for a different reason, does Arndt's curious "Let blithely savor what I boldly drew").

A somewhat longer attention span is involved when Faust, after a scene with Wagner (v. 518-601), asks "Darf eine solche Menschenstimme hier, / Wo Geisterfülle mich umgab, ertönen?" (v. 606 f.). Before Wagner's entrance, Faust had contemplated the signs of the macrocosm and of the Earth Spirit, and conjured up the latter—a "Fülle der Gesichte" (v. 520), a "plenitude of visions" that in context is obviously qualitative, not quantitative. Nevertheless, from Hayward to Jarrell most translators have pluralized the Earth Spirit—for example, Passage: "Where spirits closed around me in full ranks," and Fairley: "When the air was thronged with spirits." Those contextually alert, however, have recognized that in "Geisterfülle" *-fülle* must be qualitative, and have carefully avoided introducing a non-existing plurality of spirits. B. Taylor accordingly translated "spirit-presence fullest" and MacNeice "spiritual fulness"—which I would interpret to be "(a state of) inspiration."

Geist, whether singular or plural, is a word that must always give a translator pause. Not only must he ask if it is spirit-consciousness, spirit-mind, spirit-wit, spirit-creature (who may be natural or supernatural), *etc.*, but also whether, when it occurs as a seeming genitive plural (*Geister-*) in compounds, it does not function simply as the equivalent of a singular adjective. As Faust awakens from the spell which Mephistopheles' Spirits cast upon him, at the end of their first interview, he asks: "Verschwindet so der geisterreiche Drang, / Daß mir ein Traum den Teufel vorgelogen, / Und daß ein Pudel mir entsprang?" (v. 1527 ff.). Since Spirits have just been singing, it is impossible to read the first of these lines alone—as a translator certainly does—and not to want to render it more or less as did Hayward: "Does the throng of spirits vanish thus?" But if this is done, the two following dependent clauses (introduced by *daß*'s) have to be made into independent questions: "Was it in a lying dream that the devil appeared to me, and was it a poodle that escaped?" The "throng of spirits" are still with us in 1976 (Jarrell: "That throng of spirits comes to no more than: / That a dream lied to me about the Devil / And that a poodle ran away from me?"—in Fairley's prose: "Is this all I have from my rendezvous with spirits? Did I just see the devil in a dream and lose a poodle?"), and they are present even in translations that recognize that *so* and the two *daß*'s go together, that the last two lines are result clauses—hence Passage's "The spirit throng has fled so utterly / That I but dreamed the Devil came and stayed / And that poodle got away from me?"—in B. Q. Morgan's prose: "Is this the outcome of that spirit throng, that a dream lied to me about the Devil, and that a poodle ran away from me?") The only translator of two dozen I have examined who seems to have realized that Faust's "geisterreiche Drang" is not a reference to Mephistopheles' spirit-creatures was Bayard Taylor, who wrote: "Remains there naught of lofty spirit-sway, / But that a dream the Devil counterfeited / And that a poodle ran away?" But whether his readers understand that "spirit-sway" means the spiritual state of mind of Faust at the opening of the scene—when he felt inspired to speculate on the meaning of "In the beginning was the Word"—may well be doubted, since the last previous occurrence of *spirit(s)* in his translation has been with reference to Mephistopheles' creatures. To avoid ambiguity, and to make clear that "der geisterreiche Drang" means—as the Grimms'

dictionary states unambiguously (geisterreich = "reich an Lebens-
geistern, belebend")—"vital impulse," I would translate, in prose:
"Did life-giving forces so quickly disappear that a lying dream could
invent a devil and a dog that got away?" (in simplified syntax, and
a bit more rhythmically: "Are life-giving forces so quickly spent— /
did a lying dream invent my devil, / and did a poodle simply run
away?").

The already cited speech of Faust blinded by Care ends with
another use of *Geist*: "Daß sich das größte Werk vollende, / Genügt
ein Geist für tausend Hände" (v. 11,509 f.). The first four lines are
soliloquy:

> The darkness seems to press about me more and more,
> but in my inner being there is radiant light;
> I'll hasten the fulfillment of my plans—
> only the master's order carries weight.

The rest of his lines are addressed to his workmen:

> Up, every man,
> and make my bold design reality! . . .
> Prompt effort and strict discipline
> will guarantee superb rewards:
> to complete a task that's so tremendous
> a single mind [so I wrote in 1958] is worth a thousand hands.

Since the last four lines form a compound sentence—and since, as is
not always the case, Goethe's punctuation is here perfectly clear—
Faust's final two lines should not be read as a return to soliloquy,
or so translated as to permit the reader or listener to identify
Faust's "single mind" with his own single mindedness. One must
therefore reject Fairley's separate generalization "To complete a
great project one mind is enough for a thousand hands" or such
afterthoughts to Faust's promise of rewards as MacNeice's "That
this vast work completion find, / A thousand hands need but one
mind." Faust is still exhorting his workers, and is simply telling
them that "working as one is worth a thousand hands."

I dwell at length on this short passage, not because it presents a
particularly difficult linguistic problem, but because if it is not
translated carefully the dramatic situation, and the dramatic character of Faust at the last critical decision in his long dramatic life, are
radically distorted. Faust's impatience and irritation has just occa-
sioned the death of Baucis and Philemon, but despite physical
impairment—blindness—his resolution to create a better world for
his fellow men has not been impaired. Is his unweakened resolve
mere stubbornness, a last instance of blind, unheeding wilfulness?

Or does it contain some redeeming element of common humanity? If "*ein* Geist" is simply Faust himself, the answers to these questions will be largely negative. But if it is the spirit of genuinely cooperative enterprise, the answers become positive—and, more importantly, Faust's soon to be uttered dying wish, that he might live to stand with a free people on land unencumbered by the weight of a dead past (v. 11,580)—though perhaps self-delusion still—ceases to be the expression of an ignoble self-delusion that cynical and pessimistic interpreters have thought to discern in it.

Translation, if it is anything better than the mechanical substitution of the words of one language for those of another, is always text interpretation, and this means interpretation in context—in the context of the text itself, in the context of the language its author used, and in the context of the ideas expressed in it, whether these occur in the work or elsewhere (in other works by himself or others). In the case of Faust's "geisterreiche Drang," the supporting evidence for what best fits the immediate dramatic context—that the words mean "vital aspiration" and not a "throng of spirits"— derives from the highest lexicographical authority. In the case of "*ein* Geist," however, the immediate contextual evidence to support my interpretation "working as one" is merely punctutative, and I have already noted in passing that Goethe's punctuation is not always clear (normative). In Part Two of *Faust*, however, the importance of "working as one," of cooperative enterprise, is a concept to which steadily increasing value has been attached—most pithily in the comment made by Faust's "noble pedagogue," Chiron, on the success of the Argonauts: "Danger is best endured in company with others" (v. 7379). Although Faust has by no means become perfect when he defies Care—as the More Perfect Angels comment when, after his death, his "immortal part" is being borne heavenwards, "this remainder of earth . . . is still impure"—his errors (to paraphrase Goethe, writing to K. E. Schubarth, 3 November 1820) in Part Two are "nobler and more to be respected" ("edler, würdiger"), and a translation of "*ein* Geist" that again diminishes, however slightly, his moral stature so soon after the deaths of Baucis, Philemon, and their grateful guest almost cancels out what has just been the heroic acceptance of finitude symbolized by his challenge to Care and the price of blindness he has paid for it.

But has a translator the right to diverge as radically as I do from all his predecessors (and, I might add, from the apparent consensus of previous interpreters of *Faust* who, if they comment on "*ein*

Geist," have for a century identified it as Faust's),[7] on the basis of intratextual contexts and an extratextual statement by a Goethe whose comments (as annotators of his autobiographical writings and letters frequently demonstrate) on his own works are often inexact, if only because they are fitted to a new context or tailored to an immediate addressee? Fortunately, there is a larger context in which *Faust* belongs: German classicism, the body of ideas and values Goethe shared so closely with Schiller at almost the very time that he began composing the series of scenes which treat Faust's last mortal hours. And one—although, so far as I can discover, only one—*Faust* commentary notes a parallel to Faust's line in Schiller's cultural-historical poem "Der Spaziergang," citing only the words "Tausend Hände belebt ein Geist"[8] and leaving it to the curious reader to discover that Schiller not only uses the same emphatic form as does Goethe—"*ein* Geist," but that he too refers not to a leader, but to the spirit of cooperative enterprise: Schiller continues: "hoch schläget in tausend / Brüsten, von *einem* Gefühl glühend, ein einziges Herz, / Schlägt für das Vaterland [that is, Athenian democracy] und glüht für der Ahnen Gesetze . . . " (in Bulwer Lytton's translation: "To thousand hands a single soul gives life— / In thousand breasts a single heart is beating— / Beats for the country of the common cause— / Beats for the old hereditary laws— . . . "). A blinded Faust who speaks the language of Weimar Classicism and expresses one of its central ideas is at least somewhat more worthy of the salvation soon apparently granted him than the unregenerate egotist careless readings of his speech would have him seem.

*   *   *

Most of the time translating is simply finding a right word, or the consonant word, for the tone and rhythm of an immediate context. And this, I discovered, is usually more difficult when there is no rhyme to conceal (as it were) skewings of idiomatic expression. Like our *TLS* reviewer I have marveled—admiringly—at the skill of generations of translators who have repeatedly found clever and, I think, semantically adequate rhymes as they turned rhymed lines of *Faust* into "more or less idiomatic English doggerel" and, often, into what can be felt to be genuinely poetic English. But I have also marveled at the lapses in tone, and even sacrifices of sense, that obdurate adherence to rhyme has entailed. When Faust enters Margarete's room he exclaims "Willkommen, süßer Dämmerschein,

/ Der du dies Heiligtum durchwebst!" ("How welcome is the gentle twilight glow / that permeates this sanctuary!"—v. 2687 f.) and, rhyming, apostrophizes the pain of love "Die du vom Tau der Hoffnung . . . lebst!" The phrase "dew (or: dews) of hope" is so obviously vivid that rhyming translators may be tempted to underscore it further by placing it at the end of the verse, although most of them have been content to let some less striking sentence element bear the burden of rhyme. But two, at least, would not let well enough alone, and to prepare a rhyme for *hope* introduce off-putting elements into Faust's critical opening words: MacNeice gives us "Welcome, sweet gleaming of the gloaming / That through this sanctuary falls aslope!" (in which *aslope* is even more disturbing than the Highlands ambiance), and Arndt offers "Ah, welcome, blessed twilight haze / That hovers in this sanctuary's scope!" (into which, as any reader or hearer will know at once, *scope* has been introduced only for the sake of some rhyme still to come).

Whereas paratactic simplicity can be the verse translator's down-fall in Part One, in Part Two elliptical concentration presents almost insurmountable obstacles to the verse, and even the prose, translator anxious not to expand the text and so slow its reading or obscure its sense. I offer only one, short passage in lieu of many possible examples, above all because it occurs in lines omitted in his abridgement by MacNeice, whose explanation—"Some fine lyrical passages were hereby sacrificed but we did not wish to lose sight of Homunculus"[9]—permits me to raise a central issue of *Faust* interpretation: whether the text that Goethe calls "A Tragedy" is fundamentally lyric *drama* (that is, drama written in a variety of forms, frequently lyric—like Calderón's *comedias*), or is a drama overburdened with lyric interludes that have no significant (thema-tico-)dramatic function, that, like those of Romantic lyric drama, either represent reduplicative elaboration of elements already "dram-atically" stated or are even quasi-superfluous digressions.

It is convenient to read the Classical Walpurgis Night, in which the passage omitted by MacNeice occurs, as the successive adven-tures of Faust (who disappears one-third the way through), Mephis-topheles (who, become Phorkyas, disappears a third later), and Homunculus (whose existence as an individual is to end shortly, at the conclusion of the section with the Triumph of Galatea). But to read the last two thirds without awareness that they have to do with "Faust," as a person and as a dramatic action, is to assume, carelessly, that Goethe here is temporarily more a lyric than a dramatic poet, has lost sight of both the protagonist of his tragedy and of its structuring elements. The omitted passage contains the episode of the Nereids and the Sailor Boys they have rescued from drowning and who, although they would like to keep them as their husbands, are mortals whom they must renounce and let return to land. The episode prefigures the end of Faust's union with Helen (at a corresponding point in the action of the following act), who will simply say farewell to Faust and join their son Euphorion in the underworld; she needs give no explanation, for it has been provided here: between real and unreal beings there can be no lasting ties. The task of the conscientious translator is to make sure that the prefiguring episode is so clearly rendered that the reader will, on the one hand, not be unduly delayed while following Homunculus' adventures to their conclusion, yet not be so confused by the language in which the episode is couched that, as it were, he skips over it. The episode begins with a prayer to Diana—to the stage moon that does not change place during the whole of the scene with the Triumph of Galatea; I shall limit my comments to its opening four lines, which read:

> Leih uns, Luna, Licht und Schatten,
> Klarheit diesem Jugendflor!
> Denn wir zeigen liebe Gatten
> Unserm Vater bittend vor. [v. 8391 ff.]

A typical verse translation is B. Taylor's, who sacrifices a rhyme to sense: "Lend us, Luna, light and shadow, / Show this youthful flower and fire! / For we bring beloved spouses, / Praying for them to our sire." Revising Taylor in 1962, I also deviated from complete rhyme, and wrote: "Lend us, Luna, imperfections! / let these youths seem fully fair! / for we seek assent paternal / to the spouses whom we bear"; although this conveys the sense of the German text, the elliptical logic of the first two lines demands a reader who will pause and supply a "but" to connect them, while "imperfections" for "light and shadow" sacrifices a pictorial image and is interpretive paraphrase rather than translation; as for my second two lines, they sacrifice both idiom and exactness for the sake of a rhyme with *fair*. It might be thought that translators unfettered by verse would do better, but the sense of the lines is no more immediately clear in Fairley's translation: "Luna, lend us your light and shade, to show this galaxy of youth, these dear husbands of ours, to our father, with a request." Goethe's German is simple and immediately clear, especially to the attentive reader who has observed how frequently chiasmic patterns occur in Part Two of *Faust*: for themselves, the Nereids are content with chiaroscuro, but they want the husbands they have found to be seen by their prospective father-in-law in all their youthful splendor. And this can be said rhythmically, without rhyme, but still with economy and clarity: "Luna, half-light will suffice us; / shed on these fine youths your brilliance! / Hoping for paternal blessing, / we have brought our husbands here."

* * *

Although translating is primarily a practical art, certain general principles can be inferred from its practice—both that of others and one's own. Some are simply practical, like assuming that words may not mean what you might ordinarily expect, and that if what you produce is not quite English it is probable you have not properly interpreted the original text. Others could be called commonsensical, like not needlessly elaborating on or otherwise expanding a text which will seem frighteningly long to readers for whom *Hamlet* normally represents maximum-length drama. Adherence to these principles leads to the discovery of techniques that can, in turn, become practical principles: for example, if there does have to be expansion for clarity's sake at one point, compression usually can compensate for it at another; an affirmative formulation is often more pithily formulated in the negative or vice versa; an affective element may advantageously be shifted for the sake of idiom or tempo; *etc.* This last technique can be nicely illustrated with two lines (v. 1011 f.) usually translated in verse, as by MacNeice, more or less thus: "You great man, how your heart must leap / To be so honored by the masses!" B. Q. Morgan, recognizing that it is "un-English" for Wagner so to apostrophize a person directly addressed, accordingly changed the apostrophe to an appositive: "What emotions must fill you, great man that you are, on experiencing the reverence of this throng!" But to some English ears even this form of praise may seem fulsome, and so I shift Faust's greatness into a prepositional phrase: "What feelings, sir, you must derive / from the respect of all these people for your greatness!" [If Anglo-Americanization is made a principle by the translator of *Faust*, elements incongruous with its historical setting soon intrude themselves—for example, Fairley's Faust becomes a figure of suburbia when he speaks of himself as "sitting in his den" (v. 1194) instead, as all other translators have him do, in his "chamber" or "cell."]

But as your ears have now told you repeatedly, there is one principle I have accepted as basic for a *Faust* translation directed at readers today: that it must be in what Randall Jarrell called "metered verse," and use a minimum of rhyme. Some of my reasons for this decision have emerged from my comments on others' translations—for example, metered verse, even if not always as flexible as verse that rhymes, does not impose a straightjacket that at some point or other (in a text as long as *Faust*: at many points) entails skewings of sense or idiomaticality; it can indicate varieties of tempo and rhythm more easily than prose; it affords a context in which a great range of levels of diction is, I think, more "acceptable" than in prose; and it obviates the inevitable effect of doggerel which continuous rhyme produces on English ears. It is, moreover, preferable to blank verse, not only because blank verse drama is now itself an archaism, but also because blank verse is as great a straightjacket as rhyme for the translator and is too inflexible for a text that, like Calderonian drama, is as often lyrical as it is dramatic. (Kenneth Muir's recent translation into blank verse of *Four Comedies* by Calderón results, I think, in an unfortunate homogenization of what in the original are different, and functional, levels of tone. Translated into the ten to twelve thousand lines of blank verse that it would take in English, *Faust* would, I fear, also become hypnotically monotonous.) The reader who knows Goethe's German will sometimes miss rhyme, but he will, as I have noted, do so at some points even in translations whose authors proclaim that they have been able to keep rhyme-schemes equivalent to those of the original text.

My own choice of metered verse was determined by an almost completely extraneous circumstance: attending master-classes at which young singers first read English prose translations of the texts of the songs they were about to perform in German, I had been struck by the fact that what seemed "good" poetry in German also sounded like poetry in unrhymed, and not highly metrical, English—and more like poetry than in the rhymed translations sometimes printed in song-recital programs. As I began translating I occasionally at first wondered whether educated German readers who wished to see how *Faust* looked in English might not be painfully disappointed by the disappearance of rhyme; but when I discovered that many of them were visibly surprised to hear me estimate that as much as 80% of *Faust* is written .in rhymed verse (actually 88% is), it became clear to me that Goethe's rhymes do not strike the German with the same force that they (or their English equivalents) do the English ear. There are several reasons for this: couplets constitute only about one-third of the rhymes, or well under one-third of all rhymed passages; their rhymes are often impure or assonant and—like other rhymes as well—are quite frequently divided between two sentences or even two speakers, so that they do not necessarily link related statements and have less a semantic than a musico-ornamental function. The familiar quotations from *Faust* that occur in German speech and writing only support what I take to be a general impression that rhyme is not a dominant element in it: of the fifty *Faust* passages cited in Büchmann's *Geflügelte Worte* (the German "Bartlett"), only fifteen are two lines or more in length, and only two constitute rhymed couplets.

Having accepted metered verse as a valid substitute for rhymed verse, there still remained the problem of how to treat unrhymed verse. Since I had allowed myself irregularity of line length when translating Goethe's rhymed verses (which often vary in the number of stresses they contain), I could only assimilate his—relatively few—free rhythms to the same metrical pattern. Blank verse I kept as such, hoping that regularity would sufficiently mark the shift from metered verse to a deliberately less flexible and more "elevated" kind of versification. For the classical trimeters and tetrameters I also adopted the principle of contrastive regularity, adhering as strictly to the metrical patterns $\cup/\cup/\ \cup/\cup/\ \cup/\cup/$ and $/\cup/\cup/\cup/\cup\ \ /\cup/\cup/\cup/(\cup)$ as was possible without torturing the English language. Here my models were the translators of the University of Chicago series *Greek Tragedies*, particularly Richmond Lattimore, who by allowing himself hypermeter consistently sustains a remarkably regular English counterfeit of classical Greek stichic verse. As for the strophic verses, this time I abandoned the practice I had earlier followed, of making strophes and antistrophes metrically identical, and simply turned all strophic passages into "free rhythms"; this permitted me to make them immediately understandable, yet never confusable with stanzaic verses that, though rhymeless, I was careful to keep metrically regular.

Not only do principles of translation ultimately derive from practice, but all valid theories of translation, insofar as they are useful, also derive, I suspect, from the practice of translators. In fact, the speculations of a writer when not practicing the art will differ from his theories—and practice—when actually translating. To say (with Walter Benjamin and others) that the aim of a "good" literary translation will be to enrich and expand the target language by forcing readers to accept unfamiliar linguistic features from an alien language, is a form of alienation theory that, as you have sufficiently heard, ultimately produces translatese which only alienates the—one hopes otherwise—willing reader. In his theoretical statements Goethe repeatedly urges translators to enhance their own language by imitating features of the one they are translating from, but both in his own translations and when giving practical advice to translators, he makes or urges changes that will better please "our German ear and character" (letter 27 January 1827, to F. C. Streckfuß, as the translator of Manzoni's drama *Adelchi*, in which he expresses approval of metrical freedoms in the translation of Manzoni's choruses). If a translator believes that rhyme is the major "musical" element in *Faust*, he will argue that rhyme is indispensable. If he believes that a text can "pass wholly into the idiom and the feeling of the new language" only in prose, he will exalt the merits of his prose version (Fairley). And if he believes that rhythm is the quintessential element of all true poetry of every kind, he will praise the virtues of metered verse.

Fortunately, *Faust* survives translating if it is translated with any degree of faithfulness to its words and spirit. And so let me end by citing, with comment, the opening four lines of *Faust* in three recently published translations. First:

> Once more you near me, wavering apparitions
> That early showed before the turbid gaze.
> Will now I seek to grant you definition,
> My heart essay again the former daze? [Arndt]

To subject an eye or ear yet unprepared for "poetic" diction to *near* as a verb, to a *turbid gaze* that seems to be attached to nobody, and to a poet apparently resolved on achieving both "definition(s)" and "daze(d confusion)" simultaneously, is to discourage any reader who fears he may not be up to long works in a hermetic style.

Now in prose: "You shifting figures, I remember seeing you dimly long ago, and now I find you coming back again. I wonder should I try to hold on to you this time? Have I the inclination, have I the heart for it?" (Fairley). If read (as it can be) as verse, we have here five-plus lines of English for four German pentameters, but the expansion is not the result of translation from one language to another, and of verse into prose, but of interpretive elaboration. Still, the simple substitution of "you" for our first translator's "the former daze" nicely obviates the possible aural confusion of *daze*-singular with *days*-plural.

And now in metered verse:

> Again you come to me, faltering shapes
> Who once at morning met my somber gaze—
> Shall I try, this time, to hold fast to you?
> My heart yearns still for the old illusion? [Jarrell]

Although not much more rhythmic than our prose version, this is certainly happier than our first specimen, if only because there is no "will" that has to do double duty for both *shall* and *will*. But making "My heart yearns still for the old illusion?" a separate syntactic element (which it happens also to be in the German) forces a retardando—the rereading of a line—much too soon, I think. "At morning," like "early" in the rhymed version, is—if not a mistranslation—a metaphor for what in prose is perfectly clear, "long ago"; but this usage—of *früh*, the word of the original German, to mean "in one's youth" (very frequent in Goethe's verse and prose)—precedes any contexts that might permit inference of its meaning. As for "the old illusion" yearned for by the poet's heart, that it is the "faltering shapes" of line one is not immediately apparent. And, finally, one might ask whether "faltering" itself is not an epithet with overtones almost as negative as those of "turbid gaze" and "former daze"?

My own translation of these lines is an attempt to avoid some of the pitfalls I have pointed out, and I offer it now, well aware that equally valid objections to it may occur to you:

Once more you hover close, elusive shapes
my eyes but dimly glimpsed when I was young.
Shall I now try to hold you captive?
Do these illusions still attract my heart?

If, speaking after five decades often spent with *Faust*, I may answer in Goethe's stead and, I hope, for all its translators, these illusions indeed still do, and that is why it will be a very long time before new English versions of his most famous, and surely greatest, work cease appearing with—may I say?—alarming frequency.

University of California, Santa Barbara

Notes

[1]Anonymous review of *Faust. Der Tragödie erster Teil* (*Monthly Review*, 52 [1810], 495).

[2]Verse translations of a thousand or more lines of Part Two have been published by Walter Kaufmann, J. F. Raschen, and—in books on *Faust*—by F. Melian Stawell (with G. Lowes Dickinson) and S. Atkins.

[3]"Another Faust" (anonymous rev. of "Goethe's Faust. Translated by John Shawcross"), *TLS*, 17 April 1959.

[4]"Faust in a prose we can all understand" (anonymous rev. of "*Goethe's Faust.* Translated by Barker Fairley"), *TLS*, 31 Dec. 1971.—B. Q. Morgan's prose translation (I, 1954; II, 1964), is less consistently colloquial or idiomatic than

Fairley's, but it conveys more of the range of Goethe's levels of diction, and does not deliberately omit, as Fairley's does, details of Goethe's text that might be thought too obscure to interest an ordinary English reader.

[5] Johann Wolfgang von Goethe. *Faust. Part One.* Translated . . . by Bayard Quincy Morgan (New York: The Liberal Arts Press, 1954), p. viii.

[6] *Ibid.*, p. ix.

[7] The consensus from 1850 (Heinrich Düntzer) to 1950 (Albert Daur) was expressed by F. Melian Stawell and Lowes Dickinson, in 1928 (*Goethe and Faust*, p. 242): "What matters in the last resort is single-minded effort, and this matters so much that wisdom approves it even at the cost of blindness."

[8] Th. Friedrich and L. J. Scheithauer, *Kommentar zu Goethes Faust* (Stuttgart, 1959), p. 293. (Even Léon Polak, in his otherwise almost impeccable essay, "Faust's verblinding," *Neophilologus*, 32 [1948], 161-73, interprets *"ein* Geist" as "mijn geest *alleen"* [p. 167, n. 2].)

[9] *Goethe's Faust Parts I and II* (New York: Oxford Univ. Press, 1952), p. 306.

Goethe's house in Weimar. (Courtesy Walter Wadepuhl)

Heroic Egotism: Goethe and the Fortunes of *Bildung* in Victorian England

David J. DeLaura

Abstract

From the time of Carré's *Goethe en Angleterre* (1920), the widespread impression has been that Thomas Carlyle, from the late 1820s, fabricated a "heroic" and "moral" reading of Goethe and the Goethe canon that set the tone of English Goethe criticism for several decades. But extensive reading in English reviews reveals a much more contentious critical situation. Beyond the familiar objections raised against Goethe by Menzel and others, such as his immoral treatment of women and his alleged lack of patriotism, the larger issue arose of Goethe's conscious, lifelong efforts at "self-cultivation"—in a word, his theory and practice of *Bildung*.

Important critics of the period—including J. S. Mill, David Masson, and R. H. Hutton—participated in the running debate, which was also a running criticism and correction of Carlyle. In each case, Goethe is found at the center of far-reaching ethical, social, and literary changes with which the most alert readers had to come to terms. The debate culminates, though it does not end, in 1855 with the well-received *Life of Goethe* by G. H. Lewes, who labors to present Goethe's personal life and his conception of the privileges of the artist in a favorable light. W. H. Bruford may be correct that Goethe's influence in England "was never really fundamental." But a new dimension of nineteenth-century English culture emerges in these previously unexplored materials. Discussions of Goethe, from the 20s to the 50s, provide an extensive background for the debate over "culture" that we associate with Matthew Arnold and Walter Pater in the 60s and 70s, and with the later rhetoric of aestheticism in the final two decades of the century. (DJD)

Throughout the nineteenth century in England, Goethe remained, as an admiring critic said as early as 1836, "a puzzle." For one party, he was "the impersonation of calm and dignified poetic wisdom"; for the other, "the public symbol of all that is weak and trifling, cold and indifferent in human character."[1] As we shall see, there was also a third sort of critic, the most interesting, for whom this bifurcation existed as a disquieting division within the individual consciousness.

Goethe received a great deal of attention in England: in the 10,000 pages of periodical criticism of German literature recently gathered in ten fat volumes by Boening, fully 2,700 pages are devoted to Goethe and his works.[2] And nothing more sharply divided this small host of reviewers than the precise issue I am addressing here: that of the idea of *Bildung*, or "self-development," as that is revealed in the life and works of Goethe. And I believe no other issue in the Goethe reviews is of greater intrinsic and long-run importance for the understanding of Victorian ethics, literature and general "culture." The controversy over self-development has not been specifically detected by earlier surveys of "Goethe in England," because it was largely confided to periodicals and only a few of the important statements were later presented in book form. But the continual debate, as it proceeds in the highly centripetal world of Victorian "higher" journalism, does indeed form a distinct "tradition": in some cases a dialectical series of statements and counter-statements, sometimes by writers of notable gifts, that occasionally reached memorable definition.

Of course some of the fire which this theme tended to draw from the reviewers was more a matter of bluster and abuse than of deep knowledge of Goethe and German literature. But it is not surprising that the most alert commentators, in a period inundated by new, usually post-Christian ideals, should have responded strongly, if complicatedly, to the challenge represented by Goethe. The Goethean "view of life," with a strong sense of the privileges of the "Artist," was a deeply attractive alternative; but the "temptation of Art," as I think it should be called, was also a fearful prospect for most. Every serious writer felt obliged to come to terms with it.

A word first about terms. The German word *Bildung* and its cognates is not, I believe, used before 1860 in England—or even thereafter. In the 60s and later, and especially in the writings of Matthew Arnold, the notion of development is indissolubly tied to the word "culture." Before that time, "culture," used in an absolute sense, surfaces rarely and notably in Carlyle; but the standard expression is self-development or self-cultivation—and both, as is immediately evident, bear with them a problematic ethical coloration.

The semantic extension of the key terms remains difficult to grasp and control.[3] W. H. Bruford, in his indispensable book *Culture and Society in Classical Weimar*, distinguishes three principal meanings

of "culture" in late eighteenth-century German thought, "all connected with the notion of tending and improving by training." The
sense most relevant here is *Bildung* as "the result, in an individual,
of the process of cultivation, as in [and Bruford is using Arnold's
1853 phrase for Goethe] 'a man of widest culture.' " (The modern
sense of culture, referring to a whole civilization or to the way of
life of a less developed society—usually *Kultur* in German—was not
widespread in England until the rise of anthropology later in the
nineteenth century.)[4]

The notion of personal "cultivation," not to speak of the special
graces bestowed by "polite letters," was widespread in early nineteenth-century England, and was always viewed favorably. But from
the 1820s on, a "Goethean" self-development or self-cultivation—
with its implication of a personal discipline concentrated above all
on the arts and literature—achieves high visibility and creates a
kind of "crisis" for many literary intellectuals, many of them already
pushing beyond the older clericalized classicism of the schools to
more "modern" forms of consciousness. Because attention was at
once focused on Goethe's personal development as an Artist and on
what one critic called his "artistic views of life,"[5] the Goethe-debate
gave a strongly "aesthetic" twist to the understanding of modernity
itself, and made the high creative artist, after the Goethean
example, privileged and problematic, a kind of glamorous model of
an adequate "modern" consciousness—even when, as frequently
happened, the Goethe "temptation" was finally rejected, and with a
kind of delicious shudder.

It is not easy to trace the process by which the specifically
aesthetic issues concerning Goethe and self-development achieved a
certain distinctness. The bulk of English reviewers, rather depress-
ingly, parroted the broader charges leveled in Germany after 1820,
notably by Menzel: as one English reviewer put it, Goethe's "want
of heart, laxity in morals, [and] indifferentism in politics."[6] Certainly the objections, of both the general and the "aesthetic" sort,
were rarely based, inevitably at the time, on a knowledge of the
precise scope and dynamics of Goethe's career. Carlyle translated an
early form of the *Wanderjahre* in 1827, and his early essays and
Sartor Resartus find in *Meister* a plan of *practical* activity; and we
know that the generation of Matthew Arnold in the 40s viewed
Meister as a manifesto of liberation. *Faust* II, moreover, was widely
discussed and translated. And yet virtually none of the reviewers
glimpsed the modern view that Wilhelm was in fact moving *away*
from ego and an "overly conscious self-culture to a [more]

spontaneous understanding of life"[7]; and *Faust* II, despite its humanitarian ending, was regularly and irritably dismissed as "mystical" and symbolical. The charges arose largely from scattered hints regarding Goethe's personal and creative life, repeated often and usually out of context. Particularly damaging was the famous letter to Zelter, in which Goethe announced: "The desire to raise the pyramid of my existence, the basis of which is already laid, as high as practicable in the air, absorbs every other desire, and scarcely ever quits me."[8] The 1824 English version of *Dichtung und Wahrheit*, though done from a wretched French version, provided even more ammunition, with Goethe's account of his developing ideal of moderation, tolerance in religious and moral matters, the avoidance of politics, and an "ironical indifference" in observing human life, as well as his turning inward, and with "zeal and unremitting activity" cultivating his "mental faculties," "in order to render them useful to others."[9] Equally provocative was Goethe's much-cited remark to Falk: "Religion and politics are a troubled element for Art: I have always kept myself aloof from them as much as possible."[10]

It was that note of "usefulness" that Goethe's English critics tended either to ignore or doubt. His self-development was in any case open to conservative religious charges of being a kind of this-worldly parody of the traditional Christian struggle for "perfection." For many, the continuous reference to "self" seemed a deep-running ethical flaw; his "indifference" seemed a prideful contempt for ordinary men and ordinary reality; his elevation and detachment lacked the balancing note of universal sympathy that the English and German Romantics attributed to the equally lofty Shakespeare. For the most perceptive, there is an appalled fascination with the notion that Goethe "used" other people and his relations with them for his art, that he drew back from intimacy lest his "development" be injured, and, perhaps most prophetically, that some of his works were experiments in unfettering the artist from the "moral perspective" altogether.[11] Goethe's aversion to politics in the era of revolution and reform caused him to be pictured regularly as poised with Olympian calm overlooking the maelstrom of modern European history. In all of this there was the added stigma of an excessive intellectuality and rationalism. More pervasively, there was that disturbing and attractive "blurring of the edges between the good and the beautiful" that Bruford detects among a number of German figures of the great Weimar period.[12] The figure that half-emerges is that of the sinister "connoisseur" of people and the arts, at its best the "glorious Devil" of Tennyson's "The Palace of Art" in the early 30s (and I believe that poem to be a portrait of Goethe—or at least of a current caricature of the Goethean poet):[13] at any rate, it is predictive of a type not common in English culture until the era of Walter Pater and Henry James's "aesthete" figures. Obviously, early Victorian England was—with some significant exceptions—unprepared to embrace such notions.

I believe that the extensive evidence—some of it newly available—on which I am drawing requires that we reshape a number of the generalizations we have accepted about Goethe, Carlyle, and Culture in the Victorian period. First, Raymond Williams's essential work, *Culture and Society*, attempts to work out the English tradition almost exclusively from "native" sources; indeed, an improbable amount of weight is placed on a single sentence in Coleridge's *On the Constitution of Church and State* (1830), on the need to ground a "progressive civilization" "in *cultivation*, in the harmonious development of those qualities and faculties and characterise our humanity."[14] I am claiming that if we take the intensive public debate of the 60s over Arnold's conception of culture as an inevitable climax, the "prehistory" of the topic is simply unintelligible except in terms of the widespread earlier discussion of culture and self-development, especially centering on Goethe. (It should be noted in passing that the significant development of the notions of *Bildung* and *Humanität* in Wieland, Herder, Humboldt, and Fichte was surprisingly unknown in England, especially during this earlier period. Even Schiller, who *was* discussed frequently, was known almost exclusively as a poet and a playwright—and not in his character as a literary and cultural thinker.) The new approach I am suggesting provides for the first time the missing "German connection."

Second, I believe Goethe was more significant, and more widely so and in different ways, than we have assumed. In a quick survey, Bruford announced that "Goethe's influence in England even in Victorian times was never fundamental." And he is echoed even more strongly by William Rose: "Goethe has had an insignificant part in the shaping of English culture."[15] Both men understate the case, for even apart from the great number of translations that accumulated during the century, there are the major careers of Carlyle and Arnold, for whom Goethe *was* "fundamental," and a number of important artists (for example, Bulwer-Lytton, Meredith, Wilde, Symonds) and some notable secondary figures (e.g., John Sterling, J. A. Froude, and G. H. Lewes) who were in varying ways deeply affected by the example of Goethe. Although I agree with Rose that Goethe has been appreciated by comparatively few in English-speaking countries, even in our own time, we may need a new model of "significance"—and "influence"—to do justice to the extensive attention given to Goethe in nineteenth-century England. Perhaps we should call it "negative influence." For Goethe is a surprisingly pervasive "presence" in Victorian higher journalism for several decades, even if often misrepresented or put under a false light; the issues raised in the best reviews, especially in the tradition of debate over self-development, besides being of intrinsic interest, helped writers clarify the central issues in their own careers—issues of art and of life. Some of the most alert artists and critics discovered their own position by "triangulating" with Goethe, even as a temptation, and even if one at length put aside. For some Goethe remained a kind of "secret" source, a temptation not quite firmly renounced, even in the more public and "moral" phases of their development.

And third, this large body of Goethe commentary, elaborately interconnected and almost antiphonal, helps us put aside once and for all the nearly universal truism—it is in fact a falsism—that (as one reader puts it) "the whole nineteenth century [in England] looked at Goethe largely through Carlyle's eyes."[16] I do not wish to imply that there were not appreciative—and even informed— estimates of Goethe's poetry and drama in the period: there were a good many, and especially a rather extensive discussion of translations. But even among the admirers, very few were as uncritically worshipful as Carlyle, and virtually no one rose to Carlyle's heights in defining Goethe's merits. I want to suggest here the outlines of a revised approach to the much-mooted question of Carlyle's relationship to Goethe and German literature, and of Carlyle's role in mediating Goethe to the English public.

Carlyle, to begin with, is the first great virtuoso of "culture" in its various meanings, and long before Matthew Arnold made it a standard part of the English critical glossary. The verb "cultivate" was in wide use, as was the adjective "cultivated" (men/mind; even "cultivated Europe"); but the standard usage of the word "culture" in the period was prepositional: the culture *of* the mind, *of* the faculties, *of* the poet, etc. Carlyle's chief innovation in his early essays was his frequent addition of adjectival qualifiers. There is a large sense, implicitly educational and developmental: human, humane, universal, or solid culture. Sometimes the context is that of specific kinds of development: moral, philosophical, intellectual, mental, spiritual, or poetic culture. Occasionally he rises into a range of meaning near to both "civilization" and the modern anthropological sense: national, or Grecian, or German culture. Less common, but more prophetic, is Carlyle's use of "culture" as an *absolute* term, though not quite yet in its later Arnoldian sense as a kind of independent *force* in social and intellectual life. In Carlyle, the term is usually applied to the personal and spiritual development of a creative personality: we hear at one point that "Goethe had outgrown his generation; his culture was too high for its apprehension" (XXIII,22)[17] and even more globally, that Mme. de Staël sought "not for this or that object of culture, this or that branch of wisdom; but for culture generally, for wisdom itself" (XXVI, 503).

But only once does Carlyle reach for a high generalization of great force, and that is in the 1827 Richter essay, which looks back to the German tradition and anticipates Arnold more fully—and this is three years *before* the much-cited Coleridge passage referred to above. In this German context, which nevertheless carefully avoids mention of Goethe, we hear that "the first and last of all culture" is a "harmonious development or being": "the great law of culture is: Let each become all that he was created capable of being; expand, if possible, to his full growth; resisting all impediments, casting off all foreign, especially all noxious adhesions; and show himself at length in his own shape and stature . . . " (I, 20, 19). I take this to be the normative and benign sense of self-development or *Bildung* which establishes itself later in the century, for example, in John Stuart Mill and Arnold.

The fact is, however, that although Carlyle decisively advances—indeed, does much to initiate—the development-debate, centering it on Goethe, he not only generally avoids the ethically loaded terms "self-development" and "self-cultivation" but is even a bit gingerly about using the apparently unexceptionable emergent term "culture." The reason, I think, is that for the pattern of development Carlyle attributed to Goethe and to some extent Schiller, the word *culture*, even during this early "German" period, finally seemed too constricting, too intellectual, too "modern." The "ethereal" realm of values to which Goethe and Schiller ascended—associated with such terms as Poetry, Religion, and Genius—impiies in its highest reach a movement *beyond* the effortful, the willed, even the *moral* in the limited sense.[18]

The sequence that Carlyle ascribes to Goethe's progressive "spiritual development," his desire for a "thorough universal culture of all his being," was undoubtedly familiar to all educated Victorians.[19] The stages of Goethe's personal development, we learn, can be followed in his works: an "earnest," "toilsome" Goethe suffers through blackness, denial, and despair, up to light and better vision—a process begun in *Werther* and climaxed in the *Wanderjahre*, the *West-Östlicher Divan*, and other late works. In place of this supposed *progress* from Unbelief to Belief, Carlyle often resorts to a more static paradox: Goethe somehow unites "the belief of a Saint" with "the clearness of a Sceptic"—a combination of Fénelon and Voltaire! Carlyle's boldest stroke is to suggest that Goethe is indeed a new Christ who "suffered" modern doubt *for us*, who thus becomes "the Redeemer of the time," who underwent a "transfiguration," and who finally "rose victorious"!

Now this almost hagiographical reading of Goethe's life, far from at once becoming canonical, was challenged from an early time[20]— and even Goethe's defenders, though full of admiration for his "unwearied" efforts, stopped far short of such high-flown rhetoric. I do not call in question the sincerity of Carlyle's lifelong insistence that his early reading of *Meister* was a kind of conversion- experience, and that in the book he found "true wisdom."[21] But it is dispiriting (and inevitably suspicious) that the man who subjected everything else in heaven and on earth to the most excoriating "descendental" analysis, should remain so obstinately uncritical and unironic about Goethe, and in the process even deny Goethe those humanizing touches that are so striking in Carlyle's other portraits. There is in fact a good deal of complicating evidence that cries out for analysis, and that I can only briefly indicate here. For example, though he confined his doubts to his notebooks, he was both fascinated and repelled by the running implication in Goethe and Schiller that the Beautiful might eventually "supersede" the Good, and that "Art is higher than Religion."[22] These troubled question- ings (in 1831) coincided with Carlyle's highest flights of panegyric regarding Goethe, on the one hand, and on the other with the decisive "moralization" of the Goethe-Schiller pattern in *Sartor Resartus.*[23] For with the death of Goethe in 1832, Carlyle shifts rather abruptly from Culture to Prophecy; almost as suddenly, notions of "self-development" drop out of his preferred lexicon, as he moves toward admiration of heroes of vehement *action*, the Cromwells and Fredericks. He also begins to speak more candidly of Goethe as a "Heathen"—though not in public;[24] even when he speaks of the Fichtean "Scholar" or "Man of Letters," as he does in *Heroes and Hero-Worship* (1841), we are told of their struggles, but we hear next to nothing about the details or stages of their "culture" or any culminating "victory"; and the most eloquent testimony to Carlyle's doubts is the virtual silence he keeps, after 1832, regarding Goethe.

So far did Carlyle move from his "German" dreams of the 1820s—the ideals of cosmopolitanism, tolerance, and detachment, and the hopes for personal and social revival through internal and "aesthetic" means—that he denounced "high art" to Emerson during the latter's visit in 1847: " 'Yes, [Carlyle insisted] *Kunst* is a great delusion, and Goethe and Schiller wasted a great deal of time on it.' "[25] This revulsion from the "Goethean" point of view reaches a climax in 1851, in *Life of John Sterling*, when during his great "shouting-out" period, Carlyle finally declares: "It is expected in this Nineteenth Century that a man of culture shall understand and worship Art: among the windy gospels addressed to our poor Century there are few louder than this of Art." It was this delusion that led the tragic John Sterling into the "temporary dilettante cloudland of our poor Century" (XI, 174). It is worth noting, however, that in this public statement Goethe's name is not introduced. I suggest, though cautiously, that there is an uncomfortable running hint, in Carlyle's treatment of Goethe, of evasiveness bordering on dissimulation and a lack of candor that is a near neighbor to suppression of the truth. If that is so, then Carlyle's "arduous admiration" for Goethe, though less perhaps a matter of ethics than of systematic self-delusion (of "*engouement,*" as Matthew Arnold later judged), inevitably throws a shadow across a career in many ways notable for its courage—though courage is not quite the same thing as honesty.

Carlyle had one important ally in his missionary work for Goethe, and that is the three-volume *Characteristics of Goethe,* published by Sarah Austin in 1833. Her sources, especially Falk and Müller, far from apologizing for or explaining away Goethe's alleged "apathy" and "selfishness" with regard to morals and politics, rather agressively interpret his "tolerance" and "indifference" as the very signs of his exalted character as "*the Artist.*" In her Preface, Austin puts aside Carlyle's mollifying "moral" tone, and adopts a surprisingly defiant new tone of her own. Goethe, she insists, sees art as inherently "moral, humanizing, beneficent"; therefore, for Goethe, the "confusion of the province of ethics and esthetics which reigns [in England]" is a most "vulgar mistake." This dextrous juggling of categories reaches a climax when, against the charge that Goethe is indifferent "to the moral tone and tendency of a work," she loftily replies: "such an objection implies a belief that moral truth and beauty may be violated without injury to aesthetical perfection;—a mistake into which no true Artist could fall."[26] This too much neglected work is far and away the fullest high-aesthetic document of its era in England, long before the bulk of English readers were ready for it. It is important as a treasure-house for the early nineteenth-century promiscuous "mixing" of religious and aesthetic categories; it proved to be a rich and specific quarry for a well prepared reader like the young Matthew Arnold in the 40s.

Characteristics was rather extensively reviewed, and most responses, though refusing to confront directly the more unsettling problems of Goethe's life and career, were cautiously favorable. The significant exception was Goethe's old skeptical adversary, the Whiggish *Edinburgh Review*, which spoke scornfully, concerning "the primary motives of Goethe's mind," of his determination "to attend to his own aesthetic development" and his view that art should be substituted for religion and politics as "the great engines of [social and moral] improvement."[27] But the 30s, a time when translations of *Faust* were discussed widely and even judiciously, was in general an era of good feeling toward Goethe in England.

By the late 30s, however, a shift is detectable in English attitudes, a new phase that moves beyond the polarization of worship and defamation. The view that has prevailed for the last sixty years, in Jean-Marie Carré's standard work *Goethe en Angleterre* (Paris: Plon, 1920), is roughly that Carlyle's misinterpretation of Goethe as Saint and Sage was the view held by his English admirers for some years, alongside the attacks of ignorant and moralizing detractors; but that with greater knowledge both attitudes were eventually superseded by the vindication of the "true" Goethe in G. H. Lewes's famous *Life of Goethe* in 1855. I suggest a revised picture, again roughly. I do not deny that a depressing amount of casual obloquy regarding Goethe can be found in many journals of the period, along with much dull eulogy. And aspects of the "ideal" Goethe concocted by Carlyle in the 1820s, for purposes of his own, *were* attractive to the young, especially to some in Arnold's Oxford circle in the 40s; but from the first, as we have seen, such "religious" adulation was complicated by another and more disturbing construction of the hard "aesthetic" sort found in Austin's volumes. In short, Goethe, even for his more percipient admirers, was inevitably a "temptation"—a "glorious Devil." Even more importantly, the most interesting treatments of Goethe, from the late 30s on, are

precisely those, sometimes well informed and by no means reaction-
ary, that most candidly face the disturbing issues raised by the very
existence of Goethe as a phenomenon—whether the controlling
point of view is finally friendly or not.

One of the most able and most honest of Goethe's critics was
John Stuart Mill, who throughout his career was fascinated and
disturbed by Goethe's doctrine of "self-development." In the 1830s
he had (as he later explained) for the first time begun to "give its
proper place, among the prime necessities of human well-being, to
the internal culture of the individual," and to regard "poetry and art
as instruments of human culture"—in short, to add "the cultivation
of the feelings" to "intellectual culture."[28] In reaction against the
partisanship of the times and of his own party, and under the
tutelage of the "Germano-Coleridgians" and Carlyle's early essays,
Mill in effect adopted for himself at this time "Goethe's device,
'many-sidedness' " (*Works*, I, 171). Indeed, we now know that Mill
had a hand in the preparation of Sarah Austin's *Characteristics of
Goethe.*[29] For a while, in 1832, in one of the comic misunderstand-
ing of modern cultural history, Carlyle accepted Mill as a fellow
"mystic" and Mill offered to act as a "logical expounder" to more
average men of the "Truth" intuited and expressed "impressively" by
Carlyle the "artist" and "poet." Mill soon enough discovered his
misapprehension and withdrew his offer to act as Carlyle's "auxil-
iary," although he continued to insist that he and Carlyle agreed
that, if "the good of the species" is the "*ultimate* end," the *means* to
that end is "by each taking for his exclusive aim the development of
what is best in *himself*" (*EL, 12,* 113, 155, 161, 206-208). But Mill
had never hidden from Carlyle his doubts about Goethe; even
during the time of his most open discipleship and Carlyle's wildest
flights of panegyric, in 1832, Mill gently insisted: "I do not myself,
as yet, sufficiently know Göthe to feel certain that he is the great
High Priest and Pontiff you describe him" (*EL, 12,* 111-12; see also
p. 119).

But none of this background quite prepares us for an outburst in
1838, where Mill is defending Alfred de Vigny's *Cinq-Mars*, with its
unpleasant subject matter that violates the canon of "the intrinsi-
cally beautiful" upheld "by the ancients and by the great German
writers" (*Works*, I, 476). Mill suddenly turns to Goethe and, quite
uncharacteristically, raises his voice:

it is not possible for the present generation of France to restrict the purposes of
art within this limit. They are too much in earnest. They take life too much *au
sérieux*. It may be possible (what some of his most enthusiastic admirers say of

Goethe) that a thoroughly earnest mind may struggle upwards through the region of clouds and storms to an untroubled summit, where all other good sympathies and aspirations confound themselves in a serene love and culture of the calmly beautiful—looking down upon the woes and struggles of perplexed humanity with as calm a gaze (though with a more helping arm) as that of him who is most placidly indifferent to human weal.[30]

But the "great majority of persons," he insists, will be more morally "militant," and will pursue some end "different from the Beautiful, different from their own mental tranquillity and health" (*Works*, I, 478).

The editors of the splendid Toronto edition of Mill's works fail, rather surprisingly, to detect the topical reference to the reading of Goethe preferred by Carlyle and, I think, by Sarah Austin's German apologists. We catch Mill here in the process of moving back toward a more orthodox Utilitarianism, as well as revealing his own "romantic" sympathies with an art of struggle and imperfection. That process culminates in the *On Liberty* (1859), the central doctrine of which (as Mill explained soon thereafter in his *Autobiography*) is the "rights of individuality" and development, a doctrine "pushed by a whole school of German authors even to exaggeration"—and only Pestalozzi and Humboldt are approved heartily. Most fascinatingly, Mill pauses to say that Goethe's writings "are penetrated throughout by views of morals and of conduct in life, often in my opinion not defensible, but which are incessantly seeking whatever defense they admit of in the theory of the right and duty of self-development" (*Works*, I, 260). Indeed, there is evidence in a cancelled passage of the *Autobiography* that the regenerate Mill held for the rest of his life the conviction that the "kind of German religion" sponsored during the *Goethezeit*, was too "comfortable" to be "virtuous"—as Carlyle might have said, too much "at ease in Sion" (see *Works*, I, 184).

With more time, we could consider Giuseppe Mazzini, the exiled Italian patriot, who in a London journal in 1839 expanded the familiar charges against Goethe as the poet of "individuality" and "indifference" into a comprehensive reading of modern culture.[31] It would take even longer to do justice to the most notable piece of English Goethe criticism of the period, by the young G. H. Lewes, in 1843, which advanced English understanding well beyond the stage reached by Carlyle and Sarah Austin.[32] Far better informed than earlier critics, and himself moving from an early predilection for Comte to the harder, "scientific" rationalism of his later career, Lewes opens with a tone closer to Sarah Austin's than to Carlyle's.

He begins with the familiar tactic of denying Goethe's alleged "coldness" and "egotism" in personal relations ("it is an excess of sympathy"! p. 307). But he soon moves boldly to an unapologetic exposition of Goethe's "living the life of an artist, subjecting the whole world to his dominant feeling, *Art*." His approach is insistently paradoxical: "Renounce all" for art, he summarizes, "but develope yourself to the utmost limit. . . . This is Goethe's egotism—cruel, immovable, intense. Those who loved him must demand no return of love!" The article almost revels in such disturbing epithets: cruel, brutal, terrible, frightful; and by using the terms "intense egotism" and "marvelous greatness" in the same phrase (p. 318), Lewes very perceptively sees that Goethe's problematic "detachment" and "egotism" are the very reflex and condition of his *kind* of achievement.

Such flagrant paradoxes about morality and art were quite unwelcome in early Victorian England. Lewes chooses to present Goethe as a kind of antinomian hero of the creative process, a hero quite outside the confines even of Carlyle's cautious yoking of opposites: Lewes ends by finding "something inconceivably grand in contemplating this wonderful man" who preached the egotistical "dogma of self-culture." Had *any* creative personality in history suggested so complex and yet so subtly convincing a set of disturbing epithets? Lewes carefully avoids the tempting distortion of calling Goethe's heroism Promethean; though he does not use the term, his portrait comes closer to Goethe's own view of the "demonic." Indeed, Goethe as presented by Lewes brings to mind a figure that is itself largely "literary": I am referring to Milton's Satan. And one thinks yet again of Tennyson's paradoxical "glorious Devil," itself a version (as I believe) of the Goethe-conundrum. By developing through Goethe an unprecedented "heroic" egotism of the creative powers, Lewes was in effect sighting a new region of creativity previously unglimpsed: again, it recalls Tennyson's figure, who thinks, "I have found a new land, but I die" (11. 283-84). Lewes's impressive definition of a sort of creative "ruthlessness" would have been welcomed by Nietzsche, had he known it—the Nietzsche for whom, it has been suggested, Goethe himself was an exemplar of the "über-mensch." And Lewes's amazingly cool presentation of Goethe's Spinozistic treatment of good and evil, and right and wrong, as purely subjective judgments based on the pleasant and the hurtful, inevitably brings to mind Nietzsche's own forays "beyond good and evil."[33]

Very little English criticism of Goethe, before or after, reaches so high a level of interest and originality, and we can only make a quick guided tour of the years following. Among the New England Transcendentalists in the 1830s and 40s, the "culture" theme was a binding thread; the word became a kind of vogue-term in Boston and Concord, a vague floating "something" that gathered together the spiritual and intellectual yearnings of these religiously oriented men and women, seeking a European—well, *culture*. Goethe was, as he was in England, at the center, and the discussion reaches a climax in the first two years of the *Dial*, in 1840-42. Emerson and Margaret Fuller subject the notion of self-development to searching scrutiny—indeed, Fuller's superb and sustained insight into the issues makes her treatment, I believe, the most permanently valuable written in English during that generation.

The Puritan Emerson, though at one time deeply impressed by *Meister*, complained to Carlyle, as early as 1834, of Goethe's "velvet life," his "bad morals," his "genius [too much] acknowledged, pampered, crowned."[34] Emerson's tangled responses to Goethe reach an important moment of definition in the *Dial*, in 1840.[35] He struggles to give due praise to Goethe's realism, his "industry of observation," his "greatness of mind." More ambiguously, he notes that Goethe's "bright and terrible eyes," his imperturbably "lifting the veil" from every object, constitute a standing challenge for all modern minds. But Emerson cannot refrain from registering his disapproval of "the subtle element of egotism," as well as the "absence of the moral sentiment, that singular equivalence to him of good and evil in action," and his acceptance of "the base doctrine of Fate."

Margaret Fuller takes some of her cues from Emerson, but the much bolder welcome she extended to Goethe in the late 30s and early 40s is, like Lewes's, solidly based on the premise of Goethe's greatness. Her own brief and deeply moving career was torn between morality and art, between (in the words of a recent critic) "Goethe's example of increasing intellectual and emotional mastery of the world," and "Channing and Emerson's ideals of spiritual development and moral improvement."[36] As the first translator of Goethe's conversations with Eckermann, Fuller knowledgeably and ungrudgingly salutes Goethe's "life of severe labor, steadfast forbearance, and an intellectual growth almost unparalled," and she disdainfully pushes aside the familiar charges, too often heard in the New World, of Goethe's being an "epicurean" and a "sensualist." But "still," she declares, "I doubt. . . . He does not warm me"; and she ends by speaking of Goethe as a kind of "failure": "he might have been a priest; he is only a sage." The Goethe of *Meister*, a man whose "intellect is too much developed in proportion to [his] moral nature," is no longer like Faust an "impassioned and noble seeker" but a disciple of "circumstance" with "a *taste* for virtue and knowledge." She wishes "that he had not so variously unfolded his nature, and concentrated it more." Once we deduct for the early Victorian pitch of her rhetoric, I submit that—although there is very much more to be said about Goethe—Fuller's wrestlings exhibit genuine passion, wisdom, and telling truth, earned as part of her own striking "self-development." She is in effect one of the first to go through and "beyond" culture in Goethe's sense of the term.

Emerson was well known in England, the *Dial* was perhaps read by more in London than in Boston, and through the *Dial* at least Fuller's work was known.[37] We have not yet calculated, in short, the extent to which the American engagement with Goethe and with the notion of self-development contributed to English understanding of the issues. Certainly, the culmination of the American reaction to Goethe, in Emerson's *Representative Men* (1850), was widely read in England. In that book, as part of his own movement from self-culture to a more humanistic ideal of "culture,"[38] and perhaps emboldened by Carlyle's private outburst of 1847, Emerson, though paying passing tribute to Goethe's realism and labor again, stingingly lashed out at a Goethe "incapable of a self-surrender to the moral sentiment," a man whose devotion was not "to pure truth; but to truth for the sake of culture."[39] The word "culture" itself is beginning, in more and more contexts, to take on an embarrassing and even sinister tone that became more common later in the century. Goethe was a man, Emerson suggests, perhaps too much acquainted with "libraries, galleries, architecture, laboratories, savans [sic] and leisure," and a man "who did not quite trust the compensations of poverty and nakedness" (*ibid.*, p. 288). Indeed, in 1850 and just after, the generation of Carlyle and Emerson and a younger one too seemed all at once eager to disenthrall themselves of a Goethe they still respected, and to declare the "age of mere self-culture . . . over."[40]

The attempt to wave off the stage of history what one critic dismissed as "the old [Greek and German] dream of the omnipotence of *Künst*" was no doubt premature; that notion from "the brief splendour of the Weimar days"[41] recurs, in diminished form, in that lesser phenomenon we call English Aestheticism. But I want to end with a glance at G. H. Lewes's celebrated *Life of Goethe* in

1855. For both English and German readers, it was the first successful attempt to lay out the elements of Goethe's life and career with some fulness and justice; and one must not call its importance into question. But its *manner* requires a word of comment. Lewes's tactic, familiar among Goethe's defenders, is to overstate the ethical and aesthetic objections, so as to permit a vaguely honorific reply. Almost offhandedly, Lewes treats Goethe's "political indifference" and his unrelenting program of self-culture unproblematically, as the result indeed of Goethe's "earnestness in Art" and "a spirit deeply religious"![42] In this bland defense of Goethe the "Artist," Lewes not only suppresses the candid and challenging language of his 1843 review, but systematically avoids all occasions for examining the serious issues of Goethe's creativity. The approach is unlike Carlyle's in "regretting" Goethe's later, Olympian phase; to that extent it serves as a partial corrective. But the book is a kind of poor parody of Carlyle in its tone of almost absentminded piety.

There is a "failure of nerve" here, I suggest, and perhaps a failure of conviction about Goethe, after a decade's lapse, and Lewes's splendid anonymous review of 1843 is the best standard by which to judge the smooth surfaces of the more public *Life*.[43] The reviewers were also alert to the book's problems of tone and approach, and— Carré notwithstanding—the book, though contributing to informed judgment, by no means put to rest doubts regarding Goethe. The most fascinating review for us in the judicious but thoroughgoing attack made by none other than Sarah Austin, who had done so much to inform the British public over twenty years before, and in the most assertive tone. Her running implication now is that Lewes's "euphuistic language" regarding Goethe, and his sneers at all those who raise the question of Goethe's "moral indifference," are signs of a similar moral quality in Lewes himself.[44]

And so Goethe remained a daunting challenge to English intellectuals, right up to the threshold of the Matthew Arnold era. His defenders had been driven to either sophistical evasion or bold paradox. He remained for almost everyone a "puzzle"—but a puzzle frustrating all attempts at solution. The weariness with Goethe on the part of so many is of a piece with a widespread fear among later intellectuals regarding the self, the will, and even the intellect. There is still a lingering feeling, as Dmitri warns in Dostoevski's *The Brothers Karamazov*, that "too much breadth can destroy a man."

University of Pennsylvania

Notes

[1] J. S. Blackie, *Foreign Quarterly Review*, 16 (Jan. 1836), 360.

[2] *The Reception of Classical German Literature in England, 1760-1860*, ed. John Boening, 10 vol. (New York: Garland, 1977). Referred to hereafter by volume and page number: for example, Boening, 7, 300. When I also cite the source, I give it first, with full pagination, because Boening's format makes it difficult to determine page numbers in the original.

[3] See Raymond Williams's *Keywords* (New York: Oxford Univ. Press, 1976), where the range of meanings I am explaining is not even noted.

[4] Bruford, in *Culture and Society in Classical Weimar, 1775-1806* (London: Cambridge Univ. Press, 1962), and I think Williams, in *Keywords* and *Culture and Society, 1780-1950* (London: Chatto & Windus, 1958), miss one vital, "Arnoldian" sense of culture: that is, not only the "product" as a quality of mind, but the acquisition of mastery of a certain *content*—Arnold's "the best that is known and thought in the world"—an implied canon, mostly literary, partly religious and philosophical, and neglectful of science and the fine arts: in effect, the range of the early-modern liberal arts curriculum.

[5] *Bentley's Miscellany*, 39 (1856), 96-110; Boening, 7, 400.

[6] *Spectator*, 28 (1835), 1138-40; Boening, 7, 398.

[7] The words are Jerome Buckley's in *Season of Youth: The Bildungsroman from Dickens to Golding* (Cambridge, Mass.: Harvard Univ. Press, 1974), p. 11. Goethe's own later views on the balance of general and particular development were evident in *Eckermann's Conversations with Goethe* (1836, 1848), trans. by John Oxenford in 1850; cited here in the Everyman's Library edition (London: J. M. Dent, 1930), p. 103 (entry of April 20, 1825): "It is justly said that the communal cultivation of all human powers is desirable and excellent. But the individual is not born for this; everyone must form himself as a particular being—seeking, however, to attain that general ideal of which all mankind are constituents."

[8] Cited here from G. H. Lewes, *The Life of Goethe*, 2nd ed. (London: Smith, Elder, 1864), p. 260.

[9] *Memoir of Goëthe [sic], written by himself*, 2 vols. (London: Henry Colburn, 1824); for the phrasing here: I, 205, 259, 324-25; II, 121.

[10] Available early in Sarah Austin's *Characteristics of Goethe. From the German of Falk, von Müller, &c.* (London: Effingham Wilson, 1833), I, 18.

[11] The last phrase is from R. H. Hutton's 1856 review of Lewes's *Life of Goethe*; cited here from Hutton's *Literary Essays* (London: Macmillan, 1888), p. 39. In 1872, Hutton spoke of Matthew Arnold's "calm egotism" as modeled on the "clear, self-contained, thoughtful, heroic egotism" of both Goethe and Wordsworth—though Hutton is not there exploring the paradoxes addressed in the present paper. See *Literary Essays*, pp. 312-13.

[12] Bruford, pp. 286-87.

[13] I give some of the evidence for this claim in my "The Future of Poetry: A Context for Carlyle and Arnold," in *Carlyle and His Contemporaries*, ed. John Clubbe (Durham: Duke Univ. Press, 1976), pp. 168-75.

[14] Raymond Williams discusses the passage (which occurs early in Ch. V of *On the Constitution of Church and State*) in Part I, Ch. 3 of *Culture and Society*. Another too "English" reading of the history of "culture" appears in John Burrell's introduction to Coleridge's book, Everyman's University Library (London: Dent, 1972). Humboldt is mentioned passing (p. xxix), but with no other "German" context.

[15]Bruford, "Goethe and Some Victorian Humanists," *Publications of the English Goethe Society*, NS 18 (1949), 65. William Rose, "Goethe's Reputation in England During His Lifetime," in *Essays on Goethe*, ed. William Rose (London: Cassell, 1949), p. 142.

[16]F. Norman, Henry Crabb Robinson and Goethe, *"Publication of the English Goethe Society*, NS 8 (1930-31), 115. And Bruford, in "Goethe's Reputation in England After His Death," in *Essays on Goethe*, ed. Rose, p. 188: "Carlyle's view [of Goethe] was generally accepted."

[17]Carlyle's works are cited, by volume and page numbers only, from the 30-vol. Centenary Edition (London: Chapman and Hall, 1896-99).

[18]*The Life of Schiller* (in book form 1825) is a kind of first attempt at developing the pattern; the effort is extended in the Schiller essay of 1831.

[19]The phrases I use are culled from the following: the Translator's Preface to the first edition of *Meister's Apprenticeship* (1824), the 1827 Preface to *German Romance*, "Goethe" (an essay of 1828), and three essays of 1832: "Goethe's Portrait," "Death of Goethe," and "Goethe's Works."

[20]Hutton's 1856 review (n. 11 above) draws together long-standing doubts about Carlyle's "arduous admiration," and seems to hint at some dissembling on Carlyle's part.

[21]For evidence late in his life, see Arthur Adrian. "Dean Stanley's Report of Conversations with Carlyle," *Victorian Studies*, I (1957), 74.

[22]*Two Note Books of Thomas Carlyle*, ed. Charles Eliot Norton (New York: Grolier Club, 1892), p. 158. The possibility is once cautiously advanced in public, early in Lecture III of *Heroes and Hero-Worship*, in a passage that begins with the unexceptionable notion that the Good and the Beautiful "cannot be disjoined": "a saying of Goethe's, which has staggered several, may have meaning: 'The Beautiful,' he intimates, 'is higher than the Good: the Beautiful includes in it the Good' "—"The *true* Beautiful," Carlyle hastily explains (V, 81-82).

[23]It seems not to have been noticed that the famous three-part process of *Sartor* (Everlasting No/Centre of Indifference/Everlasting Yea) recapitulates the spiritual sequence first worked out in the careers of Schiller and Goethe, but with a decisive move away from Art and aesthetic "culture" toward morality, action, and society. Such a perspective invites a rereading of the significance of *Sartor* (finished in 1831) as a correction of the "aesthetic" mode that Carlyle has uneasily essayed throughout the 1820s. In this view, *Sartor* would be both a culmination of Carlyle's transcendentalist phase and a set of clear signals of a shift in a new direction. By 1830, e.g., Carlyle felt, "I have now almost done with the Germans. . . . I must turn me to inquire *how* true they are." *Notebooks*, p. 150.

[24]See *Reminiscences*, ed. Charles Eliot Norton, Everyman's University Library (London: J. M. Dent, 1972) p. 306; and a letter of 1840 to Geraldine Jewsbury, in S. H. Nobbe, "Four Unpublished Letter of Thomas Carlyle," *PMLA*, 70 (1955), 879: Carlyle speaks defensively but candidly of "the godless old-Heathen world" of *Meister's Apprenticeship*.

[25]*English Traits* (1856), in *The Complete Works of Ralph Waldo Emerson*, ed. Edward Waldo Emerson, Concord Edition (Boston: Houghton, Mifflin, 1903), V, 274. Emerson adds provocatively: "[Carlyle] thinks . . . that old Goethe found this out, and, in his later writings, changed his tone. As soon as men begin to talk of art, architecture and antiquities, nothing good comes of it." Presumably this implies that the "reverence" Carlyle detects in the later Goethe 1) had little to do with "high art," and yet 2) provided elements that Carlyle *could* continue to draw on. But the harshly

deflationary tone of much of Carlyle's writing after 1831 makes such continuing influence highly suppositious.

[26]See n. 10 above; the phrases cited here are all Austin's own, from pp. xx-xxvi of her Preface.

[27]*Edinburgh Review*, 57 (1833); Boening, 7, 213; the reviewer was the dry but able Herman Merivale.

[28]*Autobiography and Literary Essays*, ed. John M. Robson and Jack Stillinger, vol. 1 of *Collected Works of John Stuart Mill* (Toronto: Univ. of Toronto Press, 1981), p. 147. Hereafter cited as *Works*, I.

[29]*The Early Letters of John Stuart Mill, 1812-1848*, ed. Francis E. Mineka, Vol. XII of *Collected Works* (Toronto: Univ. of Toronto Press, 1963), p. 129. Hereafter cited as *El*, XII.

[30]*Works*, I, 476-78. 1838 has "most"; later changed to "more."

[31]"Byron and Göthe," *Monthly Chronicle*, 4 (Sept. 1839), 242-54; rpt. in *Life and Writings of Joseph Mazzini* (London: Smith, Elder, 1870), VI, 61-94.

[32]*British and Foreign Review*, 14 (1843), 78-135; Boening, 7, 300-28.

[33]Of course Lewes's portrait may be seen as partly an enlargement and complication of the conflict between Heroism and Culture in Carlyle's then recent words in *Heroes and Hero-Worship* (1841) about Goethe: "a great heroic ancient man, speaking and keeping silence as an ancient Hero, in the guise of a most modern high-bred, high-cultivated Man of Letters" (V, 158). In effect, Lewes projects Carlyle's "courtier" hero under a new and more glaring light.

[34]Emerson's *Works*, IV, 368-69.

[35]"Thoughts on Modern Literature," *Dial*, 1 (October 1840), 151-57; cited here from rpt.: New York: Russell and Russell, 1961.

[36]David M. Robinson, "Margaret Fuller and the Transcendental Ethos: *Woman in the Nineteenth Century*," *PMLA*, 97 (January 1982), 83-93. I have gathered Fuller's views from the following: the Preface to her translation of *Conversations with Eckermann* (Boston: Hilliard, Gray, 1839), and three articles in the *Dial* (in rpt. ed.): "Menzel's View of Goethe," 1 (January 1841), 340-47; "Goethe," 2 (July 1841), 1-41; "Bettine Brentano and Günderode," 2 (January 1842), 313-56. Her paradoxical approach is nicely caught in a letter of 1833: "I don't like Goethe so well as Schiller now. That perfect wisdom and merciless nature seems cold. . . . " *Memoirs of Margaret Fuller Ossoli*, ed. R. W. Emerson, W. H. Channing, and J. F. Clarke (1884; rpt. New York: Burt Franklin, 1972), I, 117.

[37]On the extensive notice taken of Emerson in England, see William J. Sowder, *Emerson's Impact on the British Isles and Canada* (Charlottesville: University Press of Virginia, 1966).

[38]Self-culture and culture are the terms used by Sherman Paul in his introduction to Emerson's *Nature, Conduct of Life, and Other Essays*, Everyman's Library (London: J. M. Dent, 1963), p. x.

[39]Emerson's *Works*, IV, 284.

[40]The phrase in Maurice's in a letter to Kingsley in 1855: *The Life of Frederick Denison Maurice*, ed. Frederick Maurice, 2 vols. (London: Macmillan, 1884), II, 266. And see his letter of February 1851, also to Kingsley: II, 59.

[41]*London Quarterly Review*, 14 (1860), 109-48; Boening, 9, 537.

[42]For these phrases, see *Life of Goethe* (n. 8 above), p. 575.

[43]There is fascinating evidence that George Eliot did not share her husband's unbounded enthusiasm for Goethe. See, for example, J. W. Cross, *George Eliot's Life*, 3 vols. (Edinburgh and London: William Blackwood & Sons, n.d.), I, 252-53.

[44] *Edinburgh Review*, 106 (1857), 194-225; Boening 7, 482-98. Even stronger are the words in *Titan*, 24 (1857), 97-108; Boening, *3*, 527: "We are far from being idolators of Goethe. We consider the excessive worship of him by Carlyle and Lewis [sic] as, in the first, a mental, and in the second a moral, derangement."

Frame, Instance, Dialogue: Narrative Structures in the *Wanderjahre*

Alexander Gelley

Abstract

In relation to *Wilhelm Meisters Lehrjahre* (1796), the *Wanderjahre* (first version, 1821, revised and expanded version, 1829) represents a marked divergence from the model of a *Bildungsroman*, that is, a narrative focused on a single protagonist and utilizing encounters and illustrative tales to mark the stages of his development. In the *Wanderjahre* the frame story, with Wilhelm at its center, is of course still operative, but instead of the teleological progression of the earlier novel, we now have a series of episodes and interpolated texts whose relation to the main strand is by no means self-evident. The very status of the frame has been put into question by the fact that many of the stories occupy an intermediate position, both inside and outside. In calling attention to the hybrid structure of the *Wanderjahre* I do not intend to make a value judgment but to explore ways of identifying and analyzing its diverse generic and formal elements.

The function of a story as *exemplum*, as illustration or instance, becomes problematic in a work like the *Wanderjahre* where the principal narrative strand, what should be the authoritative level of meaning, is ambiguous or weakly articulated. But such a problematization itself gives rise to a different kind of thematic focus, one involving the production and dissemination of narratives rather than their truth value or ethical import. Here Walter Benjamin's discussion of the storyteller is pertinent. Further, Mikhail Bakhtin's concept of the dialogic novel, of the medley of styles and attitudes that constitute the fabric of a certain kind of prose fiction, will help us to consider some of the narratives in the *Wanderjahre* not so much in terms of their content—what the story is about—but of their modes of enunciation and transmission—how they are told, by whom, and for what purpose. (AG)

> Mit solchem Büchlein aber ist es wie mit dem Leben selbst: es findet sich in dem Komplex des Ganzen Notwendiges und Zufälliges, Vorgesetztes und Angeschlossenes, bald gelungen, bald vereitelt, wodurch es eine Art von Unendlichkeit erhält, die sich in verständige und vernünftige Worte nicht durchaus fassen noch einschliessen läßt[1]

More than once Goethe spoke of the symbolic method of his later work in terms of a multiperspectivism, of "contrastive and mutually reflective forms" designed to disclose a "more secret meaning" ("durcheinander gegenüber gestellte and sich gleichsam ineinander abspiegelnde Gebilde den geheimeren Sinn . . . zu offenbaren)."[2] In statements like these regarding the method of his later work Goethe projects an ideally suited instance of reception, an audience or readership capable of penetrating the complexities of this body of work. Of course, such remarks should not be taken too strictly in a poetological sense. They were oriented to a specific correspondent or interlocutor, and may have expressed also a wish that Goethe saw little likelihood of being realized in the German public of the last twenty years of his life. Nonetheless, the formulations I have cited represent a useful heuristic model for the kind of reading of the *Wanderjahre* that I propose.

Many interpreters have sought to specify the kind of adequate reader that Goethe occasionally evoked (e.g., in such formulations as "der echte Leser," "der Aufmerkende," and "[der] einsichtige[ ] Leser"),[3] and to make this the basis of a determinate interpretation of the work, usually in terms of some thematic or philosophic thesis. But I would suggest that Goethe does not so much project a model of total comprehension, of crystallized meaning (at the level of the signified), but rather a process of signification (at the level of signifiers) that the work in itself cannot altogether anticipate or circumscribe. "Jede Lösung eines Problems ist ein neues Problem," he remarked to the Kanzler v. Müller in connection with the *Wanderjahre*.[4] And in the passage already cited where he ascribed to the work "eine Art von Unendlichkeit," we may take this not necessarily as a kind of infinity but as a principle of seriality, of propagation and dispersal.

This, I trust, will help to situate my method in what follows. Instead of drawing on a type of interpretation based largely on themes or ideas, or even a kind of formal analysis based on accredited genre concepts (for example, of the novella), I have tried to adapt elements of a narrative pragmatics, utilizing principles of communications theory and of a reader-oriented aesthetics.

* * *

Near the beginning of the *Wanderjahre*, in Wilhelm's first letter to Natalie, he mentions the obligation of his journeymanship as determined by the Society of the Tower, including the requirement that he change his locale every three days. It appears at this point that we may expect a continuation of the pattern of the *Lehrjahre*, that is, a period of searching and testing in which the chance experiences of the journey will serve as instruments of formation. But the impulse to journey is not long sustained. In Wilhelm's first encounter with a member of the Society, Montan-Jarno, he asks to be relieved of this obligation since he wants to devote himself to learning a craft, and his request is eventually granted. In spite of its title, the *Wanderjahre* is not, like *Don Quixote* or *Tom Jones*, structured in terms of the hero's peregrination. The road with its potential for incidents and encounters does not serve as an integrating narrative device. As a recent interpreter of the novel puts it, "Die Absage an den romantischen Wander-Topos ist unüberhörbar."[5]

Alternatively, a unifying principle for the novel has been sought in Wilhelm's personal project of growth and self-realization. Thus H. M. Waidson argues, "the structural centre of the *Wanderjahre* lies in Wilhelm's decision to become a surgeon in order to place his new skill at the disposal of the community . . . ."[6] Certainly, this decision is enunciated early in the work and two narrative segments mark stages of the project—the story of the drowning of the fisher boy, which Wilhelm gives as the earliest motivation for his choice of a profession; and the account of his anatomical studies in Book III. The concluding incident of the novel shows Wilhelm treating his son Felix after the youth has lost consciousness through an accidental fall, and this is undoubtedly meant to demonstrate what Wilhelm has achieved since the tragic episode of the fisher boy, when he could only embrace the body of the drowned boy in impotent grief. But a link between these episodes does not yet give us a means of unifying the work as a whole. It is true that in reworking the *Wanderjahre* for the second and final version between 1821 and 1829 Goethe took pains to elaborate the frame story, thus significantly transforming what had been more a collection of tales in the Boccaccian sense than a novel.[7] The relations among Hersilie, Felix, and Wilhelm, on the one hand, and Wilhelm's choice and attainment of the surgeon's craft, on the other, represent the major elements in this elaboration of the frame action. But these two strands, separately or in combination, are still far from integrating the diverse segments and themes of the novel, whether the unity is sought at the level of the novellas and other interpolations or of the figure of Wilhelm. Such a judgment could, of course, only be substantiated by means of a detailed interpretation of the whole work. I can do no more here than indicate the general tendency of the argument through a discussion of the fisher boy story.

This incident stands out in the novel not only as the sole reminiscence on Wilhelm's part of his childhood, but also for the intensity of the recital (in a tone that recalls *Werther*) and the passionate nature of the experience itself. The reenactment of an overpowering childhood experience, the fused themes of friendship, erotic attraction, and death, the sense of proximity to a paradisic, preternatural state of being—all these give the episode a quality that is unique in the novel. "Unerwartet, in demselbigen Augenblick," Wilhelm writes, "ergriff mich das Vorgefühl von Freundschaft und Liebe" (p. 273).[8] And he goes on to underscore the direct link between this experience and the emotional and imaginative powers that will find an outlet in his theatrical career, "Das Bedürfnis nach Freundschaft und Liebe war aufgeregt, überall schaut' ich mich um, es zu befriedigen. Indessen ward Sinnlichkeit, Einbildungskraft and Geist durch das Theater übermässig beschäftigt . . . " (p. 279). In the aftermath of the catastrophe, Wilhelm writes, he heard of forms of rescucitation that might have helped in such a case and he resolved then to learn about them. The letter goes on to justify his decision to abandon the journeymanship and to apply himself to the study of surgery. Here, however, Wilhelm's application of the fisher boy story is far from doing justice to the quality of the episode itself as he had delineated it earlier. What was revealed there was a psyche in a formative stage, open to the influences of a primal natural environment and of a spontaneous, still undifferentiated erotic drive. The encounter with Adolf (the fisher boy) represented, as Wilhelm puts it, "jenes erste Aufblühen der Außenwelt," and he identifies this with "die eigentliche Originalnatur . . . , gegen die alles übrige, was uns nachher zu den Sinnen kommt, nur Kopien zu sein scheinen . . . " (p. 273 f.). In the later part of the letter, when he draws a lesson from the episode, Wilhelm stresses the relative and indeterminate nature of any single motive in shaping his future. He has distanced himself from the intense childhood experience and, writing in a much cooler tone, seems intent on assimilating that episode to the requirements of a rational life plan. The letter itself reflects a shift from the sphere of "eigentliche Originalnatur" to that of "Kopien." Karl Schlechta has argued that after the attachment to Mariane early in the *Lehrjahre*, Wilhelm falls increasingly under the sway of a petrifying, authoritarian spirit, a spirit typified by members of the Society of the Tower.[9] This leads to a progressive suppression of Wilhelm's affective and imaginative impulses. While I cannot altogether subscribe to this position, Schlechta's study represents a serious challenge to any overly positive or unproblematic view of Wilhelm's career. As my discussion of the one letter has tried to show, there are striking shifts in perspective, in voice, and in narrative form that make it difficult to view the action in terms of a linear, teleological pattern.[10]

The evolving, cumulative form of self-consciousness that is characteristic for the *Bildungsroman*, and that is to some degree present in the *Lehrjahre*, is markedly absent in the *Wanderjahre*. Let us briefly sketch this pattern by way of contrast. What is typical for the protagonist of a story of growth and formation is that his most significant acts involve not what he does in direct commerce with individuals and circumstances but what he comes to know through a retrospective interpretation of his acts. Greimas and Courtès have put forward a structural narrative model that tries to establish a common ground for action and for the attainment of knowledge by narrative agents, an approach that is most pertinent to our topic.[11] They posit first an elementary level, a "simple narrative," where "there is no distance between the events and the knowledge about the events," and then proceed to develop various forms of "cognitive action" that constitute a second degree of narrative. This level may take the form of an interpretive investment on the part of the protagonist, an investment that adds the new function of being a recipient (of knowledge) to that already operative of being the agent of action (or "the subject of doing," in their terminology). The protagonist realizes that actions undertaken for apparently self-evident motives must be revised in the light of his new stage of self-understanding. But the earlier, unreflective agent of action is not thereby simply eliminated and supplanted. Rather, the split in the subject is itself now thematized and this brings about a transformation of the narrative form. The shift is from a first level of narrative whose pivots are the acts of a unified protagonist, a single "subject of doing," to a second order of pivots (such as dissimulation, self-deception, recognition, peripeteia) which specify the mode of action of the "cognitive subject." In adapting this model I have sought to identify the principal elements of a *Bildung* narrative in structural rather than historical terms. The model proves to be perfectly congruent with an analysis that Goethe offered regarding the *Lehrjahre*. In it he speaks of the errors and false turnings that seem to pursue his protagonist during his life, and concludes, "Und doch ist es möglich, daß alle die falschen Schritte zu einem unschätzbaren Guten hinführen: eine Ahnung, die sich im 'Wilhelm Meister' immer mehr entfaltet, aufklärt und bestätigt, ja sich zuletzt mit klaren Worten ausspricht: 'Du kommst mir vor wie Saul, der Sohn Kis, der ausging seines Vaters Eselinnen zu suchen, und ein Königreich fand.'"[12]

But in the *Wanderjahre*, Wilhelm, though involved throughout the frame action and privy to all of the interpolated texts, rarely assumes the function of a cognitive subject in the sense just discussed. In the letter to Natalie that includes the fisher boy story Wilhelm, of course, serves as narrator. More often his part in the action is rendered by a third-person narrator, but this does not bring a greater focus on stages of growth and self-awareness. Thus the diverse forms of aesthetic experience evoked in the episodes of Saint Joseph the Second, the trip on Lago Maggiore, and the visit to the Artists' Province do not seem to affect Wilhelm in a cumulative manner. He takes in the system of instruction in the Artists' Province without giving the slightest indication that, only a little earlier when he was in the company of the painter on Lago Maggiore, he had been in contact with a conception of art that represented its very antithesis.[13] One could almost speak of a kind of amnesia on Wilhelm's part, or at least of a disinterestedness which makes him eminently adaptable to the various situations in which he finds himself but, correspondingly, leaves him relatively immune to being strongly affected by them.

We do not find in the *Wanderjahre* the kind of passionate self-scrutiny and projection of purpose as in the long letter to Werner in the *Lehrjahre*, where Wilhelm stated, "Daß ich Dir's mit *einem* Worte sage: mich selbst, ganz wie ich da bin, auszubilden, das war dunkel von Jugend auf mein Wunsch und meine Absicht."[14] What corresponds to this in the *Wanderjahre* is perhaps the parable of the rudder peg (*Ruderpflock*—see p. 268), though it projects a far more tenuous and indeterminate path. Though he is the nominal hero of the *Wanderjahre* Wilhelm does not provide the kind of unifying thread that we might expect from a general account of the frame story or from the antecedent patter of the *Lehrjahre*. Although the dispersal of personal identity is not so extreme in the *Wanderjahre* as in the second part of *Faust*, there is a marked loosening of structure in the second part of both works. Goethe's well-known characterization of Wilhelm as "armer Hund" was made in 1821 when he was just putting out the first version of the *Wanderjahre* and it seems more applicable to the Wilhelm of that work than of the *Lehrjahre*: "Wilhelm is freilich ein armer Hund, aber nur an solchen lassen sich das Wechselspiel des Lebens und die tausend verschiedenen Lebensaufgaben recht deutlich zeigen, nicht an schon abgeschlossenen festen Charakteren."[15] But while this remark supports us in not looking for a structuring principle for this novel at the level of character or psychology, it does not provide any indication of what to look for. We still need to find a way of converting "das Wechselspiel des Lebens und die tausend verschiedenen Lebensaufgaben," into a principle of narrative sequence and linkage, and for this we will do well to turn to a consideration of the narrative structure in its own right.

* * *

It is not easy to characterize the novellas in the *Wanderjahre* as a group. Most interpretations underline certain consolidating themes that tie them to one another and to the frame story.[16] But I would stress their open-ended, discontinuous features, their tendency to dispersal and fragmentation. Some break off unexpectedly. Some introduce new narrative strands that displace the original focus. Some cross over into the frame action in ways that leave one uncertain regarding the link between novella and frame. There are abrupt transformations in figures who appear in both a novella and in the frame action (for example, the Beautiful Widow). This is true too of figures who tell stories about themselves in which they appear very different than in the main strand (for example, Wilhelm, Odoard).

Telling a story about oneself rarely serves as a means of self-revelation (as in the fisher boy episode) but is more often a kind of strategy, a modus of behavior adapted to the given situation (for example, the burlesque romance that the Foolish Pilgrim sings as payment for her reception; the Barber's storytelling for the amusement of the company). We are not generally given finished life stories but images or episodes of a life in progress (for example, Leonardo, Makarie), and often the recital of such an episode itself contributes to the furtherance of a more general process whose outcome remains unarticulated. Leonardo's words at the beginning of "Das nußbraune Mädchen" have a more general application: "Ich darf Ihnen wohl vertrauen und erzählen, was eigentlich keine Geschichte ist" (p. 129). What he recounts is indeed not a unified narrative but the inaugural episode of a circuitous search involving mistaken identity, diversionary materials, and breaks in the manuscript.

The search is for a woman who herself undergoes a series of transformations, from the intense, passionately pleading child who first arrests Leonardo's attention to the shadowy, recessive figure dubbed "die Gute-Schöne." (This kind of fading from a proper name to an epithet says much about the conception of character in this novel.) Her eventual union with Leonardo is evoked but left unresolved and she is left in the end in the role of Makarie's assistant. Everything about her—the multiple names and epithets, the indeterminate fate—confirms Leonardo's impression of her as "die Ersehnte," (p. 416) the wished-for but never altogether palpable goal of his quest.

The *Wanderjahre* is composed of an assemblage of text forms that represent a great variety of language uses, and these uses or pragmatic functions cannot be readily reconciled to one another or made to depend on a single, authoritative narrative principle. To be attentive to the pragmatic dimension of a text means that we attempt to situate it in terms of its intended application, that we discern in its very form a directive or mode of transformation that implicates all the instances of a communicative process. Of course, the question of the application of a text, of its pragmatic dimension, is one that may be posed for all types of texts, fictive or non-fictive, narrative or nonnarrative. And we cannot overlook that the structure of the *Wanderjahre* is perplexing in part because it includes a great heterogeneity of textual forms—novellas, letters, monologues, collections of maxims, scientific discussions, aesthetic speculations, accounts of dreams, data regarding techniques and crafts, pedagogic theory, etc.[17] All these forms are, of course, to some extent modalized by their inclusion in the novel, and yet they may still be analyzed by means of pragmatic models appropriate to each of them.

Walter Benjamin sought to define the pragmatic dimension of storytelling—"die Kunst des Erzählens"—by underscoring its usefulness—"ihren Nutzen"—its tendency to convey what we would term home truths, words of wisdom—"Rat," "Weisheit."[18] What is basic to the traditional story in his sense is that it draws on a stock of communal experience—"Erfahrung"—and is thus capable of fashioning exemplary cases, that is, such as replenish and extend a communally accredited image of man. Benjamin's argument is designed to set off the traditional, orally-based story from one of its modern derivatives, namely, the novel, which is deprived of an exemplifying function through the solitude, the infertile inwardness of its protagonist. "Die Geburtskammer des Romans," he writes, "ist das Individuum in seiner Einsamkeit, das sich über seine wichtigsten Anliegen nicht mehr exemplarisch auszusprechen vermag, selbst unberaten ist und keinen Rat geben kann." The exemplary function that Benjamin assigns to the story, and which differentiates it from the novel in the modern sense, can help us to identify the *Wanderjahre* as a hybrid form occupying an intermediate place between *Novellenkranz* and novel.

The storyteller, Benjamin writes, "weiß Rat—nicht wie das Sprichwort: für manche Fälle, sondern wie der Weise: für viele." When Benjamin speaks of "Rat" as one of the effects of storytelling, he allows for a transformation of the exemplary function of narrative (in the traditional sense, the story as an illustration of proverb or maxim) into a more fluid principle of form. The level of proverbs, the explicit condensation of wisdom and good counsel, is obviously very important in the *Wanderjahre*, but we cannot always assume that the "truths" enunciated in this form are intended as propositional statements. There are in fact so many "truths" strewn through the multiple, interrelated stories that they contravene any fixed application. The overdetermination of the level of wisdom and good counsel becomes veritably dizzying if we include the extranarrative collections of aphorisms and notations, "Betrachtungen im Sinne der Wanderer" and "Aus Makariens Archiv." Within the narrative proper a saying often stands in an oblique relation to the action and may be enunciated primarily in order to be tested.

The clearest case involves the Uncle whose estate Wilhelm and Felix visit early in the book. This typical Enlightenment figure is in the habit of affixing maxims on the gates and entryways of his estate, a penchant that is wittily subverted by his niece, Hersilie. During a conversation between Wilhelm and the two sisters, Hersilie and Juliette, Wilhelm notices one of the maxims that the Uncle has had posted in the garden, "Vom Nützlichen durchs Wahre zum Schönen" (p. 65). And although we are told that Wilhelm undertakes to interpret it "in his manner" (which must be appropriately moralistic since it gains the approbation of the gentle Juliette), Goethe does not actually give us this interpretation but a much less orthodox view offered by Hersilie, an explicitly feminine exegesis:

Wir Frauen sind in einem besondern Zustande. Die Maximen der Männer hören wir immerfort wiederholen, ja wir müssen sie in goldnen Buchstaben über unsern Häupten sehen, und doch wüßten wir Mädchen im Stillen das Umgekehrte zu sagen, das auch gölte, wie es gerade hier der Fall ist. Die *Schöne* findet Verehrer, auch Freier, und endlich wohl gar einen Mann; dann gelangt sie zum

Wahren, das nicht immer höchst erfreulich sein mag, und wenn sie klug ist, widmet sie sich dem *Nützlichen*, sorgt für Haus and Kinder and verharrt dabei. (p. 66)

A feminine exegesis, as I have said, and at a number of levels: First, in that Hersilie takes a general rule, supposedly operative at a universal level, and demonstrates its specific applicability for a subclass of the social body, for a minority not usually taken account of in the principles of the Enlightenment. And then feminine also in the rhetorical sense—in the supple, ingratiating, yet basically subversive manner in which the language of authority is turned against itself.

Benjamin's study suggests that the "moral" of a story, its pragmatic point, may be understood not only as an effect of summation and closure but also as a kind of propagating energy that connects the single tale with a larger narrative current. This may take two forms. One involves the principle of linkage among stories, the network of what he terms narrative remembrance ("Gedächtnis") or "das Netz, welches alle Geschichten miteinander am Ende Bilden." And he goes on, "Eine schließt an die andere an, wie es die großen Erzähler immer und vor allem die orientalischen gern gezeigt haben. In jedem derselben lebt eine Scheherazade, der zu jeder Stelle ihrer Geschichten eine neue Geschichte einfällt." The other form this energy takes involves the formation of a body of auditors, "die Gemeinschaft der Lauschenden," a communality specifically constituted by its receptivity to the story. Here too Benjamin utilizes an image from textile manufacture. The art of telling stories, he writes, "verliert sich, weil nicht mehr gewebt und gesponnen wird, während man ihnen lauscht. Je selbstvergessener der Lauschende, desto tiefer prägt sich ihm das Gehörte ein. Wo ihn der Rhythmus der Arbeit ergriffen hat, da lauscht er den Geschichten auf solche Weise, daß ihm die Gabe, sie zu erzählen, von selber zufällt. So also ist das Netz beschaffen, in das die Gabe zu erzählen gebettet ist."

The association of spinning and weaving with the formation of stories is, of course, an ancient one—its mythological prototype is the three Fates. In the *Wanderjahre* we find more than one variant of this theme. In the case of the Beautiful Widow (in "Der Mann von Fünfzig Jahren") it is adapted to the luxurious world of an eighteenth-century salon. The Widow, in connection with an elaborately embroidered portfolio she has made, speaks of her handiwork in these terms: "Als junge Mädchen werden wir gewöhnt, mit den Fingern zu tifteln und mit den Gedanken umherzuschweifen; beides bleibt uns, indem wir nach und nach die schwersten und zierlichsten Arbeiten verfertigen lernen . . . " (p. 189). The musing, uncommitted play of fancy expressed here suggest a Penelope function, the weaving of an endless tapestry, perhaps a metaphor for a protonarrative source from which every story is derived and to which it refers through some loose ends, some trace of its connection to other stories, to all stories.

By drawing on Benjamin's analysis we have been able to relate certain formal elements of narrative to a communal practice that brings into play the circuit of narrative transmission. "So haftet an der Erzählung," Benjamin writes, "die Spur des Erzählenden wie die Spur der Topferhand an der Tonschale." Now this foreign element in the tale, the trace of its origin, of who made it and for what purpose, should be projected forward as well, toward the recipient. When this is done we have all of the constituents of narrative structure in a pragmatic sense—the telling, the listening, the passing on.

*   *   *

Recent theoretical work has shown that the narrating process is itself a modus of action within narrative forms, perhaps the most basic and pervasive of all. Far from placing it outside the form, as a kind of source or cause, critics have begun to demonstrate how this process (the "discours du récit," as the French structural critics term it) is perfectly assimilable to those signifying elements that have generally been considered the primary content or subject matter of narrative, such as action, character, or description. Since, in the *Wanderjahre*, the narrating instance is distributed among many figures, the circuit of narrative transmission[19] is complex and exceptionally significant for the work's structure. The novel includes, as I have already indicated, a great multiplicity of text forms, and not only does each one involve its distinct mode of enunciation, transmission, and reception, but their copresence within the same narrative further complicates the communicative circuit. This explains why I have been led to focus on the pragmatic dimension of the text—on the modes of transmission rather than on some definitive message.

Mikhail Bakhtin's work allows us to extend the notion of a narrative pragmatics by offering a model of dialogue or intertextuality designed specifically to account for the heterogeneous materials that enter into the structure of the novel. Of the various terms that

Bakhtin utilizes, "heteroglossia" is perhaps the most suggestive for the medley of styles and attitudes that make up the fabric of prose fiction. In Bakhtin's view the multiplicity of discursive modes that make up a text are not simply citations or remnants of antecedent speech forms, as Barthes interprets them in the context of his "referential, endoxal" code.[20] Rather, Bakhtin underscores a dynamic interplay, a collision of singular, though not necessarily personal, "voices," and through the conjunction which the novel brings about a new form of meaning emerges, an authentic signifying operation. The dialogic novel, as he conceives it, has the capacity of assimilating these heterogeneous elements but without altogether normalizing them. They retain to some degree the force of their various origins. Furthermore, Bakhtin makes us particularly attentive to the specific stance, the intentional vector, one may say, encoded in every statement, the very quality that makes it a voice in an active dialogue. But to call it a voice does not mean to make it dependent on a character. The polyphony of voices derives from a prepersonal discourse level which frequently but not invariably utilizes anthropomorphic agents as instances of enunciation. The speech of characters in a novel represents a secondary operation and it presupposes a repertoire of registers, what has been termed "normative genres of discourse,"[21] whose ultimate basis is social and cultural.

What is especially relevant for us in Bakhtin's notion of dialogue is that every word, or speech segment, is to be taken not as an invariant unit of meaning but as enunciatory act, an act which betrays the pressure of other speech acts. "The word is not a thing," he writes, "but rather the eternally mobile, eternally changing medium of dialogical intercourse. It never coincides with a single consciousness or a single voice. The life of the word is in its transferral from one mouth to another, one context to another, one social collective to another, and one generation to another. In the process the word does not forget where it has been and can never wholly free itself from the dominion of the contexts of which it has been a part."[22]

Bakhtin's categories refer to different levels of the narrative process in ways that he himself did not fully indicate, thus any effort to apply his ideas to a work involves certain interpretive choices regarding the theory. I would suggest three ways in which the *Wanderjahre* exemplifies a dialogic practice: first, in destabilizing genre forms; then, in orienting representational devices toward the instance of reception; and finally, in thematizing the channels of communication as such.

Let us first examine heteroglossia at the level of genre, as a loosening of, a playing with a given generic formula. The pattern that Goethe had available in constructing the stories for the *Wanderjahre* was that of the Renaissance novella, a form in which exemplarity and entertainment, moral point and witty pointe, are subtly interwoven. As a background to this form we may take, as Karlheinz Stierle has argued,[23] the medieval fable, where the narrative sequence is unequivocally oriented toward an apothegm or maxim, a *sententia*. Conversely, this moral point may be viewed as the kernel that gives rise to a narrative expansion. Now in various Renaissance forms the expansion went well beyond the limits implicit in the didactic or moralistic kernel, without, however, altogether obliterating the initial pragmatic orientation. What is noteworthy about the Boccaccian novella, Stierle argues, is the way that the exemplum, the illustrative narrative, wins a certain autonomy, establishing an oblique relation to the pragmatic context on which it is based. The exemplum is overdetermined; its applicability in moral or social terms is no longer self-evident though the field of that applicability remains as a point of reference. The problematization of the exemplum in the novella may be viewed not only in terms of the narrative form (at the level of the sender) but also of the intended audience (or receptor). In fact, it is often the frame structure that makes this feature most explicit. "The new mode of representation of the novella," Stierle writes with respect to Boccaccio, "is thematized as a function of the self-understanding of the kind of society that is delineated in the frame."

One could find numerous instances in the *Wanderjahre* where the exemplifying function typical of the novella form is put into question, instances both at the level of the stories (as in "Die gefährliche Wette," where a farce takes an unexpected tragic turning) and of the frame (as in various episodes where there is a disequilibrium between what we know of the speaker and what he recounts about himself—for example, the case of Wilhelm already discussed, or Odoard recounting "Nicht zu weit"). In a pioneering study Ernst Friedrich von Monroy showed that many of the novellas displace the basic narrative pattern by introducing contrastive devices characteristic of other literary forms, such as legend, comic drama, or fairy tale.[24]

A second way of approaching the dialogic mode in the *Wanderjahre* is to note the frequency of speech forms, whether in monologue or dialogue, that are markedly oriented toward their reception. This might be viewed as a thematization of the dialogic by means of dramatic or theatrical devices. In such utterances the intention to affect or influence the auditor is clearly exhibited by way of manner and gesture. But there is also in the substance of the enunciation a strategy aimed at forestalling and modifying the anticipated response. Bakhtin speaks of the "alien words" which inhabit all our utterances and which we, consciously or not, take account of in all communicative acts. This alien word, he writes, is "in the consciousness of the listener, of his apperceptive background, pregnant with responses and objections. And every utterance is oriented toward this apperceptive background of understanding, which is not a linguistic background but rather one composed of specific objects and emotional expressions."[25]

A number of episodes in the *Wanderjahre* hinge not on what is directly stated in a speech or dialogue, but rather on a strategy oriented to the act of reception. This is patent in instances where a speaker directly manipulates an interlocutor, as in the Foolish Pilgrim's half-veiled, deceiving intimations to Herr von Revanne and to his son that she has become pregnant through the other. But it is operative too in less overt instances where we become attentive less to the motives of the speaker than to the effects of the speaking—thus, in the Foolish Pilgrim's ballad, in Nachodine's plea to Leonardo, in Lucidor's monologues in "Wer ist der Verräter?" (whose plot turns on their being overheard), in the echo effects of the poems which Flavio and Hilarie exchange, not to mention the *Wechselgedichte* which they read together and which serve to kindle their love. Of course, each of these instances viewed in the context of its episode fulfils a traditional pattern of dramatized representation. But, through its repeated, cumulative use in the novel, this kind of strategic address in monologue and dialogue must be accounted a basic structuring principle, subverting the authority of a single narrative persona and shaping the reception of the work as a whole.

Finally, I see the dialogic principle operative in the *Wanderjahre* in a recurrent focus on the communicative channel as such, or rather on the interferences or blockages that impede the full circulation of narrative information. An important recent study of the novel is entitled *Wilhelm Meisters Wanderjahre oder, die Kunst des Mittelbaren; Studien zum Problem der Verständigung in Goethes Altersepoche.*[26] In it Manfred Karnick deals with what may be termed Goethe's communicative reticence, and he offers some excellent analyses of its implications for the mode of indirect and symbolic presentation characteristic of the *Wanderjahre*. What for him, however, are privative categories at a biographical, existential level—such as secrecy and hiddenness ("Verschlossenheit")—I would take more as strategic choices which open up new possibilities of form. I can only sketch what I have in mind by touching on the role of Hersilie in the action.

Hersilie provides her own character, and that of her household, in a consciously parodistic listing of the cast of characters that Wilhelm meets on the Uncle's estate: "ein wunderlicher Oheim, eine sanfte und eine muntere Nichte, eine kluge Tante, Hausgenossen nach bekannter Art . . . " (p. 68). She, of course is the "muntere Nichte." Her first letter to her aunt Makarie opens with a complaint that strikes us as singular when we consider the highly disciplined, well-neigh ritualistic pattern of intercourse practiced in her house. "Ich will und muß sehr kurz sein, liebe Tante," Hersilie writes, "denn der Bote zeigt sich unartig ungeduldig" (p. 75). How could a messenger from Makarie's household be so impertinent? Later in the letter she writes, "Der Bote! der Bote! Ziehen Sie Ihre alten Leute besser, oder schicken sie junge. Diesem ist weder mit Schmeichelei noch mit Wein beizukommen" (p. 76). We never hear again about this annoying courier. Now if we attempt to assign him a function in the action we hardly know what to do with him. He is a kind of noise, an intrusive, unassimilable element in the communicative circuit. But the insistent, thrice-reiterated reference to the messenger—"Der Bote! der verwünschte Bote!"—foregrounds a meta-narrative function that we cannot altogether ignore.

Later in the novel a young courier does in fact appear. This one bears a message ("eine Botschaft") from Felix, who at this point is in school in the Pedagogic Province. The whole episode is recounted by Hersilie in a letter to Wilhelm. (It's worth noting that her sole entry into the novel after her initial appearance at the Uncle's estate is by way of a series of letters which she addresses to Wilhelm, though we never learn that he replies to any of them.) What is it that the courier brings from Felix? A slate school tablet with the rudimentary inscription,

> Felix
> liebt
> Herselien.
> Der Stallmeister
> kommt bald. [p. 265]

Herselie is perturbed, baffled, uncertain how to reply. In the end the young itinerant merchant gives her a similar tablet on which she traces a response, a slightly askew mirroring of Felix's words designed both to satisfy him and to show her good-humored reception of his message,

Hersiliens
Gruß
an Felix.
Der Stallmeister
halte sich gut.

Goethe here undoubtedly alludes to far more exalted instances of a courtship carried on by an exchange of verse where each partner echoes the other—there is his own cycle, the *West-östliche Divan*, and in this novel there is the exchange of poems between Flavio and Hilarie already mentioned. The exchange of messages on slate tablets between Hersilie and Felix appears to be a kind of parody of such a courtship.[27]

It serves, though, to introduce another courier figure, another passing intermediary—gypsy or Jew, perhaps, "etwas Orientalisches," is how Hersilie characterizes him. Typically, he is gone before she can get a clear image of him, and she muses, "Allerdings etwas Geheimnisvolles war in der Figur; dergleichen sind jetzt im Roman nicht zu entbehren, sollten sie uns denn auch im Leben begegnen? Angenehm, doch verdächtig, fremdartig, doch Vertrauen erregend; warum schied er auch vor aufgelöster Verwirrung? warum hatt' ich nicht Gegenwart des Geistes genug, um ihn schicklicherweise festzuhalten?" (p. 267).

Hersilie and the elusive courier—here is a motif that does not fill out into a story. It is a narrative kernel of indefinite mass. Hersilie, of course, is a figure who tries to resist typification. She knows the stereotypes of fiction all too well. Her own story, her attachment to Felix or to his father, never quite gets off the ground. She is the guardian of the mysterious little box that Felix had found, but she never gets to see what's in it, even when the key is finally restored to her. Her plea to Wilhelm regarding this box—"daß es ein Ende werde, wenigsten daß eine Deutung vorgehe, was damit gemeint sei, mit diesem wunderbaren Finden, Wiederfinden, Trennen und Vereinigen," (p. 378)—remains unanswered. If Makarie is the repository of everyone's secrets, the wise counselor, the secular mystic, what is Hersilie, who can't decide between father and son, whose letters go unanswered, who remains in posession of a mysterious box that she can't or won't open?

There seems to be a function in the communicative channel that facilitates narrative without being altogether part of it. We hardly have a name for it. Its agents have no great dignity in the roster of narrative roles. Perhaps we touch here on an emergent stage of the narrative impulse, one not yet fully conscious of itself, not yet informed by a narrative subject. If so, Hersilie names it since she is akin to it—"Der Bote! der verwünschte Bote!"

University of California, Irvine

Notes

[1]To Johann Friedrich Rochlitz, November 23, 1829. Cited in the edition of the *Wanderjahre* in *Goethes Werke*, Hamburger Ausgabe, ed. Erich Trunz (Hamburg: Christian Wegner Verlag, 1950) VIII, 578. Hereafter cited *GW.*

[2]To Iken, September 23, 1827. Cited in *GW*, III, 448.

[3]"Der echte Leser," *GW*, VIII, 575; "der Aufmerkende," *GW*, III 448; "Dem einsichtigen Leser," *GW*, VIII, 578.

[4]June 8, 1821. Cited in *GW*, VIII, 574.

[5]Heidi Gidion, *Zur Darstellungsweise von Goethes 'Wilhelm Meisters Wanderjahre'* (Göttingen: Vandenhoeck u. Ruprecht, 1969 [Palaestra, Bd. 256]), 27 f.

[6]"Death by Water: or, The Childhood of Wilhelm Meister," *Modern Language Review*, 56 (1961), 44-53; this passage p. 50.

[7]Cf. Hans Reiss, "'Wilhelm Meisters Wanderjahre'—Der Weg von der ersten zur zweiten Fassung," *D.V.L.G.*, 39 (1965), 34-57.

[8]All page numbers in the text from *GW*, VIII.

[9]Karl Schlechta, *Goethes Wilhelm Meister* (Frankfurt a.M.: V. Klostermann, 1953). Cf. Arthur Henkel's review, *G.R.M.*, 36 (1955), N.F. 5, 85-89.

[10]The overwhelming tendency of modern interpreters to understand the Wilhelm Meister novels in this progressive manner can be traced back at least to Max Wundt's *Goethes Wilhelm Meister und die Entwicklung des modernen Lebensideal* (Berlin and Lepzig: G. J. Göschen, 1913). But recent studies like those by Gidion (see note 5 above), Karnick (see note 26 below), Heinz Schlaffer ("Exoterik and Esoterik in Goethes Romanen," *Goethe Jahrbuch*, 95 [1978], 212-226), and Hans Vaget ("Recurrent Themes and Narrative Strategies in Goethe's Novels," a paper delivered at the Irvine Goethe Symposium, April 8, 1982, forthcoming in proceedings of the Symposium, Walter de Gruyter, Berlin) have moved in an opposite direction. Schlechta, in spite of the extreme thesis he maintains, can be viewed as their pioneer.

[11]A. J. Greimas and J. Courtès, "The Cognitive Dimension of Narrative Discourse," *New Literary History*, 7 (1975-76), 433-47.

[12]From *Tag-und Jahreshefte*. Cited in *GW*, VIII, 519.

[13]Cf. Gidion, p. 30.

[14]GW, VII, 290.

[15]In conversation to Kanzler v. Müller, January 22, 1821. Cited *GW*, VIII, 519.

[16]One of the most discerning studies in this vein is Arthur Henkel, *Entsagung, Eine Studie zu Goethes Altersroman* (Tübingen: Max Niemeyer, 1954 [Hermaea, Bd. *3*]).

[17]Hans Reiss's comparison of the style of the two versions of the *Wanderjahre* is illuminating. In contrast to the relative homogeneity of the first he lists some of the new stylistic registers of the second: "In der zweiten Fassung aber gibt es jene intensivierte Dichte der Makarie-Kapitel, wo wissenschaftliche Sprache und Darstellung in einer wohl höchsten Steigerung der Goetheschen Erzähler-Prosa verbunden

sind. Es gibt außerdem noch eine an der Sturm und Drang erinnernde Sprache, in der Flavios leidenschaftliche Erregung geschildert wird;... Außerdem gibt es noch den lakonisch abrupt konzentrierten Stil des zusammenfassenden Berichts, welcher, ähnlich wie in Goethes *Annalen* viele Ereignisse zusammenrafft und knapp angibt. Schließlich noch die prägnante Form der Sprüche und die symbolische Ausdrucksform der beiden weltanschaulichen Gedichte." op. cit., p. 56 f.

[18]"Der Erzähler," in *Gesammelte Schriften*, II, 2.

[19]I adapt this notion from an analysis by Jean-François Lyotard that develops certain issues of the tradition of storytelling in a manner similar to Benjamin's essay. Lyotard suggests that one way a culture stores and transmits its customs and wisdom ("savoir") is through its techniques of narrative construction. "A generally acknowledged property of traditional knowledge," he writes, "is that the narrative positions or stances (sender, receptor, hero) are so distributed that the right to occupy that of the sender is based on the double condition of having occupied that of the receiver and of having been, by virtue of his name, already the object of a narrative, that is, placed in the position of a diegetic referent of other narrative occurrences." *La Condition post-moderne* (Paris: Editions of Minuit, 1979), p. 40. My translation.

[20]See *S/Z—An Essay*.

[21]John Frowe, "Voice and Register in *Little Dorrit*," *Comparative Literature*, 33 (1981), 263.

[22]M.M. Bakhtin, *Problems of Dostoevsky's Poetics* (Ann Arbor: Ardis, 1973), p. 167.

[23]"Geschichte als Exemplum—Exemplum als Geschichte—Zur Pragmatik und Poetik narrativer Texte," in *Text als Handlung* (Munich: W. Fink, 1975), pp. 14-48.

[24]"Zur Form der Novelle in 'Wilhelm Meisters Wanderjahre,'" *G.R.M.*, 31(1943), 1-19.

[25]M.M. Bakhtin, *The Dialogic Imagination—Four Essays*, ed. Michael Holquist (Austin: University of Texas Press, 1981), p. 281. I have already spoken in connection with Benjamin and Lyotard of the ways that the context of reception is constitutive for the form of a narrative. For Bakhtin too a narrative event cannot be established in abstract terms, as part of some self-contained logic of narrative. There is an "evaluative function" encoded in the telling without which there would be no story. (I cite this phrase from the stimulating article by Rolf Kloepfer, "Dynamic Structures in Narrative Literature—'The Dialogic Principle.'" *Poetics Today*, [1979-80], 118.)

[26]Manfred Karnick, *Wilhelm Meisters Wanderjahre oder, die Kunst des Mittelbaren; Studien zum Problem der Verständigung in Goethes Altersepoche* (Munich: W. Fink, 1968).

[27]I note two recent essays focusing on the figure of Hersilie, though neither parallels my discussion: Marianne Jabs-Kriegsmann, "Felix und Hersilie," in *Studien zu Goethes Alterswerken*, ed. Erich Trunz (Frankfurt a. M.: Athenäum-Verlag, 1971); Françoise Derré, "Die Beziehung zwischen Felix, Hersilie and Wilhelm in 'Wilhelm Meisters Wanderjahre,'" *Goethe Jahrbuch*, 94(1977), 38-48.

Goethe's Theory of Literature

Victor Lange

Abstract

Literary scholars have often maintained that Goethe avoided specific and unequivocal poetological definitions and, where these are offered, he remained strictly within the given conventions of his time. The predilection of nineteenth century readers, historians and critics for poetic pathos rather than reflections has reinforced this view.

It is true that Goethe's place within the tradition of eighteenth century aesthetic theory determines the general tenor of his judgments of poetry and criticism. As he remains committed to a unitary or monistic philosophy which is differentiated by his scientific convictions, Goethe maintains, historically, a position midway between normative and post-normative poetics.

Two sets of criteria may help to define the character of Goethe's notions of literary judgment: one concerns the relationship of the writer (and his essential instability) to a world of presumed coherence, patterned order and "meaning," comprehensible in the terms of Goethe's philosophy of nature. An understanding of Goethe's conception of language leads to the second category, that, generally speaking, of "reading." This concerns the quality of poetic perception, the functioning of poetic devices, the individual and collective effect of poetry and the role, ultimately, of poetry as an experiential and cognitive tool.

Both sets of criteria lead to the issue of Goethe's view of "time" (history and mortality) and of the feasibility of transcending discontinuity in writing. (VL)

We have in recent years become accustomed to speak of theories of literature as systematic approaches not so much to an understanding of a given literary document as to an analytical view of how literature operates. We have been urged to define the features and impulses that give to a text its "literary" character, to determine what it is that literature requires of its readers, or presupposes of their participation, and how literature can or should be related to the larger philosophical issues, to theories of knowledge or understanding, to linguistic, semiological or hermeneutical enquiry. Indeed, a powerful phalanx of literary theorists have disavowed *interpretation* altogether as the central purpose of dealing with a text; it has rejected the commitments to the autonomy of the literary artefact, its potential authority as to its goals and means.

It would take me too far afield to do more than suggest the directions in which the doubts in the efficacy of "interpretation" and the interest in de-stabilizing the literary work of art and its innocent reading has proceeded. Jonathan Culler has, in his *The Pursuit of Signs* (1981) given a useful account of some of these efforts and has identified the codes and assumptions that subordinate works of literature to a dynamic pluralism of meaning. Others have thought of the canon of literature as a succession of misreadings, as a history of constant deformation of predecessors, and of an inevitable, perhaps fruitful misconstruing of texts. Derrida, to name only the most resolute, has deliberately rejected any presumed integrity of the text, any binding unity of purpose, of theme or form. What he has instead urged is a "description of the general processes through which texts undo the philosophical system to which they adhere by revealing its rhetorical nature."[1]

If we accept these central tenets of much contemporary criticism we are bound to find ourselves in a climate of opinion and in a topography of judgment that is far removed from that of the late eighteenth century and from the critical convictions of one of its most articulate figures, from Goethe's theory of literature.

For anyone familiar with the remarkable body of Goethe's poetry, his fiction, his plays, it must seem inappropriate to use the term "theory" of literature in relation to the work of a man of letters whose mode of writing, whose view of the literary process, indeed, whose explicit notion of the interplay of theory and practice in his scientific as well as his poetic work, tends to subordinate theory as incidental to the creative performance.

It is not surprising that the academic assessment of his critical work has ranged from impatient dismissal to unqualified admiration: George Saintsbury, one of the most interesting surveyors of theoretical positions, roundly declares in his *History of Criticism* (1899), that the notion of Goethe's originality as a critic is a "stale superstition"; Ste. Beuve, on the other hand, who—unlike Saintsbury—had actually read Goethe's writings on art and literature, revered him (in 1858) as "the greatest of all critics."[2] René Wellek describes Goethe's literary views as derivative on the one hand, and blurred by a lack of precision in concepts and terminology, as superimposing the organistic convictions that sustain Goethe's studies in natural history upon a differently motivated aesthetic practice.[3]

I suspect that both views, the negative and the positive, are in some measure justified: Goethe was by no means an original critic, nor one of preeminently technical interests such as Dryden or Friedrich Schlegel. His critical efforts almost invariably are the result, and not the premise, of his work as a poet, and nothing is therefore less rewarding than to make a reading of his poetry or his plays dependent upon his incidental, and almost entirely occasional, criticism. Just as his poetry is, in the sense of the eighteenth century—not that of the Renaissance or the Baroque—the product of specific incidents, of occasions that brought his imagination and his desire for cognitive scrutiny into play, so must his criticism be tested and understood as an (usually defensive) articulation of concrete challenges. From his early expressions of distaste for doctrinaire poetics to the later thoughts on the relationship between observation and speculation, Goethe himself never failed to stress the primary importance of practice over theory. It would be easy to assemble a long list of considered statements in which he argues that "all theorizing suggests a lack, or a stoppage, of productive energy,"[4] or, more bluntly, that "the fact itself implies a theory."[5] "Theories," he thought, "are usually the product of a hasty, impatient mind, who is eager to get rid of a particular phenomenon and in its place to put images, concepts, or merely words."[6]

This stubborn notion of a theory of art as a grammar of only limited usefulness is, of course, not merely a Goethean whim but the conviction of an age, the late eighteenth century, which was inclined, more and more categorically, to reject the *normative* implications of all theories of judgment or of conduct which the previous generation had produced in such profusion. He considered one of his distinguished older contemporaries the greatest master of technical perfection as well as an exemplary critic: of Klopstock he said in a letter of June 1774 that one of his works, curiously entitled *The Republic of Learning*, had poured fresh blood into his veins and that it contained "the only poetics of any age or nation, the only kind of rules that are admissible."[7]

Goethe's early distaste for what seemed to him the atrophied rules of classicist poetics remained alive throughout the more sophisticated and differentiated aesthetic thinking of his later years, though the recognition of the great classical models and their living presence became the premise of his subsequent views of art and literature. His ample reflections on poetry, on sculpture and painting, (this we should keep in mind), were not, at any rate, intended to form a coherent system of aesthetic principles, a system resting upon logical propositions such as Kant's or Schiller's or Hegel's. Like his poetry itself, like his fiction or his studies of natural history, his critical pronouncements were corollaries of a mind of increasing, even compulsive, productivity. He liked to conceal the calculated interplay in his writing of spontaneity and analytical discipline by suggesting, half mockingly, that creativity is the signature of genius and that even his most complex pieces were the product of something like a somnambulist state. In 1806 one of his close collaborators reports his statement that, while he may have thought a good ideal about the principles that guide the sculptor or painter, he had never seriously or systematically thought about the theory of poetry: of all his literary works, none had come about as the result of clear thinking of how it should be put together; without much reasoning, he had been guided by feeling and an instinctive assurance that he was doing the right thing.[8]

Nevertheless, critical reflection, this we cannot doubt, was at all times part of Goethe's exuberant efforts at clarifying, in aesthetic or scientific terms, the place and function of a questioning mind within a universe of fundamentally intelligible coherence. It is this large assumption of a comprehensible universe—which the writer inhabits and which it is his task to illuminate—that determines the main impulses of Goethe's practice, as well as his general view of literature. Literature has for him an eminently cognitive purpose within a unified, cohesive and resonant totality of life. We would do well to recognize that such a conception, however carefully argued, is far removed from our own, and that any effort at deriving exemplary relevance from Goethe's critical system may well present nearly insurmountable difficulties.

Yet, however disinclined we may be to grant the validity of his universalist presuppositions, many of the questions and topics which his criticism raises and examines seem remarkably close to the concerns of our own critical discourse. An idealistic framework certainly determines the essentially mimetic character of Goethe's theory of art in which the particular phenomena of experience, accidental and fragmentary as they may appear, can—by a process of elucidation and artistic transformation—be shown to convey their telling function within the total universe of meaning. In such a scheme the concrete figure, the graspable object, must assert its superiority as a vehicle of meaning over the more elusive configurations of language. The pictorial arts are, therefore, throughout Goethe's life, the preeminent means of aesthetic representation— "art," wherever its characteristics are closely defined, is for Goethe not primarily poetry but those forms of art in which the palpable, the visible, the infinitely perfectable object is the vehicle of significance. In the artist's progression from "mere imitation" to a skill of suggesting a particular point of view, and a specific manner of rendering his world, to that highest form of an artistic *style* in which the most intelligent, cognitive perception discovers and conveys intelligible structures and functions, Goethe suggests an aesthetic procedure which corresponds to his scientific convictions.[9] In science as he understands it and in art, it is *observation*, reflection and an ultimate recognition of a fully developed and richly telling "Gestalt," that indicates the means of access, not to any metaphysical harmony but to a natural order of ever increasing complexity.[10]

But we are here not so much concerned with Goethe's notion of "art" as with his views of the functioning of literature. Literature or poetry, Goethe knew well enough, is a far more elusive and inherently ambiguous enterprise than the figurative or visual arts. It was an axiom of eighteenth-century criticism that poetry, though still within the mimetic framework, should let us share in the inner workings of the human mind, "so as to lay open," as one critic, James Harris, puts it, "the internal constitution of man, and to give us an insight into characters, manners, passions and sentiments."[11] This, within an aesthetic scheme that seeks to differentiate rather than—like the romantics—to synthesize the resources and effects of art, remains one of the preconditions of Goethe's reflections on the various facets of literature. While the human body, that central medium in Renaissance aesthetics of a potential equilibrium of visible form, continues to provide the topic and focus of Goethe's theory of the visual arts, literature, at once inferior in its capacity to evoke the concentrated pictorial image of perfection or of beauty, offers the means of exploring and analyzing the infinite scope of human thought and feeling. Goethe's exuberant literary productivity before Weimar testifies beyond question to his early awareness of these special resources of literature. He had learned to recognize in literature a vehicle of mimetic specificity, powerfully enhanced by its abstracting or reflective capacities. Literature, he knew, must respect the fundamental descriptive imperative while questioning as well as the adequacy of language. This double capacity of literature led him to the writing of *Werther*, to the choice of so hybrid or so fascinating a form as the novel, in which truth and fiction, narration and introspection, make equal claims on the imagination. If he remembered James Harris's injunction that the poet should lay open the internal constitution of man, he was clearly intent on representing in an involved narrative, the perplexity of human intentions as they emerge in ambiguous actions. This was not a topic that any theory of the visual arts could have dealt with—it was rather a matter of language, of language stretched to the limits of its syntactical, its discursive scope. Here, for the first time, Goethe uses language with that extraordinary instinct for its metaphorical wealth and power that remains the signature of his poetry, and with the care and scrutiny of a writer who is at every moment aware of the responses or the doubts or the counterarguments of his readers.

An instinct for exploiting the give and take of dialogue remains the characteristic quality of Goethe's writing, whether narrative, argumentative or scientific; this judicious and persuasive management of language is his way of coping with what he never ceased to regard as the essentially ambivalent nature of speech, its indeterminacy, its dependence upon two conflicting modes of judgment—that of careful delimitation, definition and precision, and that of the imagination, of fantasy, of the poetic energy.

If for a brief moment in the days of his first acquaintance with Herder he had been intrigued by Hamann's deeply religious belief in language as a vehicle of divine meaning, he recognized, even at that time, the risks involved in utterance, the difficulties in achieving an adequate reading and a conclusive sort of interpretation. This doubt in the reliability of speech continues long after *Werther* to be a source of profound concern. The word, he was soon to conclude, is a sign that can merely approximate the dense reality of the object, the resonance of an idea or the intended implications of a pronouncement. "We never quite realize," he was to say in his *Science of Color*, "that language is, strictly speaking, a system of symbols ('bildlich') which can never immediately convey the concrete character of an object, but can offer only a reflected image of it."[12] While he recognized, in the tradition of Baroque poetics, two levels of linguistic functioning, a purely descriptive or common use and the more elevated possibilities of carefully organized poetic speech, he thought of both as essentially metaphorical. During his incomparably important two years in Rome, he had come to be interested in notions of language formulated by a curiously inventive friend, Karl Philipp Moritz, who proposed to interpret linguistic signs by means of what he called an alphabet of thought and feeling. Here, he found his convictions of the allusive and metaphorical nature of language confirmed. While the use of language for descriptive purposes seemed limited, its potential for speech with specific strategic intentions was obvious. Whatever the reliability of simple utterances, their range is restricted by the demands of *what* is to be conveyed: "as soon as complex relationships are to be conveyed, another linguistic level—the poetic—must be employed."[13]

It is these "complex relationships" that only language and not the devices of the figurative arts, however sophisticated, can fully render. The goal of the pictorial arts, of *Kunst*, is to objectify the experience of beauty in its fullest sense, aesthetic as well as moral; the chief impulse of the literary mode is not so much to crystallize experience as to bring subjective energies into play, to portray states of mind, however puzzling or contradictory, and to use a multitude of available devices, rhetorical or metrical, to illuminate and communicate processes of feeling and thought. Not to recognize the essential difference between the two aesthetic modes seemed to Goethe a deplorable sign of muddle-headedness, for each has its own kind of impact upon the recipient: "No genuine work of the figurative arts should try to affect the imagination; that is the job of poetry." ("Kein echtes Kunstwerk soll auf die Einbildungskraft wirken; das ist die Sache der Poesie.")

These distinct purposes of separate if complementary systems must not be confused or glibly fused by an imprecise aesthetic terminology. Both depend, in Goethe's view, upon a clear understanding of the structure of the natural world and of the means of defining and representing it; every aesthetic act at once renders and transforms the objective world, but while the sculptor should aim at achieving an object of the most rarefied coherence and logic, the poet must ultimately create a work, not of "beauty" but of intellectual and emotional fascination. Goethe provides one of the key concepts of romantic theory when in a critical discussion of Diderot's essay on painting he suggests that unlike the sculptor, the poet is bound to aim not at beauty but at what is "interesting."[15]

Let me pursue two major aspects of Goethe's theory of literature: the first concerns the *means* by which the "interesting" work is brought about, the other the *effect* which it may, or should, produce; the one concerns, if you like, the implications of *writing*, the second those of *reading*.

If literature produces *fascinating* discourse that renders alternatives of human behavior or the intricacies of intellectual, aesthetic and moral propositions, it must make the fullest possible use of the powerful and essentially unsettling energies of the *imagination*. Imagination, "Fantasie" or "Einbildungskraft" (terms used by Goethe almost interchangeably), an impulse so dubious in the pictorial arts, is the specific resource of the literary performance. It has an incomparable evocative power, and can be called upon, as Goethe puts it, to play its daring games "between Heaven and Earth, the possible and the impossible, the coarsest and the most delicate."[16] Far from being restricted by the material and formal requirements of the sculptor, the poet must, on the contrary, communicate that mobility and ubiquity of the mind which is, in the procedure of the sculptor, entirely ingested. Insofar as he is concerned with moral conflicts, he cannot, and need not, resolve these in any harmonizing configuration of beauty, but must explore their alternatives and the impact of emotions and impulses upon the directives offered by philosophical propositions.

There is no doubt that the lines of demarcation between the imagination and reflective behavior were for Goethe clarifed in his reading of Kant's *The Critique of Judgement*. We know that he read it with considerable sympathy—quite different from the chill he felt when he looked at *The Critique of Pure Reason*—and that he welcomed the clear distinction which Kant made between scientific and aesthetic judgments, between, as he puts it, the operations of rational enquiry and those of the genius, that paradigm of imaginative power and originality. "The great central ideas of the work," he confessed, "were congenial and analogous to my own work, my practice as well as my thinking."[17]

Systematic philosophical reflection, especially if it tended to resort to what he considered speculative waffling, had for Goethe only limited legitimacy: while it might help to discipline thought and discourse, it could not adequately deal with the tensions undeniably inherent in the human condition. The imagination makes us aware of these tensions and imbalances, but it is at the same time and in its most sophisticated form, itself an element of a profoundly unsettling kind: whatever its power of illumination, it may deceive and confuse, and in transcending the coherent order of the natural universe, creates fictional constructs of devious and troublesome challenge. "The imagination," Goethe notes in a remarkable sentence in 1805, "is the all-powerful antagonist of rational behavior, it has an inherent and irresistible drive towards the absurd." ("Die Einbildungskraft lauert als der mächtigste Feind, sie hat von Natur einen unwiderstehlichen Trieb zum Absurden.")[18]

Writing, then, through the imagination, offers access to a kind of sensibility which disposes the mind to an understanding of complexity, of ambiguity, even of the destructive element. But despite its admitted power of penetrating surfaces and of laying bare the contradictory features of the human mind, the imagination must be controlled if it is not to degenerate into a totally subjective energy, unsettling rather than offering insight and understanding.

Ordered in a variety of rhythmical patterns and with constant reference to the universe of experience, the language of the poet can give concreteness and direction to the volatile element of the imagination. Poetic speech, he argued, is our defense against the accidental, the contingent, the temporal, the destructive element of our life. It represents the linguistic medium with the greatest power to give structure to the imagination. The contemporary—romantic—tendency to give equally expressive resonance to prose, he felt, can have only the deplorable result of releasing the imagination, of confusing the distinction between a descriptive and an evocative manner, of abandoning the intellectual advantages of poetic concentration and discipline.

It was this concern for the most effective and economical use of speech and writing that led Goethe to engage in a most lively and revealing discussion with Schiller on the tradition of literary forms, of metrical devices and, above all, of those definitions of genres, of modes of communication, that the Greeks had practiced with such intelligence and tact. At no time were Goethe or Schiller interested in merely *reiterating* the canon of Greek poetics, being "classicists" in the narrow academic sense of superimposing ancient forms and attitudes upon contemporary subject matter. What mattered was the testing of traditional literary concepts for the use of the modern poet. If in their correspondence Goethe and Schiller return almost daily to the Greek conventions of poetics and prosody, they do so in the conviction that such conventions, the recognition of genres in particular, give continuity to the enterprise of literature.

Together with Schiller, Goethe examines ancient and modern dramatic forms, the structure of tragedy and comedy, the effect on literature of the loss of such stern religious sanctions as the Greek concept of fate, the pathetic inadequacy altogether of a consensus of taste in the contemporary German audience. To obtain a clear view of the various genres seemed, during the last decade of the century, of overriding importance: to disregard them is ultimately to blur the difference between a merely spontaneous or descriptive way of writing and the supreme thrust of a specifically designed sort of statement.

The most important of these genre concepts seemed to Goethe the epic and the dramatic—two kinds of writing which he distinguished by defining the poet's corresponding attitudes towards his audience. The dramatic poet is the mime who relates a present and immediate action to an audience of impatient and critical listeners. The epic poet is envisaged as the "rhapsodist" who gives to a calmly listening audience an account of events wholly past.[19] He deals with spacious external realities, with adventures, battles or travels, while the dramatist creates figures whose actions reveal their characteristic disposition and who must be shown within a limited space and through a plot designed to demonstrate the particular disposition of the dramatic hero. As a result of these discussions, Schiller wrote a series of meticulously organized plays, the most impressive body of German drama; and these reflections led Goethe to a number of splendid novels and novellas, all reflecting in their topics and their lively and elegant prose, Goethe's narrative talent and his sense of a modern and critical sort of fiction.

The dramatic form struck Goethe and Schiller as perhaps the most effective way of involving an audience much in need of intellectual and, indirectly, political education. In the theater they hoped to lead an ill-equipped public to an awareness of the great issues of time and of the resources of judgment and reflection that were required for their understanding.

Genres codify the reader's or listener's expectations. Yet, Goethe was not inclined to deal in any systematic fashion with the *lyrical* mode; wherever he speaks of it as part of an assessment of literary devices, he speaks of the poet's gift, of his subjective genius, that seizes upon the incidents of experienced life in order to give them an aura of general, of symbolic meaning.

It is in the narrative mode that Goethe offers examples of a radically modern point of view. His *Wilhelm Meister's Apprenticeship*, that prototype of much European nineteenth-century fiction, far from the mixture of adventure and didactic reflection of earlier narratives, shows us the almost fortuitous process of a young man's gradual maturing, his orientation in the social matrix of his time and the inevitably inconclusive ending of his progression towards self-awareness. The central figure of Goethe's novel loses, in a later continuation, his specific individuality and in the experimental design of *Wilhelm Meister's Travels*, becomes merely the witness of any increasingly technological and collective world that can only be shown in a series of soberly offered documentary scenes linked in a system of mirrored and mutually illuminating episodes. For the young romantics, the first *Wilhelm Meister*, the *Apprenticeship*, represented by its open poetic designs, the epitome of a characteristically modern literary work.

It is certainly in his novels and novellas that he strikes us as most modern in topic and in an allusive, even symbolist technique. *Elective Affinities*, for instance, gives us an extraordinarily subtle and moving account of the destructive impact of impulse and wilfulness upon an aristocratic society no longer assured in its beliefs and its conduct.

Central to all writing for Goethe is the use of language as a *metaphorical* instrument, as an essentially pictorial tool—the German term *Bild* seems explicitly to point to the metaphorical image as the most telling vehicle of the imagination. Its allegorical or symbolic use is for Goethe the criterion of effectiveness. Both of these terms point to the evocative use of the word: in the one, in the allegorical mode, we interpret the image within the relatively narrow context of a particular system of faith or ideology; in its most powerful and suggestive *symbolic* sense, the word points to the comprehensive meaning which we derive from our understanding of the *natural* order of a meaningful universe. Goethe follows the practice of his time when he insists on a sharp distinction between allegory and symbol:[20] his devaluation of the allegorical mode was in keeping with his strong dislike of poetry with a narrow, didactic or ideological base. But it is precisely the modern doubt in broad, universal idealistic assumptions and altogether the ideological character of modern life that has for us restored the usefulness of the allegorical mode, while *symbolic* speech has, in the poetics of the past century, become increasingly suspect. Its range of possible meanings has become so broad and arbitrary as to yield less and less specific insight into the functioning of a world of nearly impenetrable complexity upon which the poet and his readers must reflect.

Symbolic poetry was, for Goethe, wholly secular: the Greek cosmos from which the sculptor could derive his figures and themes seemed to him compelling for the work of the poet as well; he had little faith in the power of Christian symbolism—whatever his own religious convictions, he preferred the rich and worldly, the human and fallible faith of the Greeks to the pale and abstract sort of imagination of the Christian tradition. In the fabulous configura-

tions of the second part of *Faust*, the two worlds suggest symboli-
cally the ancient quest for perfection in beauty and the modern
preoccupation with the haunting consciousness of lost innocence,
the infinite striving for resolution and peace.

The dichotomy of these two forms of experience, the ancient and
the modern, determines the range of poetic devices which Goethe
employed with such astonishing skill and assurance. From the
powerfully irregular hymns of his early years to the polished but
never pallid verse of his *Iphigenie*, his *Tasso*, his *Pandora*, his
"Roman" elegies and the transparent and playful approximations of
oriental poetry in his *Divan* collection, he seemed to achieve an
infinite variety of perfectly shaped statements, instinctively struck as
though to confirm the barely credible suggestion of which he was so
fond, that inspiration and the gift of genius were the undefinable
preconditions of creativity.

For himself, he knew better, and at rare moments confessed that
he could think of nothing more serious and more difficult than the
writing of sustained poetry or prose. There are no contradictions in
poetry, [21] and there is genuine method, he said at one time, *only* in
the making of the work of art: "Eigentlich haben nur Dichter und
Künstler Methode."[22] Hence, his profound dislike of dabblers in art,
those who think of art as an agreeable or profitable pastime rather
than as an immense burden of insight, of having to testify to the
barely namable range of experience. This burden he discharged with
undue confidence in the capacity of reason to achieve resolution or
harmony. Indeed, it was one of the chief convictions of his life that
reason and its tools were in the long run deceptive means of
ensuring order. He often spoke of the powerful presence of the
demonic, that incalculable source of a greatness that was to be
feared as much as admired. And no statement is more revealing of
his sense of the ambivalent and the irrational than the remark he
made after completing his novel *Elective Affinities*: "No one can for
long remain in a state of full consciousness; we must again and
again return to the unconscious, for it is there that our roots are
alive."[23]

One of his visitors reported in 1810 that Goethe invariably spoke
"quietly and in measured sentences but with incredible assurance
and flashing eyes that seem to contrast strangely with the firm
balance of his sentences."[24] His speech was incisive, always
addressed to his listener, always enhanced by the skill of his "acting
the part" of the person or the figure he spoke of. Speech was one
means by which he turned insight into expression—the other,

equally often noticed and commented upon, was the remarkable intensity of his eyes—not, perhaps, so much the sharpness of his vision, as the power of implicating his listener in the join enterprise of understanding, of "interpretation." Establishing that relationship seemed to him the very method of the man of letters towards reaching conclusions as to how the world functions.

If we look at his mature discursive prose, his essays, his autobiographical writings, even those amazing fifty volumes of letters, we shall find them nearly indistinguishable in style and purpose. Commentaries on the works of others (or of his own) seem to become part of the poetic text itself; his reflections on Shakespeare are not so much critical explications as elaborations, or extensions, of the works and passages that struck him. This is to say that his criticism is not a detached, academic, objective sort of discourse, but itself a creative product, suggested by the original text. Shakespeare scholars have often belittled the validity of his observations on *Hamlet*, on *Macbeth, King Lear* or *The Tempest*, as poetic effusions rather than scholarship. This may well be beside the point: to read, he was inclined to suggest, and thus to gain clarity and an adequate comprehension of a given work can be achieved only in a statement equal to the impression which a text makes upon us.

What seemed to him of incomparable importance in Shakespeare was not his dramatic technique but the fact that he was able to give speech to the universe. Some of you will be familiar with his two important essays on Shakespeare: one is the oration for Shakespeare's birthday in October 1771, in which the young Goethe testifies to the poet's power of illuminating the world, of curing, with his immense capacity for elucidation, the blindness of one who had so far looked in poetry only for correctness and obedience to the rules: "I learned to see," he confesses at that time, "and felt my life infinitely expanded."[25] The other piece was written more than forty years later: Shakespeare is now defined and praised as the arch-poet who makes the world intelligible and transparent, not merely by his theatrical, his visual art, but by his power of speech. "The eye," he says there in keeping with eighteenth-century aesthetics, "may well be the sharpest of our senses; but our inner sense is sharper still, and we reach it in our most effective manner through the word."[26] It is Shakespeare, he continues, whose power of language penetrates and gives linguistic reality to what the world spirit may keep from us as secret or mystery; he articulates that secret, he makes even stones testify to it; the elements, the sky, the earth, the oceans, thunder and lightning, even wild animals raise their voices;[27] Shakespeare, he concludes, is the very articulator of the universe, an articulator in speech and its infinite symbolic resources.[28]

Here we may well pause to draw our conclusion: Goethe's view of literature, his theory of writing and reading, however occasional, rests upon the presupposition of poetry as a ceaseless exploration, demonstration, revision of the energies and devices of speech. From beginning to end, from his dithyrambic hymns and the calculated inversions of *Werther* to the astonishing mastery of poetic forms in the second part of *Faust* Goethe thinks, speaks and writes with an unshakable faith in the illuminating power of shaped speech, speech not only, at its finest, clarifying life but, no less urgent, pointing to its obscurity, its contingency, its unresolvable tensions. He was one of the great poets, perhaps the last, who felt sure that the human being had the power—and the duty—to explore the world, to describe it and render it intelligible in *language*, in terms, that is to say, of a logocentric system. It is language, our use of it and our awareness of its range and its dimensions, that represents our most important philosophical, aesthetic and moral tool: it is the best and the most concentrated means of gathering our usually scattered energies. To that end, language must be dialogue and, as such, prove its value as an instrument of social consequence. To read Goethe today compels us to ask ourselves if literature has not moved from the center of our life to its periphery, if the object has not emancipated itself from speech and if, in turn, words have not at times become merely visible, perhaps powerful but single-minded slogans. Is Goethe's faith in language, illuminating the total range of our experience, still available to us and truly effective? If we cannot answer that question in the affirmative should not our growing defection from language, its replacement by signs and codes of a very different sort and power, lead us back, not in nostalgia, but from a profound sense of need, to what the great poets, Goethe among them, have left us as an opportunity and obligation?

Princeton University

Notes

[1]Jonathan Culler, *The Pursuit of Signs* (Ithaca, N.Y.: Cornell Univ. Press, 1981), p. 15.

[2]Ernst Robert Curtius, "Goethe als Kritiker" in his *Kritische Essais zur europäischen Literatur* (Bern: Francke, 1950).

[3]René Wellek, *The Later Eighteenth Century*, Vol. I of *A History of Modern Criticism, 1750-1950* (New Haven: Yale Univ. Press, 1955), p. 201-266.

[4]Johann Wolfgang Goethe, *Gedenkausgabe der Werke, Briefe and Gespräche* (Zürich: Artemis Verlag, 1948), X, 590. Cited hereafter as *GA*.

[5]*GA* IX, 574.

[6]*GA* IX, 551.

[7]*GA* XVIII, 229.

[8]*GA* XXII, 387.

[9]"Der Sammler und die Seinigen," *GA* XIII, 259-319.

[10]*GA* XVII, 13.

[11]James Harris, *Three Treatises Concerning Art: Music, Painting, and Poetry*, 4th ed. (London: n.p., 1783), p. 84.

[12]*GA* XVI, 203.

[13]*GA* XVII, 775.

[14]*GA* XIII, 119.

[15]*GA* XIII, 212.

[16]*GA* XIV, 953.

[17]*GA* XVI, 875.

[18]*GA* XI, 784.

[19]*GA* XIV, 367-370.

[20]*GA* IX, 639.

[21]*GA* XXII, 400.

[22]*GA* XXII, 597-598.

[23]*GA* XXII, 598.

[24]*GA* XXII, 600.

[25]*GA* IV, 123.

[26]*GA* XIV, 756.

[27]*GA* XIV, 758.

[28]*GA* XIV, 766.

Goethe, Klopstock and the Problem of Literary Influence: A Reading of the Darmstadt Poems

Meredith Lee

Abstract

The vexing question of literary influence is enjoying current revival as critics seek to articulate new models to describe how one artist's work affects the creation of another. The labored search for sources that characterized older studies has been replaced by interest in the psychology of the creative process, the artist's quest for identity, notions of the poet as reader, and specification of how social-historical contexts and constraints alter, impel, or otherwise affect a poet's response to the literary past.

Within Goethe scholarship tenacious notions about Goethe's "original genius" have combined with critical discomfort regarding older influence models to hinder assessment of Goethe's relationship to his literary past. Goethe's response to Klopstock, in particular, has proven a troublesome topic and one that reveals some of the difficulties common to any influence study. In this study the development of Goethe as a writer and, specifically, as a lyric poet is addressed in the question of Klopstock's "influence" on Goethe. Three poems written by Goethe in 1772— "Elisium," "Fels-Weihegesang," and "Pilgers Morgenlied"—are used to document Goethe's attention to Klopstock's writing, his creative rivalry, and the significance of his audience (the sentimental circle in Darmstadt) for the young Goethe's bid for recognition as a poet equal in stature to Klopstock. (ML)

Goethe scholarship has frequently proven uneasy with the notion that Goethe might have been "influenced" by Klopstock. The issue is a larger one, I believe, than merely a healthy distrust of the outmoded mechanistic models of older influence studies (the idea that x line, phrase, or poem by Klopstock caused y in Goethe).[1] There is a tenacious notion that Goethe, unlike most other younger poets, did not have to work to acquire his poetic identity. Other poets may learn to write by adapting the strategies of older established writers and turning them to their own purposes. Goethe, it is implied, with all the genius that the tradition has bestowed upon him as a "naive" poet, was an autonomous artist who wrote with effortless originality.[2] Furthermore, Klopstock, his reputation diminished following his eclipse by Goethe as the most important German-language poet, seems an unsuitable candidate for extended attention as a poetic precursor. The linguistic and structural innovation of his poetry and its eighteenth-century preeminence have not been forgotten, but they seem remote. Homer, Shakespeare, Pindar, and even Ossian are easily understandable as writers who claimed Goethe's admiring attention; Klopstock, much praised but little read, in Lessing's epigrammatic summary, has proven more puzzling.[3]

It is useful, therefore, to recall that Klopstock was indisputably the most important and controversial poet in Germany in the late 60s and early 70s, and one particularly admired in select circles of younger writers and critics. A recognition of Klopstock as the major lyric poet in Germany is not only explicit in Herder's critical writings at that time, for example, but also the published opinion of Johann Heinrich Merck, minor court official in the duchy of Darmstadt-Hessen and editor in 1772 of the *Frankfurter Gelehrte Anzeigen.* Herder, who proclaimed Klopstock "der erste Dichter unseres Volks"[4] and "unser größte [sic] Dichter an Empfindung,"[5] wittingly or unwittingly generated considerable pressure on the younger and eagerly receptive Goethe to come to terms with Klopstock's poetic accomplishments—not so much by direct admonition as by repeated reference to Klopstock's excellence and exemplary status and by unequivocal rejection of the gallant conventions of anacreontic verse. Merck, to whom Goethe was introduced in December of 1771 by his future brother-in-law Schlosser, proved an additional authoritative voice. It was Merck who proclaimed Klopstock in the January, 1771, review of the Hamburg *Oden:* "der Schöpfer unsrer Dichtkunst, des deutschen Numerus, der Seelensprache des vaterländischen Genius"[6] and the collection itself "ein Werk der Ewigkeit."[7] With bold judgment in an analogy suggesting Klopstock's status as the German Milton, Merck predicted Klopstock's lasting reputation not as author of *Der Messias* but as a lyric poet:

> Wir beschließen diesen Artikel mit der einzigen Anmerkung, daß eine Zeit war, wo *Waller* an *St. Evremond* schrieb: "Der Lyrische Dichter *Milton* hat auch ein Episches Gedicht, das *verlohrne Paradies* geschrieben," und wir überlassen es unsern Lesern zur Ueberlegung, ob nicht eine Zeit bey der Nachwelt möglich ist, daß das Rad der Dinge da stehen bleibt, wo es heist: *Klopstock, der gröste lyrische Dichter der Neuern, schrieb auch den Messias.*[8]

For the young and gifted Goethe, unpublished except for the *Neue Lieder*, a small collection of anacreontic verse written in Leipzig, the judgments of his two mentors were of considerable consequence. It is not surprising, therefore, that Goethe, in his 1772 review for the *Frankfurter Gelehrte Anzeigen* of a volume of verse entitled *Gedichte von einem Polnischen Juden*, alluded to Klopstock's poetry as a measure of the genuineness of poetic expression he found lacking in the poems before him.[9] Nor is it surprising that Goethe's first extended experiments with free rhythm verse fell in the months between Strassburg and Wetzlar, the months when first Herder, and then Merck, were his critical guides. I have argued elsewhere that "Wanderers Sturmlied" can be understood as a self-assertive response to Herder's praise of Klopstock's "Pindaric" odes and an attempt to rival his accomplishment by surpassing his evocation of the Pindaric spirit.[10] In this essay three other poems written at about the same time as "Wanderers Sturmlied" will provide not only further evidence of Goethe's poetic preoccupation with Klopstock in the spring of 1772, but also his creative rivalry. They are "Elisium. An Uranien," "Fels-Weihegesang. An Psyche," and "Pilgers Morgenlied. An Lila," the three poems sent by Goethe in late May from Wetzlar to Luise von Ziegler for distribution to his Darmstadt friends.[11]

The poems, admittedly minor from a literary point of view, gain in interest and importance when seen in the context of Goethe's response to Klopstock. What makes an assessment of them somewhat difficult, and, by extension, of Goethe's response to Klopstock within them, is that they are so avowedly products of a stylized sociability. In them Goethe is not engaged in a naive imitation of Klopstock's poetry, but rather in a sophisticated but rather playful appropriation of his structural and lexical strategies. One theme will be basic to our investigation of the poems: the centrality of Darmstadt and the sentimental activities of the small circle of Klopstock admirers to their interpretation. In order to understand them it is necessary to understand how Klopstock's poetry functioned in this social setting, for Goethe's poems are, in good part, an attempt to duplicate this function. A consideration of the texts of the three poems will follow an elaboration of this initial assertion.

It should be noted, at least briefly, that the limited literature on the poems has not been particularly concerned with Klopstock or with any other issue beyond biographical matters. Most discussions have focused on the personalities of Henriette von Roussillon,

Caroline Flachsland, and Luise Ziegler, the Urania, Psyche, and Lila of the titles, and Goethe's response to their sentimental activities.[12] The poems themselves have not received much close attention, in part due to an attitude most recently expressed by Erich Trunz: "sie wollen nicht Dichtung sein."[13]

But to view them merely as occasional pieces, without any claim to further interest, is to disregard, in addition to the issue of audience sketched above, the deliberate stylization of the poems, their unusually complex syntactical structures, and the occasional conspicuous allusion to Klopstock's odes. One critic has even exclaimed that "Elisium" reveals "eine Sprachmanie, eine Leiden-schaft für Klopstocks Worte."[14] Although it has not gone com-pletely unnoticed that the poems are "planvoll im Klopstockschen Odenstil angesetzt,"[15] to quote Julius Bab's characterization, there has been a tendency to oversimplify the question and to see the deliberate adaptation of Klopstock's strategies in the poems as less than creative, perhaps even as an embarrassment. Most commenta-tors, like Fischer-Lamberg, have been content with rather vague appeals to an even vaguer notion of influence. She tends to regard Klopstock more as a liability than as an asset in the matter and asserts in a general reference that the poems "stehen unter Klop-stocks Einfluß": "Dieser Einfluß ist in den drei Gedichten auf seinem Höhepunkt, klingt danach aber wieder schnell ab."[16]

I would like to suggest that the poems and the apparent allusions to Klopstock's poetry within them serve a double purpose. They are, first, an attempt to please and to flatter an audience of devoted Klopstock admirers. Second, they are an attempt on Goethe's part to redefine his relationship both to this audience and, in a sense, to Klopstock. The two points are closely related and suggest that the poems are anything but straightforward biographical documents, as has been generally assumed. Rather they document a literary experiment, a rather skillful and genial appropriation of Klopstock's poetry to ends both serious and convivial.

In the poems Goethe's relationship to the Darmstadt women, and indeed, to the entire sentimental association, is at issue. In them he evokes a number of biographical guises to characterize his relation-ship to the circle of friends. But these guises, such as "errant wanderer" and "stranger" are really in the service of a more basic identity, I believe, one asserted by the very existence of the poems. It is as "poet of sentiment," or to put it in another way, "poet of the quality of Klopstock," that the erstwhile stranger and newly departed friend presents himself. This assertion, which will need

some elaboration, obviously suggests that a recognition of Klopstock's poetic strategies in the poems is not accidental, nor simply a
sign of the young Goethe's lingering dependence on older literary
models. Goethe does not set out in the three Darmstadt poems to
imitate Klopstock, in the sense of echoing lines of his poetry, but
rather to equal his mastery of emotional effect.

But why Klopstock? Because Klopstock had accomplished, in the
judgment of Herder, the nearly impossible task of translating
emotion into language. A lament Herder voices in a letter to
Caroline Flachsland has multiple echoes in his correspondence and
critical writings: "Es ist elend, daß man das Alles schreiben muß!
Die besten Silberlaute des Herzens u. Theilempfindungen laßen sich
nicht schreiben: sie laßen sich selbst nicht dichtend sagen—o
Mädchen, sie sind die Scenen der Menschheit u. ewgen Freundschaft."[17] And again in a letter to Merck: "Sie wissen das Herz hat
keine Sprache, die sich schreiben lasse."[18] The heart, an established
metaphor for deeply felt emotion, is in the discourse of sentiment
the essential self. It is not silent; it "speaks" in various ways: "es
spricht lebendig, durch Mienen, durch Auftritte, durch stumme
Scenen, durch Bilder und Personificationen, durch einem Himmels-
anblick des Auges und durch ein Ergreifen des Felsstücks."[19]
Language is the troublesome vehicle: "die Sprache [ist] eigentlich
gar kein Ausdruck der Empfindung, sondern mehr der Begriffe."[20]

The inadequacy of language and especially written language to
the emotions of friendship and sentiment is a commplace complaint
in the mid-eighteenth century and not unique to Herder. Luise von
Ziegler's letter to Caroline Flachsland stands for many: "Unsere
Schnelle Bekantschaft und Liebe kan nur Empfunden werden, den
Erzählen kan man nicht was unsere Herzen gefühlt."[21] But coupled
with the complaint is the recognition that certain modes of
discourse do succeed, at least partially, in communicating the heart-
felt experience so elusive of verbal expression. "Die Briefe meiner
Freundin sind die Sprache, die Ausflüsse des Herzens selbst" Herder
proclaims to Merck.[22] In a letter to Caroline he bestows the highest
accolade: "Jedweder Brief mehr als eine Klopstocksche Ode! denn
er ist Wahrheit, Ausguß des schönsten, vollsten Herzens, Einfalt, Ja
u. Amen."[23] The flattering comparison of Caroline's letter to
Klopstock's poetry reveals a second possibility for language to
convey the heart's emotion—in poetry. Klopstock's poetry is "ganz
Ausguß des besten Jugendlichen Herzens, u. die schönste Seele."[24]
According to Herder, any poet who attempts to write poetry of
sentiment is to be admired for his struggle to express in words, or

more in keeping with the dynamic of Herder's language, to press into words, the fullness of human emotion. Even partial success is not to be scorned and Herder declares his pleasure "wenn ein Poet in seine Sprache nur einige lebhafte und rührende Nuancen der Empfindung hineinkämpfen kann."[25] The reader, even the poet as reader of his own verse, will never be able to recover all the emotion deposited in the text, but the better the poet, the stronger and more nuanced his originating emotion, then the better the sensitive reader's retrieval of the "Empfindung" from the text. And Klopstock is the best: "er ist in meiner Seele unser grösste Dichter an Empfindung."[26] It is in an extended defense of Klopstock's poetic schemes (in the face of Lessing's criticism) that Herder employs the paradigm for poetic expression sketched above.[27]

It is not surprising, therefore, that Klopstock's poetry was frequently at the center of the sentimental exchanges in Darmstadt. It was understood to mediate between feeling hearts, defying, as it were, the perceived limitations of language. "In Klopstock und Kleist haben sich unsre Seelen gefunden" reminisced Caroline Herder years later about her first meeting with Herder[28] and the letters that pass between them are full of allusions to Klopstock's odes and the idealized friendships within them.[29] After compilation and publication of the odes in the limited 34-copy Darmstadt edition, individual copies of the volume were exchanged as tokens of high regard between Herder and Caroline Flachsland and later Therese Heyne, whom Herder had met in Göttingen. Herder writes: "P. S. Ihren Klopst*ock* habe ich an meine Freudin Heine geschickt! daß sie die süßesten Oden *Klopstocks* lese, die sie noch nicht kennet, u. alsdenn mit meiner Carol*ine* F*lachsland* in Gesellschaft sei."[30] Klopstock's poetry became, like select geographical settings, a meeting place for the sentimental spirits and his name inseparable from the memory of time spent together. Herder recalls: "Unser Wald, und Klopstock, und Alles, was wir einander zu sagen hatten."[31] Caroline affirms the pattern in a letter to Herder, remembering his recitation of Klopstock's "Die Verwandlung":

> Dencken Sie, wie oft ich mir die ersten Zeiten erinnre, da ich die Orte so oft sehe. Wenn Sie doch wüßten, wie mir war, da ich Sie in her Fasanerie auf dem Boden sitzen sahe und Sie die letzten Worte sprachen
> > Also sang er und wurde zum Adler
> > und am Olymp zog sich ein Wetter herauf.
> Sehn Sie, süßes Kind, unter allen diesen Erinnrungen lebe ich und mache mir ein kleines Elysium daraus.[32]

and, again, as she recalls his reading from *Der Messias:*

An was für Zeiten erinnren Sie mich, mein süßester holder Freund? ich lebe und träume ganz darinnen. Denken Sie, wie lebhaft mir alles ist, da ich jeden Ort sehe, wo wir uns gesprochen. . . . wißen Sie noch, mein lieber, wie Sie uns die Geschichte von Cidli und Gedor in unsrer Stube vorgelesen, und ich, Gott weiß, wit welcher Rührung da geseßen und geweint habe . . . mir wirds ein ewiger elysischer Traum bleiben.[33]

According to their letters, Klopstock's poetry facilitated the first encounter between Herder and Caroline Flachsland. In her letters Caroline presents the recollection of these Klopstock-filled moments not only as an affirmation of the emotional link between them but more centrally as a recovery, in a sense, of their meeting. Caroline's "Elysium" is a refutation of the spatial and temporal separation from Herder. Klopstock is used to create and sustain it.

Throughout the activities of the Darmstadt group it is apparent that Klopstock is being used as a device among others to create and sustain the sentiment that is a binding element of their association. That the value of friendship is one of Klopstock's central themes undoubtedly augmented his effect in this circle of admirers. It was indeed Klopstock who had completed the transformation of friendship poetry begun by Pyra and Lange from socially conventional verse to an expression of a holy intimacy and idealized union.[34] In his odes the embrace of friendship is metaphorically linked to Elysium, and the separation of friends lamented, rhetorically intensified by visionary death scenes.[35] The poet, or rather his *Genius*, is the one who calls the friends together, overcoming in a moment of poetic evocation the separation and isolation they experience:

> Dir streut Freund, mein Genius Rebenlaub,
> Der unsern Freunden rufet, damit wir uns
>   Wie in den Elysäer Feldern
>   Unter den Flügeln der Freud' umarmen.
>   ["An des Dichters Freunde"][36]

This is the Klopstock Goethe encountered in Darmstadt.

*   *   *

Goethe's relationship to the sentimental activities in Darmstadt was apparently one of willing if somewhat playful participation. During his visits in the spring of 1772 he went on outings with the "Gemeinschaft der Heiligen" as he called the select circle; he recited poetry in the park, including one poem (not extant) written for Luise von Ziegler, recognized selected sites as places set apart for melancholy reflection, and engaged in emotional farewells.[37] Caroline Flachsland's letters to Herder, the main source of information about Goethe's relationship to the circle, appreciatively record every gesture of sentiment but attempt no more complex assessment of his responses. In the quick-witted and sometimes sarcastic Merck, who also wrote poetry for the Darmstadt women and joined in the stylized sociability (which, of course, denied all stylization, being from the heart), Goethe undoubtedly found a cautionary companion.[38] His first letter to Herder from Wetzlar clearly signals distance as well as appreciative association: "Von unsrer Gemeinschafft der Heiligen sag ich euch nichts, ich binn νεόφυτος [der Neubekehrte], und im Grund bisher nur neben allen hergegangen; mit Mercken binn ich fest verbündet, doch ists mehr gemeines Bedürfniss als Zweck" (DjG II, 257).

In this context the three poems we are considering need to be understood in somewhat contradictory terms. They are not unlike the rock that Goethe selected in the Darmstadt park and forbade anyone but himself to climb:[39] a good-natured affirmation of the sentiment cultivated by the group and at the same time a participation that underlined his individuality. There is a self-aggrandizing moment, playfully redeemed, in Goethe's claim to his rock. The poems suggest a similar claim to a unique presence in the circle of friends. They recall the encounter of the once errant wanderer and a community that welcomed him. They suggest that his physical absence has made possible a new kind of presence among them—a literary presence. As poet he returns to Darmstadt, in his poetry.

The creative rivalry with Klopstock is from the outset therefore both serious and genial. Klopstock is stylized by the Darmstadt circle even as he is celebrated as a mediator of sentiment. Goethe, in effect, accepts the stylization, rivaling in his own poems the Klopstock who is prized by his Darmstadt admirers and the poetic "Elysium" fashioned in his name. When Caroline Flachsland passed the poems on to Herder, she recognized their participation in the genre at which Klopstock excelled: "einige Empfindungsstücke von unserm großen *Freund* Göthe. . . . —jetzt sitzt er in Wetzlar, einsam, öde und leer, und überschickte diese 3 Stücke an Lilla zum austheilen."[40] It is to these three "Empfindungsstücke" we shall now turn.

*   *   *

Of the three Darmstadt poems, "Elisium" is the one most explicitly evocative of Klopstock's poetry. Not only the title of the

poem, but also its diction and structural strategies provide conspicuous allusion to Klopstock's odes.[41] "Fels-Weihegesang" and "Pilgers
Morgenlied" are much less indebted. But all three are designed to
function in the Darmstadt Community of Saints as Klopstock's
poetry has functioned—as a reminder and recovery, of sorts, of past
moments of bliss, as a generative source for renewed sentiment, and
as an affirmation of the elite community of recognized spiritual
association.

It is fundamental to the poems' fiction that they are written from
the heart and to the heart without calculation or artifice. Consequently, each of the three posits an equation of the encounters and
scenes recorded with biographical events and an explicit identification of the poems' figures—"der Fremdling," "der Freund," Urania,
Lila, and Psyche—with the poet himself and his Darmstadt acquaintances. The guises used in the sentimental circle like the intimate
"du" of the poems' address are not admitted as poetic conceit but as
a means to facilitate a confessional exchange. In the poems,
responses previously hidden in Goethe's heart in his earlier meetings
with the Darmstadt women are now ostensibly revealed and his
present feelings in his Wetzlar isolation fully conveyed. In short, the
fictive world of the Darmstadt sentimental association functions as
the "real" world of the poems, and in turn, is sustained by them.

The primary landscape of this gentle social fiction is the grove.
Within its agreeable contours friends gather and embrace one
another warmly. In both "Elisium" and "Fels-Weihegesang" the
poet is shown to be a stranger who has wandered into this amiable
landscape and benefited from its generous reception. In "Elisium"
he is the grateful recipient of friendship's kiss. In "Fels-Weihegesang"
he is the errant wanderer who has found a resting place in the new
setting.

Just as Klopstock in his friendship odes uses a visionary
reflection on separation from his friends and even the final
separation of death in order to value fully the experience of their
presence, so Goethe evokes in the three poems his departure and
existence apart from the Darmstadt circle in order to augment his
celebration of the fellowship within it. A contrasting landscape is
introduced. In a setting reminiscent of the barren shores of Ovid's
banishment, the poet in "Elisium" sees himself "verschlagen / unter
schauernden Himmels / öde Gestade."[42] In "Fels-Weihegesang" he
anticipates a distant, disagreeable land and in "Pilgers Morgenlied"
he confronts obscuring mists and blustery winds.

Despite marked differences among the three, each poem addresses
the problem of the poet's potential loss after leaving the friends. Is
the experience of welcome and the attendant happiness now beyond
reach? The answer, as one might expect, is no. The poems
appropriately suggest that the sentimental activity of the women to
whom they are dedicated has made the difference—the welcoming
embraces, the kisses of friendship, the melancholy tears and small
ceremonies of remembrance. But the poems suggest as well that the
poet has not been inactive. Removed from immediate contact with
the Darmstadt friends, he has not lost sight of them. Each of the
poems introduces a notion of visionary seeing—in "Elisium" primarily as a recollective moment, in "Fels-Weihegesang" as an anticipa-
tory one, and in "Pilgers Morgenlied" in a strategy with a bit more
complication, as a recollection of a moment of fundamental
transformation that made the present visionary reconstruction and
in this sense the poem itself possible.

Goethe, who writes to his friends in the rhymeless free rhythm
verse introduced to German poetry by Klopstock, offers them his
poems as a means to participate in his vision. "Elisium" provides an
example. The climactic moment in "Elisium" is the blissful kiss of
friendship. A recollected moment, its idyllic quality intensified by
explicit contrast with the poet's landscape of desolation, the kiss is
elaborately prepared by the mounting tension of unresolved syntactical periods until the eruptive: "Seeligkeit! Seeligkeit! / Eines Kusses
Gefühl!" gives exclamatory voice to the previous descriptive
sequence and the poet confesses direct experience of the heavenly
joy that he as a stranger at the poem's beginning, observing the
friends embrace, only beheld as an outsider: "wie ihr euch rings
umfassend / in heilger Wonne schwebtet, / und ich, im Anschaun
selig / ohne sterblichen Neid / darneben stand." The poem is so
organized that the celebrated kiss is not introduced within the initial
narrative sequence of arrival and welcome, strolling in the protected
environs and twilight leave-taking. Rather, it is recalled in a
visionary moment. The poet's newly confirmed friends depart,
leaving him in isolation in the growing dusk. The present is
achieved, in the tense system of the poem, and as visual contact
between poet and friends is lost, visionary sight is introduced. Using
a device familiar from Klopstock's odes, the two modes of seeing
are linked by repetition of select phrases ("seh ich . . . seh ich
. . . seh mich . . . seh ich"),[43] rendering somewhat indeterminate
whether the poet is speaking from the emptied grove or from a
distant shore. In one sense, there is little difference. It is the absence

of the friends that is critical. In their absence the meaning of their presence is recalled, recovered, and recreated in the poet's ecstatic vision of the kiss. The poem, which Goethe has sent to Darmstadt, gives the friends opportunity to share the vision, to perceive the full value of their generous welcome, and like him to make the past present again. The poem is designed to function in Darmstadt both as a reminder of the past association and a source of renewed sentiment. In short, it is designed to function precisely as Klopstock's poetry has functioned for the group.

But the poem does not conclude without an additional sigh, one guaranteed to stir the emotions of his audience yet further. In a variation on the refrain, the poem first concludes triumphantly:

> Mir gaben die Götter
> auf Erden Elisium!

and then somewhat unexpectedly:

> Ach, warum nur Elisium!

Repeatedly in the poem, the poet has suggested that his experience with the friends has surpassed earthly expectation. In the concluding line, however, he laments the limits of the transcendent "Elisium" he has evoked. The commemorated moment and the poem that is the recollective vehicle of this "Elisium" are less than full and present reality, however favorably the vision offered may be shown to contrast with the poet's present desolation. Similarly, the intended audience cannot but conclude that the poem is, finally, a poor substitute for the poet.

That is, of course, among the desired effects, and Caroline Flachsland's response to Goethe indicates his success:

> Werden wir Sie bald wiedersehn? o lieber guter Freund was haben Sie zurück in unsern Herzen gelaßen! wir stimmen zuweilen auf einmal an "wenn unser Goethe doch wieder hier wäre!"— . . . So oft ich zum Felsen komme stecke ich einen grünen Zweig, die ich sehr liebe, u. Blumen darauf, umarme dann alle meine Freunde, u. blicke gen Himmel— . . .
>
> Uns gaben die Götter
> auf Erden Elysium.[44]

In addition to "Elisium" Caroline's letter refers specifically to the second of the three poems, "Fels-Weihegesang." It, like "Elisium," offers a vision to link the poet and his friends. I have mentioned previously the rock that Goethe selected in the Darmstadt park as his contribution to the group's general cultivation of select sites for sentimental retreat. He engraved his name in the stone, forbade anyone but himself to climb it, and possibly organized a dedication ceremony. In the poem Goethe's rock, conceived as a well-appointed resting place for the errant wanderer, is revealed to be the site of the poem's composition, future site of Psyche's melancholy lament for those separated from the community, and in consequence, the site in which a new community of those united in their absence is recognized. In direct contrast to "Elisium," in which a recollective moment allows a celebration of community despite physical separation, in "Fels-Weihegesang" spatial community, despite temporal separation, is the organizing idea. Because only time separates the friends, the poem closes with an oblation to time itself, "ein Opfer der Zukunft." The poet's dedicatory violets and his poem, like Psyche's sentimental tears and rose, mark the site as one of anticipated recovery as well as melancholy loss.

The poem, in a manner more easily documented than in the others, draws on practices of the sentimental association: not only Goethe's rock but numerous ceremonies of dedication and remembrance, as well as Caroline Flachsland's willing confession of melancholy in the face of Herder's long absences, and the notion of a geographical location providing physical continuity. Indeed, the poem seems to draw rather explicitly on a scene first communicated to Herder by Merck and then recreated by Herder in a letter to Caroline:

> Ich sahe nur Sie, ich war mit Ihnen: ich sahe Sie den Fels umarmen, Ihren Himmlischen, naßen Blick sich erheben: unsre Seelen waren zusammen: ich war zu Ihren Füßen; ich küßte Sie ganz, meine liebe, zarte, fühlende Freundin![45]

and again in a letter to Merck:

> Ja, ich sehe sie—liebster Freund, die arme Unschuldige! wie sie in Ihrer melancholischen Zaubergegend dasteht, mit thränendem Auge den wüsten Fels umarmt, und mit leeren ausgebreiteten Armen in die Wüste des Aethers hinspricht—ich sehe die ganze rührende Scene.[46]

In "Fels-Weihegesang" Goethe has appropriated the scene and altered the site. The poem provides, a bit audaciously, instruction on how his absence, in addition to Herder's, can be commemorated, consciously vying for a portion of the melancholy previously reserved for Herder, indeed, purposefully stimulating production of the humour. In phrases with immediate allusion to idealized friendship as celebrated by Klopstock, the poet recalls how in times past he beheld from his rock "der Freunde Seligkeit." In good part it is this sight that has made the rock so special. In the present moment of the poem he is again at his rock and once more sees the friends together aglow in their fellowship. But Psyche slips away, or rather, "verliert sich," in a reference that links her both to the errant wanderer and the absent Herder, isolated from the group in her grief, "traurend/um den Abwesenden." The poet imagines her, in the indeterminate future, once again slipping away, and seeking out the very spot where he now rests:

> Wo meine Brust hier ruht,
> an das Moos mit innigem
> Liebesgefühl sich
> athmend drängt,
> ruhst du vielleicht dann Psyche.

As in "Elisium" a visionary scene follows, one in which Caroline's sadness at Herder's absence from the community is intensified by renewed thoughts of Goethe's absence. Gentle tears flow and an exhortation to place flowers in remembrance closes the poem.

In the poem Goethe has encouraged a momentary ambivalence about whom it is Psyche first laments, Herder or perhaps Goethe himself. But in another more important way Goethe has intruded on the pair, for it is no longer Klopstock's poetry alone that mediates her awareness of Herder's absence and marks the site of wistful recollection. Goethe has offered his own poem to this purpose. And Herder resented the intrusion, naming Goethe "ein irrer Götzenpriester" in his testy answering poem, not the least bit pleased by Goethe's imagined intimacy, mediated by rock and poem, with his friend.[47]

In "Fels-Weihegesang" as in "Elisium" Goethe has written a poem designed to be set beside Klopstock's within the Darmstadt circle. Goethe, writing in phrases evocative of Klopstock's poetry, implicitly suggests that his poems be used, as Klopstock's have been, in the perpetuation of the Elisium that is the recollected memory of past moments of happiness and in the cultivation of the melancholy that seeks to link separated friends by intensification of feeling. "Pilgers Morgenlied," the third poem, begins on a similar note, casting the initial encounter of the "stranger" and Lila in the religious language of exalted friendship. As in the two previous poems, the poet's visionary sight sustains him as visual contact with the world of the Darmstadt friends is disrupted. But an important contrast is evident. In "Pilgers Morgenlied," unlike "Elisium," the poet doesn't recreate in ecstatic transport a lost moment, claiming in a sense to relive friendship's bliss within it. He doesn't need to emotionally reconstruct his "Elisium" in his poetry. He has himself been reconstructed by the experience of friendship—at least, this is the claim.

The transformation of the poet is shown to be rooted in the encounter with Lila. That meeting is the turning point, and in a structural scheme not uncommon in Goethe's poetry, it is recalled in the centrally pivotal lines of the poem:

> als zum erstenmal
> du den Fremdling
> ängstlich liebevoll
> begegnestest,
> und mit einemmal
> ew'ge Flammen
> in die Seel' ihm warfst.

The poem is in two parts and it is in the second half that the full import of the initial encounter is realized. Quite unlike the first half (the recollection of the tower and Lila's welcome), the second is an apostrophe to two forces, one threatening to break the poet, one sustaining him: "Nord," personification of the antagonistic wind, and "Allgegenwärtige Liebe," which has rallied the heart. But the two parts are not without connection. In the imagery of flames and warmth linking the two, Lila, a "Genius" of sorts, is recognized as an agent of higher powers. The two previous poems were set in the fading rays of an afternoon sun where the poet lingered with his thoughts of separation. In "Pilgers Morgenlied" the separation, in a physical sense, has occurred. But a heart warmed by myriad images of friendship and by Lila's flame—that is, by "Allgegenwärtige Liebe"— leaves no doubt that not even cold blustery winds, let alone light morning fogs, can destroy him or his contact with his friends.

And what of Klopstock? In "Pilgers Morgenlied" Goethe seems to have gone his own way. The disrupted vision of Lila's tower and the final departure are set in the larger context of cosmic forces embattling and empowering the poet. The imagery is not Klopstock's. Unquestionably this poem like the other two employs language marked by the innovations of Klopstock's poetry (that is, the free rhythm verse, the omission of subject pronouns such as "du" 11. 28-30, the intensifying use of "tausend," the *composita* such as "frühwelckend,") but the poem itself is one of independent direction.

Like Klopstock, Goethe has assigned transcendent value to the encounter of friendship, but it is quite evident that Goethe does not agree with Klopstock about what this means. As a text "Pilgers Morgenlied" can be read against "Elisium." In both poems the encounter of the stranger and Lila is evoked, but "Elisium," with its appeal not only to Klopstock's diction but also the ecstatic transport of his visionary sequences, ends on a note of slight disappointment. Elisium, in a lament that Klopstock would never assent to, is "nur Elisium." In "Pilgers Morgenlied," in contrast, friendship's value is not one of transport but rather transformation. In it love's regenerating power is manifested and actively renews the human heart.

But Goethe is not offering an elaborate critique of Klopstock's friendship odes in the three Darmstadt poems. Quite to the contrary, the poems suggest a willing identification with him and his poetry to a rather specific end. I stated at the beginning of this essay that all three of the Darmstadt poems suggest a new relationship between the erstwhile stranger and wanderer recalled within them and the three women the poems celebrate for their gifts of friendship. In the poems the poet presents himself not only as the passive but grateful recipient of kisses, the one embraced, and the object of melancholy tears, but also as a bit of an outsider. Most evidently in "Elisium" and "Fels-Weihegesang," he is as much an observer as participant in the sentimental exchanges.

As a poet, however, a fuller participation in the circle is assured. Goethe's separation from the Darmstadt circle is the immediate occasion for the three poems. Within each of them he evokes the recent departure. But the poems themselves suggest that the friend who must depart from the Darmstadt fellowship is able to "return" and participate in the community—as a poet. Unlike the women, he doesn't dispense kisses or tears or flames, but he does offer his poetry as a return gift. And for his return he had donned the poetic costume most fitting for the occasion. He has returned as a poet of sentiment, a poet of the quality of Klopstock. He has set out to match his emotional effect and even to rival his reputation in this rather specific social context.

But what of Goethe and Klopstock apart from Darmstadt? Do the poems tell us anything about Goethe's response to him and his poetry beyond the Darmstadt circle? A few things can be asserted, I believe. They attest to his familiarity with Klopstock's odes, his attention to them in the spring of 1772, his willingness to allude to them and to appropriate from them. In general, Goethe affirms in the poems his loyalty to the principles of true feeling and heart-felt emotion being promoted by Herder and Merck, among others, in Klopstock's name. Goethe's three poems are no match for the best poetry by the older and established poet, but they also make no claim to be so.

Most importantly, the poems provide a useful reminder of Goethe's poetic apprenticeship. His attention to Klopstock's syntactical and lexical strategies, his awareness of how Klopstock's poetry has functioned in a specific social setting, and his ability to approximate his poetic stance, mastering his techniques even as they are altered to fit new purposes—all these are evident in the three Darmstadt poems. Because Goethe scholarship has proven susceptible to the notion that Goethe, the "naive" poet, developed his poetic abilities with little explicit attention to the strategies of older and more established writers, and particularly those writing in German, the three poems provide important testimony not only to the unavoidable presence of Klopstock, mediated by a variety of admirers, in the years Goethe struggled to develop an independent poetic voice, but also Goethe's engaged response to him and his poetry. The Darmstadt poems are one example of how Goethe came to terms with this figure of celebrated literary stature.

University of California, Irvine

Notes

[1]Recent approaches to the vexing question of literary influence and attempts to articulate suitable models for a description of how one artist's work affects the creation of another include such diverse projects as: Göran Hermerén's rigorous analysis of semantical and logical problems raised by influence hypotheses, *Influence In Art and Literature* (Princeton: Princeton University Press, 1975); Harold Bloom's neo-Freudian accounts of poetic misprision and the identity quest of the artist: *The Anxiety of Influence. A Theory of Poetry* (New York: Oxford University Press, 1973), *A Map of Misreading* (New York: Oxford University Press, 1975), *Kabbalah and Criticism* (New York: The Seabury Press, 1975), *Poetry and Repression Revisionism from Blake to Stevens* (New Haven: Yale University Press, 1976); *Agon. Towards a Theory of Revisionism* (New York: Oxford University Press, 1982), *The Breaking of the Vessels*, The Wellek Library Lectures (Chicago: University of Chicago Press, 1982); Douglas N. Archibald's appeal to a vocabulary of inter-personal relationship and a recognition of the literary imagination as both complex and autonomous, "Yeat's Encounters: Observations on Literary Influence and Literary History," *New Literary History*, 1 (1969/70), 439-69. Among the general surveys of the problem area: Erwin Koppen, "Hat die Vergleichende Literaturwissenschaft eine eigene Theorie? Ein Exempel: Der literarische Einfluß," in *Zur Theorie der Vergleichenden Literaturwissenschaft*, ed. Horst Rüdiger, Komparatistische Studien, 1 (Berlin: Walter de Gruyter, 1971), pp. 41-64; Ulrich Weisstein, *Einführung in die Vergleichende Literaturwissenschaft* (Stuttgart: W. Kohlhammer Verlag, 1968), esp. the chapters "'Einfluß' und 'Nachahmung,'" pp. 88-102 and "'Rezeption' und 'Wirkung,'" pp. 103-117; Ronald Primeau, ed., *Influx. Essays on Literary Influence* (Port Washington, N.Y.: Kennikat Press, 1977). Goethe scholarship has contributed little to the recent discussion.

[2]The most recent representative of this long tradition in Goethe scholarship is Walter Kaufmann, who has entitled a chapter in his study of Goethe, Kant, and Hegel, "Goethe at twenty-one. Autonomous from tip to toe," *Discovering the Mind. Goethe, Kant and Hegel* (New York: McGraw-Hill, 1980), p. xiii. Friedrich Gundolf's Goethe biography, *Goethe* (1916; rpt. Darmstadt: Wissenschaftliche Buchgesellschaft, 1963), is a key document in the promotion of original genius: "Dem Riesen ist das Riesenhafte normal, und nirgends hat sich Goethe vom Standpunkt der Zwerge aus geschildert, d.h. mit unsrem Staunen und Hinaufblick" (p. 628). See also Hans-Wilhelm Kelling, *The Idolatry of Poetic Genius in German Goethe Criticism*, European University Papers, Series 1, Vol. 27 (Berne: Herbert Lang & Co., 1970), esp. pp. 147-59. Gundolf, after a lengthy acknowledgement of Klopstock's contribution to German letters, hastens to add that Goethe's relationship to Klopstock is "wie der König zum Gesandten eines Königs, wie der Gott zum Priester" (p. 114).

[3]Gotthold Ephraim Lessing, *Sämtliche Schriften*, ed. Karl Lachmann and Franz Muncker (Stuttgart: G. J. Göschen, 1886-1924), I, 3. The claim is not that Goethe scholarship has failed to recognize Klopstock altogether, of course, but that inadequate models of literary influence (in which to be "influenced" is to imitate and consequently to be a "weaker" poet) coupled with the notion of poetic genius have precluded a satisfactory and fully convincing evaluation of Goethe's relationship to Klopstock.

[4]Johann Gottfried Herder, *Sämtliche Werke*, ed. Bernhard Suphan (1877-1913); rpt. Hildesheim: Georg Olms Verlagsbuchhandlung, 1967), II, 42. Cited hereafter as "Suphan."

[5]Suphan I, 522.

[6]Johann Heinrich Merck, *Werke*, ed. Arthur Henkel (Frankfurt am Main: Insel Verlag, 1968), pp. 527-28.

[7]Merck, *Werke*, p. 528.

[8]Merck, *Werke*, pp. 530-31.

[9]Johann Wolfgang von Goethe, *Der junge Goethe*, ed. Hanna Fischer-Lamberg (Berlin: Walter de Gruyter & Co., 1963-73), II, 273-75. Cited hereafter *DjG*. Goethe misquotes Klopstock's 1752 ode "An Cidli," first published in the 1771 Hamburg edition of the *Oden*.

[10]"A Question of Influence: Goethe, Klopstock, and 'Wanderers Sturmlied'," *The German Quarterly*, 55 (1982), 13-28.

[11]The texts in *DjG* II, 259-63.

[12]Valerian Tornius, *Schöne Seelen. Studien über Männer und Frauen aus der Wertherzeit* (Leipzig: Klinkhart & Biermann Verlag, 192), pp. 157-74. The book is an expanded and revised version of the author's 1910 study *Die Empfindsamen in Darmstadt*. Lilli Rahn-Bechmann, *Der Darmstädter Freundes-Kreis. Ein Beitrag zum Verständnis der empfindsamen Seelenhaltung des 18. Jahrhunderts*, Diss. Erlangen, 1934 (Erlangen: Karl Dorres, 1934). Heinrich Jacobi, *Goethes Lila, ihre Freunde Leuchsenring und Merck und der Homburger Landgrafenhof.* Mitteilungen des Vereins für Geschichte und Landeskunde zu Bad Homburg vor der Höhe, 25 (Bad Homburg vor der Höhe: 1957). Ernst M. Oppenheimer, *Goethe's Poetry for Occasions* (Toronto: University of Toronto Press, 1974), pp. 28-31. Katharina Mommsen. "'Wandrers Sturmlied.' Die Leiden des jungen Goethe." *Jahrbuch des Wiener Goethe-Vereins*, 81-83 (1977-79), 215-35. Of interest in this context: Gerhart von Graevenitz, *Eduard Mörike, die Kunst der Sünde: zur Geschichte des literarischen Individuums*. Untersuchungen zur deutschen Literaturgeschichte, 20 (Tübingen: Max Niemeyer Verlag, 1978), 124-30.

[13]Commentary in *Goethes Werke*, Hamburger Ausgabe, ed. Erich Trunz, 8th ed. (Hamburg: Christian Wegner Verlag, 1966), I, 500.

[14]Arthur Kutscher, *Das Naturgefühl in Goethes Lyrik bis zur Ausgabe der Schriften 1789* (Leipzig: Max Hesses Verlag, 1906), p. 77.

[15]Julius Bab, "Goethe's Briefgedichte," *Goethe Kalendar auf das Jahr 1930* (Leipzig: Dieterich'sche Verlagsbuchhandlung, 1930), p. 114.

[16]*DjG* II, 355.

[17](20-23 October 1771) Johann Gottfried Herder, *Briefe*, ed. Wilhelm Dobbek and Günter Arnold (Weimar: Hermann Böhlaus Nachfolger, 1977), II, 86.

[18](12 September 1770) Herder, *Briefe*, I, 216.

[19](12 September 1770) Herder, *Briefe*, I, 216.

[20]Suphan I, 552.

[21](16 February 1771) Max Morris, "Aus dem Kreise der Empfindsamen in Darmstadt," *Chronik des Wiener Goethe-Vereins* 25 (1911), 10.

[22](12 September 1770) Herder, *Briefe*, I, 216.

[23](23 September 1770) Herder, *Briefe*, II, 238.

[24](Nach Mitte März 1771) Herder, *Briefe* I, 317.

[25]Suphan I, 522-23.

[26]Suphan I, 522.

[27]Suphan I, 519-26.

[28]Caroline Herder née Flachsland, *Erinnerungen aus dem Leben Johann Gottfried von Herder*, ed. J. G. Miller (Stuttgart: Cotta, 1820), I, 151.

[29]The correspondence is reprinted in Herder's *Briefwechsel mit Caroline Flachsland*, ed. Hans Schauer, Schriften der Goethe-Gesellschaft, vols. 39 and 41 (Weimar: Verlag der Goethe-Gesellschaft, 1926 and 1928). Cited hereafter *SGG*. Caroline Flachland's allusions to Klopstock: *SGG* 39: 7, 36, 219, 279, 289, 381-83, 399-400; *SGG* 41: 48, 63, 108-09, 157, 323, 364. Herder's allusions to Klopstock: *Briefe* I, 191, 198, 201, 206, 207, 209, 210, 213, 222, 224, 232, 236, 240-42, 243, 244, 252, 254, 270, 294, 304, 306, 317; *Briefe* II, 51, 65, 77, 80, 91, 103, 109, 111, 128, 139, 148, 165, 179, 192, 238, 284.

[30](25 April 1772) Herder, *Briefe* II, 165.

[31](27 August 1770) Herder, *Briefe* I, 191.

[32](26 July 1771) *SGG* 29, 279.

[33](19 August 1771) *SGG* 39, 289.

[34]Wolfdietrich Rasch, *Freundschaftskult und Freundschaftsdichtung im deutschen Schrifttum des 18. Jahrhunderts vom Ausgang des Barock bis zu Klopstock* (Halle/ Saale: Max Niemeyer Verlag, 1936), pp. 222-63.

[35]Cf. Friedrich Gottlieb Klopstock, *Oden*, ed. Franz Muncker and Jaro Pawel (Stuttgart: G. J. Göschen'sche Verlagsbuchhandlung, 1889), I, 83-85 ("Der Zürchersee"); I, 38-43 ("An Ebert"); I, 44-45 ("An Giseke"); I, 58-59 ("Selmar und Selma"); I, 65-70 ("Der Abschied").

[36]The poem, also known as "Auf meine Freunde," is in its revised version (1767) entitled "Wingolf," Klopstock, *Oden*, I, 8-31. The text of the Darmstadt edition is quoted here: *Klopstocks Oden and Elegien. Faksimiledruck der bei Johann Georg Wittich in Darmstadt 1771 erschienenen Ausgabe*, ed. Jörg-Ulrich Fechner, Sammlung Metzlar, 126 (Stuttgart: J. B. Metzlersche Verlagsbuchhandlung, 1974), p. 116.

[37]*SGG* 41: 48-49, 91-92, 103-04, 110.

[38]Merck, *Werke*, pp. 114-16, 122-23, 127-41. See also the introduction to the volume by Peter Berglar, pp. 7-39, and Helmut Prang, *Johann Heinrich Merck. Ein Leben für Andere* (Wiesbaden: Insel Verlag, 1949), pp. 43-88.

[39]Caroline Flachsland writes: "er hat sich einen großen prächtigen Felsen zugeeignet und geht heut hin, seinen Namen hinein zu hauen, es kan aber niemand darauf als er allein" (27 April or 1 May 1772) *SGG* 41, 103-04.

[40]*SGG* 41, 120.

[41]Characteristic are the dynamic prefixes ("entgegentreten," "entgegenkeimen," "entgegenbeben"); the abundant participial constructions ("liebahndend," "umfassend," "liebend," "sehnend," "wehend," "dämmernd," "schauernd," "bittend," "hoffend"; the repeated exclamations; intensifying plurals ("Hände in Hände"); phrases directly evocative of Klopstock's diction ("wandeln," "im Anschaun selig"). The topography of the poem has multiple correlates in Klopstock's odes; cf. "Thuiskon," *Oden* I, 171-72. The extended subordinate periods demanding syntactical resolution are used by Klopstock both in his friendship odes and his free rhythm hymns: cf. "An Fanny" (I, 63-64); "Der Abschied" (I, 65-70); "Die Glückseligkeit Aller" (I, 140-45).

[42]*Cf.* Publius Ovidius Naso, *Epistulae ex Ponto* I, 3, 49-51 (orbis in extremi iaceo desertus harenis. / fert ubi perpetuas obruta terra nives. / non ager hic pomum, non dulces educat uvas.") The settings of isolation also have equivalents in *Der Messias* II, 534-35 "im einsamen Wald, am öden Gestade, / wo er oft war."

[43]The opening lines of "Frühlingsfeyer" provide an example. Klopstock, *Oden* I, 133-34 (II. 1-16). See also: "An Fanny," I, 63-54; "Dem Allgegenwärtigen," I, 124 (11. 45-46); "Die Glückseligkeit Aller," I, 140 (11. 5-16). Examples of visionary seeing include: "Auf meine Freunde," I, 22 (11. 201-12); "Die künftige Geliebte," I, 33 (11. 37-40).

[44](13 June 1772) "Zwei Briefe an den jungen Goethe/mitgeteilt von Max Morris," in *Insel-Almanach auf das Jahr 1912* (Leipzig: Insel-Verlag, 1912), p. 136.

[45](12 September 1770) Herder, *Briefe* I, 211.

[46](12 September 1770) Herder, *Briefe* I, 214.

[47]"Antwort auf die Felsweihe an Psyche," Suphan 29, 511-13.

Absolute and Affective Music: Rameau, Diderot, and Goethe*

John Neubauer

Abstract

Goethe's translation of the dialogue *Rameau's Nephew* by Diderot is annotated with some important comments on music and music history, which allow us to consider Goethe's view in light of the eighteenth-century French debates between Rameau on the one hand and Rousseau, Diderot, and d'Alembert on the other. Rousseau and the encyclopedists insisted that music was an imitative art, and that, consequently, melody and vocal music were superior to harmony and pure instrumental music. Rameau, in turn, wanted to construct harmonic principles for music, derived from the natural phenomenon of the overtones.

Like Diderot and Rousseau, Goethe preferred melody and voice to instrumental music: his gloss on Rameau in the Diderot translation is a critical passage on him adopted from Rousseau. However, Goethe's correspondence with Zelter and Schlosser, and his sketch for a *Tonlehre* indicate that he was genuinely interested in Rameau's project of establishing the major and minor scales as the fundamental and natural bases of music—even though he disagreed with Rameau's mathematical method.

Goethe's remarks on these theoretical issues indicate how far he was willing to depart from the mimetic principle in the arts towards absolute music and formalism.(JN)

The concept of "absolute music" was first used by Wagner, but elaborated on by Eduard Hanslick, better known as Wagner's Beçkmesser, to characterize the non-representational instrumental music of the classic-romantic age. Hanslick's famous formula, "Tönend bewegte Formen sind einzig und allein Inhalt und Gegenstand der Musik," inaugurates a formalistic and texture-oriented approach: defining music as a language "which we speak and understand yet cannot translate," Hanslick seems to draw on the Goethean symbol; attacking biographical, genetic, and psychological interpretations he already anticipates New Criticism and text-immanent interpretations during the heydays of positivism.[1]

Now, Goethe had conceived of autonomous music as early as 1805:

> Alle neuere Musik wird auf zweierlei Weise behandelt, entweder daß man sie als eine selbständige Kunst betrachtet, sie in sich selbst ausbildet, ausübt und durch den verfeinerten äußeren Sinn genießt, . . . oder daß man sie in Bezug auf Verstand, Empfindung, Leidenschaft setzt und sie dergestalt bearbeitet, daß sie mehrere menschliche Geistes-und Seelenkräfte in Anspruch nehmen könne.[2]

We have to attend carefully to Goethe's meaning. Autonomous music appeals to the senses, "äußere Sinne," only; and these, even if "refined," cannot match the higher pleasures afforded by the intellect and the imagination. I hasten to add that Goethe does not draw this idea of autonomous music from his acquaintance with the art of Haydn, Mozart, or Beethoven. In a passage that I have omitted, Goethe exemplifies autonomous music with the eighteenth-century opera, where music has emancipated itself from the insipid librettos and appealed only via sweeping melodies. Though Goethe acknowledges the power of such pure music, he considers it ultimately inferior to that second kind which appeals to "intellect, sensibility, and passion." The conflation of the intellectual and emotional powers in this latter category glosses over some highly problematic issues in music theory, but it makes evident that Goethe wants meaningful music to reach beyond the senses.[3]

Actually, eighteenth-century critics routinely condemned nonimitative instrumental music for appealing to the senses only. According to Diderot, for instance, such instrumental music is like the rainbow which gives us only the pleasure of "pure and simple sensations."[4] Beautiful chords, he said, may please his ears; they are "independent of all sentiments in my soul, all ideas in my mind. But, to tell the truth, I would not listen long to a music which had only this merit. I never listened to a good symphony, above all to an adagio or an andante, that I did not interpret, at times so happily that I guessed exactly the painting proposed by the musician. . . . immediate sensation . . . means very little to me" (*Oe*, VIII, 508).

In this typical enlightened view, music acquires intellectual respectability by painting concrete meanings. The concomitant belittling of mere instrumental music is echoed by Wilhelm Meister: "Das Instrument sollte nur die Stimme begleiten; denn Melodien, Gänge und Läufe ohne Worte und Sinn scheinen mir Schmetterlingen oder schönen bunten Vögeln ähnlich zu sein, die in der Luft vor unsern Augen herumschweben, die wir allenfalls haschen und uns zueignen möchten; da sich der Gesang dagegen wie ein Genius gen Himmel hebt und das bessere ich in uns ihn zu begleiten anreizt" (*BA*, X, 132). Goethe recognized, however, that Italian opera, usually praised for its successful fusion of language and music, actually appealed by a similar superficial but ebullient force: "Der Italiener wird sich der lieblichsten Harmonie, der gefälligsten Melodie befleißigen, er wird sich an dem Zusammenklang, an der Bewegung als solchen ergötzen, er wird des sängers Kehle zu Rate ziehn . . . und so das gebildete Ohr seiner Landsleute entzücken. Er wird aber auch dem Vorwurf nicht entgehen, seinem Text, da er zum Gesang doch einmal Text haben muß, keinesweges genuggetan zu haben" (*BA*, XXI, 681). As music overpowers the text, Italian opera turns into a species of "senseless" instrumental music. Indeed, Goethe weakens his earlier north-south distinction by comparing the Italian opera to German instrumental music: "Wie der Italiener mit dem Gesang, so verfuhr der Deutsche mit der Instrumentalmusik. Er betrachtete sie auch eine Zeitlang als eine besondere, für sich bestehende Kunst, vervollkommnete ihr Technisches und übte sie, fast ohne weitern Bezug auf Gemütskräfte, lebhaft aus, da sie denn bei einer, dem Deutschen wohl gemässen, tiefern Behandlung der Harmonie zu einem hohen, für alle Völker musterhaften Grade gelangt ist" (*BA*, XXI, 682). Since Goethe ascribes this music to the past, he probably thinks of baroque contrapunctal music rather than the chamber or symphonic music of the Viennese classics.

Goethe considers, then, three different types of autonomous music: 1) the older contrapunctal music of Bach and Händel, 2) Italian opera and virtuoso instrumental music, and 3) the instrumental music of the classic-romantic age. It was perhaps the greatest limitation of his musical taste not to recognize that the pleasure derived from the imaginative grasping of formal relationships in fugues or sonatas is fundamentally different from "gut-reactions" to sheer melodic beauty or showmanship. In contrast to the romantics, who constructed a rationale and a metaphysics for instrumental music, Goethe remained essentially faithful to the enlightenment concept, not, as usually thought, because that taste dominated his formative years, but out of a reasoned ethical conviction. In the following pages I intend to explore Goethe's relationship to the French Enlightenment by way of two problematic notions of musical imitation: the relationship of music to language, and the roots of harmony in nature. The topic is of historical interest, but it also raises fundamental aesthetic questions.

*   *   *

Goethe's distinction between pure and representational, or pleasing and meaningful, music appears in his annotated translation of Diderot's satire, *le Neveu de Rameau*. It was Schiller who acquired the unpublished French manuscript from the imperial archives in Moscow through the mediation of Klinger, the *Sturm und Drang* poet now turned into a Russian officer. Goethe was taken by Diderot's irreverent dialogue, and upon Schiller's instigation he set out to translate it; when he recognized that the German audience would not understand the satire on the Parisian scene, he prepared annotations which make up almost a third of the published text.

While the fascinating fortunes of Diderot's manuscript have often been told, music's role in the satire and Goethe's response to it has been little appreciated, though Rameau, a major composer and the greatest theoretician of music in the eighteenth century, appears in its very title.[5] The nephew, Jean-François Rameau, wasted his life away as a buffoon and a sycophant at the dinner tables of the Parisian aristocracy, to achieve finally a dubios immortality not only in Diderot's satire, but, via Diderot and Goethe, as the symbol of modern alienated consciousness in Hegel's *Phenomenology* (Ch. VI, Sect. B). We shall do well to remember that this fame attaches to Diderot's fictional figure and not to the historical person. At the time of translating the satire Goethe was actually unaware of the existence of the historical Jean-François, and this enabled him to appreciate the irony of the piece. Jean-François is Diderot's fictive counter-self; he is also a mouthpiece to satirize Diderot's enemies and a means to settle accounts with the uncle, Jean-Philippe.

Let me offer a model for musical history as a background to *Rameau's Nephew*. The Goethean distinction between autonomous and representational music applies to the later eighteenth century, but earlier music was always imitative in terms of two broad paradigms, a verbal and a mathematical one. The mathematical approach originated with the Pythagorean notion that musical harmony reflected cosmic, social, and psychic harmonies. This concept dominated the Middle Ages, where music was considered to be a mathematical science within the trivium of the liberal arts. The great Renaissance and seventeenth-century syntheses by Fludd, Kepler, Mersenne, or Kircher continued to associate musico-mathematical harmony with the universe; later, in the works of Descartes, Leibniz, Rameau, and Euler, mathematics becomes fused with the emerging science of physical acoustics. The verbal paradigm subordinates music to language and ascribes to it moral or didactic meanings. It leads from Plato and Aristotle through the medieval use of music in church service to the birth of the opera around 1600; the tradition continues throughout the seventeenth and eighteenth centuries, in rhetorical approaches to music.

The history of music may, then, be described in terms of two traditions that constantly interact and conflict with each other. The pivotal significance of the later eighteenth century is to bring about a two-fold emancipation of music: in the mathematical paradigm the metaphysical ballast of the Pythagorean tradition is jettisoned, allowing for the emergence of harmonic and formalist theories; in the verbal paradigm the relationship between music and language becomes inverted: from Romanticism onward and throughout symbolism *la musique avant toute chose* becomes the model of poetry.

The clash between Rameau and Diderot ought to be understood in the context of these radical changes. Starting with the epochal *Traité de l'harmonie* (1722), Rameau attempted to demonstrate that the principles of harmony were rooted in nature, and music was therefore a science as well as an art. Relying on Sauveur's discovery that the notes of the perfect major chord (c-e-g- in the key of C-major) were among the overtones, he sought to deduce that all permissible chords and chord-combinations were somehow natural. Rameau's harmony aspired to the status of science. In practice, Rameau established tonality as a kind of gravitational center: he saw music as a series of brief excursions into dissonances whose sole function was to enhance the listener's pleasure upon hearing the cadential returns to the tonality. This theory prepared the ground for musical formalism, although Rameau continued to believe that music represented and elicited the emotions, and he assigned specific affects to intervals, keys, and other elements in music.

Rameau's opaque writings had difficulty in gaining recognition, but by mid-century his authority reached its apogee. In 1749 he prepared, perhaps with the editorial help of Diderot, a *Mémoire,* which was warmly endorsed by a committee of the Academy headed by d'Alembert, In fact, d'Alembert immediately set out to publish an *haute vulgarisation* of Rameau's theory entitled *Elemens de musique, theorique et pratique, suivant les principes de M. Rameau,* and the composer publicly expressed his thanks for this "most glorious testimony to which an author could ever aspire."

Like d'Alembert, Diderot was originally a disciple of Rameau. In 1748 he published an essay on music following Euler's and Rameau's mathematical approach; in his subsequent *Lettre sur les sourds et muets* (1749) as well as in the Encyclopedia article *beau* he made aesthetic quality a function of the tonal relations in music, and this lent itself well for a harmonic theory of music. But trouble was already brewing. For reasons that are not quite clear, the Encyclopedia articles on music theory were not commissioned to Rameau but to Rousseau, who bore a grudge against him. Though they turned out to be quite favorable to Rameau in the end, perhaps under the moderating influence of d'Alembert, they eventually unleashed a quarrel between the composer and the philosophers. The true irritant was probably an open but anonymous letter by Rousseau, published in 1752, which contained a lengthy critique of Rameau, including a passage on his theory which Goethe adopted in his Diderot translation as his gloss on the composer:

> Die theoretischen Werke Rameaus haben das sonderbare Schicksal, daß sie ein großes Glück machten, ohne daß man sie gelesen hatte, und man wird sie jetzt noch viel weniger lesen, seitdem Herr d'Alembert sich die Mühe gegeben, die Lehre dieses Verfassers im Auszuge mitzuteilen.[6] Gewiß werden die Originale dadurch vernichtet werden, und wir werden uns dergestalt entschädigt finden, daß wir sie keinesweges vermissen. Diese verschiedenen Werke enthalten nichts Neues, noch Nützliches, als das Prinzip des Grundbasses; aber es ist kein kleines Verdienst, einen Grundsatz, wär er auch willkürlich, in einer Kunst festzusetzen, die sich dazu kaum zu bequemen schien, und die Regeln dergestalt erleichtert zu haben, daß man das Studium der Komposition, wozu man sonst zwanzig Jahre brauchte, gegenwärtig in einigen Monaten vollbringen kann. [*BA*, XXI, 695]

I must add that Rousseau destroys this concluding praise by blaming the simplicity of the new theory for the wave of mediocre composers and compositions.

*   *   *

Goethe's annotations have the double purpose of providing personal information on the major figures and clarifying the key theoretical issues.[7] He sided with Diderot, Rousseau, and d'Alembert, though he questioned musical mimesis. Batteaux, who wanted to reduce the arts to the single principle of imitation, is glossed by Goethe as the "apostle of the half-true gospel of imitating nature, which appeals to all those who trust only their senses and remain unaware of what lies beyond them" (*BA*, XXI, 668). To be sure, Rousseau and the encyclopedists also criticized Batteux,[8] but for the weakness of his arguments instead of his basic principles.

Goethe first criticized Diderot's notion of mimesis in a translation and discussion of the philosopher's *Essai sur la peinture* (1795): "Die Neigung aller seiner theoretischen Äußerungen geht dahin, Natur und Kunst zu konfundieren, Natur and Kunst völlig zu amalgamieren; unsere Sorge muß sein, beide in ihren Wirkungen getrennt darzustellen" (*BA*, XXI, 735); "Der Künstler strebe nicht, ein Naturwerk, aber ein vollendetes Kunstwerk hervorzubringen" (*BA*, XXI, 775). In the annotations to *Rameaus Neffe* this point reappears as a criticism of the mistaken French preference for the simplicity of the Italian opera: out of dislike for mannerism and convention, Diderot and his friends came to favor the pleasing superficiality of Italian music, though intellectually they should have preferred "meaningful" French music (*BA*, XXI, 683).

The point is well taken, though it does not recognize the complex situation of Diderot's generation. At the transition from Rationalism to Romanticism, *Rameau's Nephew* documents the blurring of the meaning of meaning in music. Rationalism assigns musical meaning to the imitated external objects, events, or words. The imitation of objects and events leads to naturalistic depictions of thunders, murmuring brooks, posthorns, earthquakes, or chirping birds that are ubiquitous in the music of Vivaldi, Bach or Handel. The imitation of language is justified in Gottsched's dictum, "Das Singen ist doch nichts als ein angenehmes und nachdrückliches Lesen eines Verses."[9] Diderot's generation continues to believe that music ought to imitate, but it depreciates the musical portrayal of the external world as a species of naturalism and it finds language too conceptual for the emotional nuances that music is now supposed to express. Rousseau bewails the separation of language and music, but regards it as an inevitable consequence of the gradual rationalization of language, its shift from accent to articulation. Hence he advocates the musical expression of the inarticulate cries of passion. A version of his view is carried to its logical if absurd conclusion by *Lui* in *Rameau's Nephew*, who undermines his ideas on musical imitation by working himself into a frenzy:

> He was getting into a passion . . . he gesticulated, made faces and twisted his body, . . . He jumbled together thirty different airs, French, Italian, comic, tragic—in every style. Now in a baritone voice he sank to the pit; then straining in falsetto he tore to shreds the upper notes of some air, imitating the while the stance, walk and gestures of the several characters; being in succession furious, mollified, lordly, sneering. First a damsel weeps and he reproduces her kittenish ways; next he is a priest, a king, a tyrant; he threatens, commands, rages. Now he is a slave, he obeys, calms down, is heartbroken, complains, laughs; never overstepping the proper tone, speech, or manner called for by the part . . . he kept on, in the grip of mental possession, an enthusiasm so close to madness that it seemed doubtful whether he would recover. He might have to be put into a cab and be taken to a padded cell. . . . His art was complete—delicacy of voice, expressive strength, true sorrow . . . With swollen cheeks and a somber throaty sound, he would give us the horns and bassoons. . . . He whistled

piccolos and warbled traverse flutes, singing, shouting, waving about like a madman, being in himself dancer and ballerina, singer and prima donna, all of them together and the whole orchestra, the whole theater; then redividing himself into twenty separate roles, running, stopping, glowing at the eyes like one possessed, frothing at the mouth. . . . He wept, laughed, sighed, looked placid or melting or enraged. He was a woman in a spasm of grief, a wretched man sunk in despair, a temple being erected, birds growing silent at sunset, waters murmuring through cool and solitary places or else cascading from a mountaintop, a storm, a hurricane, the anguish of those about to die, mingled with the whistling of the wind and the noise of thunder. He was night and its gloom, shade and silence—for silence itself is depictable in sound. He had completely lost his senses. [*OE*, V, 463-65][10]

The brilliance of Diderot's verbal performance highlights *Lui's* inarticulateness: the rational principles of mimesis have been turned here into parodies of uncontrolled passion, which slide from imitation of speech to imitation of instruments, and, after brief pantomimes of human behavior, into the portrayal of natural events. Mimesis, which Diderot originally considered as a rational comparison of signifier and signified, turns into a sheer virtuoso performance. If *Lui's* show involves some imitations of human passion in Rousseau's sense, it also mocks Rousseau's theory, because it dehumanizes the voice by aping the instruments and the sounds in nature. In baroque music the imitation of natural sound was usually the task of the instruments. *Moi's* fascination with *Lui's* mad outburst reveals Diderot's sense for the dark powers dormant in music. Goethe, who was more wary than fascinated by the demonic in music, underestimated this irrational element in Diderot. Believing that Diderot was always in search of "meaning" and reason in music (*BA*, XXI, 683), he imputed Diderot's contradictions to an excess of wit rather than to fundamental tensions in his personality.

In Goethe's own theory, musical imitation was perhaps more deeply moored to articulate language than in Diderot's. As late as 1829, Goethe would best understand quartets as conversations: "man hört vier vernünftige Leute sich unter einander unterhalten, glaubt ihren Discursen etwas abzugewinnen und die Eigenthümlichkeiten der Instrumente kennen zu lernen" (Zelter, III, 194). In this sense he expected that composers serve the poets, and he depreciated through-composed songs for abandoning the strophic structure of the poem.

As to the imitations of physical objects and events, Goethe preferred indirection and suggestion to naturalism. Responding to Zelter's setting of his poem, *Johanna Sebus*, Goethe wrote on

March 6, 1810: "Es ist eine Art Symbolik fürs Ohr, wodurch der Gegenstand, insofern er in Bewegung oder nicht in Bewegung ist, weder nachgeahmt noch gemalt, sondern in der Imagination auf eine ganz eigene und unbegreifliche Weise hervorgebracht wird, indem das Bezeichnete mit dem Bezeichnenden in fast gar keinem Verhältnisse zu stehen scheint" (*WA*, Ser. 4, XXI, 204).

There is a certain evident parallel between this passage and the indirection and symbolic representation that Goethe derives from his visual experience and advocates for literature. But a moment's reflection will indicate, how much more radically he departs in music from the principles of concretion and imitation. In the painterly symbol the idea is infinitely effective and elusive; the concrete signifier is itself an ineffable general signification. In music, the signifiers have almost no natural tie to the objects signified, they function semi-independently, as if emancipated from nature and merely triggering the imagination.[11] The letters to Adalbert Schöpke on February 16, 1818 and Zelter on May 2, 1820 reinforce this point:

Auf Ihre Frage zum Beispiel *was der Musiker mahlen dürfe?* wage ich mit einem Paradox zu antworten *Nichts* und *Alles.* Nichts! wie er es durch die äußern Sinne empfängt darf er nachahmen; aber *Alles* darf er darstellen was er bey diesen äußern Sinneseinwirkungen empfindet. Den Donner in Musik nachzuahmen ist keine Kunst, aber der Musiker, der das Gefühl in mir erregt als wenn ich donnern hörte würde sehr schätzbar seyn. So haben wir im Gegensatz für vollkommene Ruhe, für Schweigen, ja für Negation entschiedenen Ausdruck in der Musik, wovon mir vollkommene Beispiele zur Hand sind. Ich wiederhole: das Innere in Stimmung zu setzen, ohne die gemeinen äußern Mittel zu brauchen ist der Musik großes und edles Vorrecht. [*WA*, Ser. 4, XXIX, 53-54]

Die reinste und höchste Malerei in der Musik ist die welche Du [Zelter] auch ausübst, es kommt darauf an den Hörer in die Stimmung zu versetzen welche das Gedicht angibt, in der Einbildungskraft bilden sich alsdann die Gestalten nach Anlaß des Textes, sie weiß nich wie sie dazu kommt. [Zelter, II, 56][12]

In both of these letters the central purpose of music is the creation of *Stimmung*. While Goethe nominally adheres to the principles of imitation, he has no advice on how to achieve it, and, in fact, there is no insistence here that the mood should correspond to the object represented.

*   *   *

So far I have discussed Goethe's view on the musical imitation of verbal or physical subject matters. But we can conceive of musical imitation in a different manner as well, if we assume that its modalities are determined by nature. In this case, music becomes an expression, a language of nature. This was, of course, Rameau's premise when he attempted to derive the musical modes from principles in nature. Given Goethe's reservations about mimesis in Diderot's and Rousseau's sense, we would expect him to sympathize with Rameau's undertaking; but it is not easy to determine how much he actually knew about this technically complicated issue. From Diderot's satire he could gather only negative information about Rameau: his theory and music were ephemeral; *Moi* describes him as a "hard man, brutal, inhuman, miserly, a bad father, bad husband, and bad uncle," and *Lui* adds that he was a "man of stone" who "could see my tongue hanging out a foot long and still not give me a glass of water" (*OE*, V, 395 and 460). This image, carved in stone, contrasts curiously with the soft, angelic countenance in Lavater's *Physiognomische Fragmente*, written about the same time:

> Sieh diesen reinen Verstand! . . . Sieh diesen reinen, richtigen, gefühlvollen Sinn, der's ist, ohne Anstrengung, ohne unseliges Forschen; Und sieh dabei diese himmlische Güte!
> Die vollkommenste, liebevollste Harmonie hat diese Gestalt ausgebildet. Nichts Scharfes, nichts Eckigtes an dem ganzen Umrisse, alles wallt, alles schwebt ohne zu schwanken, ohne unbestimmt zu sein. Diese Gegenwart wirkt auf die Seele wie ein genialisches Tonstück, unser Herz wird dahingerissen, ausgefüllt durch dessen Liebenswürdigkeit, und wird zugleich festgehalten, in sich selbst gekräftigt, und weiss nicht warum?—Es ist die Wahrheit, die Richtigkeit, das ewige Gesetz der stimmenden Natur, die unter der Annehmlichkeit verborgen liegt.
> Sie diese Stirne! diese Schläfe! in ihnen wohnen die reinsten Tonverhältnisse. Sieh dieses Auge! es schaut nicht, bemerkt nicht, es ist ganz Ohr, ganz Aufmerksamkeit auf innres Gefühl. Diese Nase! Wie frei! wie fest! ohne starr zu sein—und dann, wie die Wange von einem genüglichen Gefallen an sich selbst belebt wird, und den lieben Mund nach sich zieht! und wie die freundlichste Bestimmtheit sich in dem Kinne rundet![13]

One is reluctant to believe the evidence in Goethe's correspondence which suggests that he authored this embarrassing piece of trash, for even at the peak of Storm and Stress he employed a more forceful style, and some of the other pieces attributed to him in Lavater's work are of an incomparably higher quality. Whatever the case may be, Goethe surely read this ode to Rameau's physiognomy, and it may have been his only information on the French composer until the translation of Diderot's satire. Neither the annotations for the translation nor Goethe's later writings make any significant reference to Rameau, which may well be the reason why Rameau is among the last major figures of the eighteenth century not yet honored with a study on his relation to Goethe. Yet, important aspects of Rameau's harmonic theory were debated between Goethe, Zelter, and Christian Heinrich Schlosser, and they form the nucleus of Goethe's ideas for a *Tonlehre*. While these ad hoc writings cannot match the sustained effort of the *Farbenlehre*, Goethe considered the topic important enough to post his outline for the *Tonlehre* in his study. Indeed, musical structure is such an important aspect of his notion of musical mimesis that I will trace his thoughts on the matter for the remainder of my paper.

*   *   *

The status of the minor chords and keys was a central issue between Rameau, Rousseau, and the encyclopedists. Having found the notes of the major chord both by dividing a vibrating string and by analyzing the overtones, Rameau thought he had demonstrated its natural origin, and he set out to find a similar natural justification for the minor chord. But after arduous and stubborn attempts he had to admit of a certain asymmetry: while the major chord was produced by nature, the minor was merely "indicated" by it. Rameau's failure to offer a convincing derivation for the minor chord eventually endangered his whole enterprise of establishing natural laws for music; d'Alembert, Diderot, and Rousseau all came to the conclusion that music was an artifice invented by man and developed in the course of history.

When Goethe asked Zelter on April 20, 1808, why composers were inclined towards the use of the minor mode (Zelter, I, 219), Zelter, far from offering an explanation, responded that the minor chord was actually derivative: "die kleine Terz [ist] kein unmittelbares donum der Natur, sondern ein Werk neuerer Kunst und man muß sie wie eine erniedrigte große Terz betrachten" (Zelter, I, 214). Goethe, who was working on the *Farbenlehre* at the time, replied with a line-by-line refutation of this claim. He saw no justification for deriving the minor from the major: instead of diminishing the major third one could just as well augment the minor one and thus reverse the priorities. If the minor chord could not be derived by dividing a vibrating string, this merely disqualified the experiment.

This seems to be a defense of Rameau, though Goethe's superficial agreement with him on the equality of the modes belies their fundamental differences on the status of theories, on the role of mathematics in science, and on the relationship between nature and art. Rameau thought that musical harmony had its objective "Newtonian" laws that were independent of the observer. If the historical practice of music showed a development which culminated, as he thought, in the parity of the major and minor modes, the modes had to be rooted in the sound producing body (*corps sonore*), not in the accidental auditory mechanism of man. Now, Goethe agreed that the evolution of compositional practice could not have been a mere accident. If composers have treated the minor chord as a consonance, though it is not contained in the overtones or the vibrating string, it must be naturally harmonious and cannot be a dissonance (Zelter, I, 231). But the similar convictions sent Rameau out to nature and referred Goethe back to man himself. Hence the famous concluding passage in the cited letter to Zelter:[14]

> Der Mensch, an sich selbst, in sofern er sich seiner gesunden Sinne bedient, ist der größte und genaueste physikalische Apparat den es geben kann. Und das ist eben das größte Unheil der neuern Physik, daß man die Experimente gleichsam vom Menschen abgesondert hat, und bloss in dem was künstliche Instrument zeigen die Natur erkennen, ja was sie leisten kann dadurch beschränken und beweisen will. Eben so ist es mit dem Berechnen. Es ist vieles wahr was sich nicht berechnen läßt, so wie sehr vieles, was sich nicht bis zum entschiedenen Experiment bringen läßt. Dafür steht ja aber der Mensch so hoch, daß sich das sonst Undarstellbare in ihm darstellt. Was ist denn eine Saite und alle mechanische Theilung derselben gegen das Ohr des Musikers? ja, man kann sagen, was sind die elementaren Erscheinungen der Natur selbst gegen den Menschen, der sie alle erst bändigen und modificiren muß, um sie sich einigermassen assimiliren zu können?

Zelter's conciliatory response brought the debate to a halt; but Goethe returned to it shortly before his death, on March 31, 1831, fanning his still smouldering anger "daß Ihr theoretischen Musik-hansen sie [die klein Terz] nicht wolltet als ein *donum naturae* gelten lassen. Wahrhaftig eine Darm- und Drahtsaite steht nicht so hoch, daß ihr die Natur allein ausschließlich ihre Harmonien anvertrauen sollte. Da ist der Mensch mehr werth, und dem Menschen hat die Natur die kleine Terz verliehen, um das Unnenn-bare, Sehnsüchtige mit dem innigsten Behagen ausdrücken zu können; der Mensch gehört mit zur Natur, und er ist es, der die zartesten Bezüge der sämmtlichen elementaren Erscheinungen in sich aufzunehmen, zu regeln und zu modificiren weiß" (*WA*, Ser. 4, XLVIII, 169).[15]

*   *   *

Diary entries, letters, and other biographical documents testify that the 1808 debate with Zelter continued to occupy Goethe throughout the completion of the *Farbenlehre*, culminating in an 1810 sketch for a *Tonlehre*. This Goethean acoustics was designed to have three parts, each accommodating an important dimension of sound: 1) the organic, subjective, and physiological one, 2) the mathematical or objective one, and 3) the mechanical or instrumental one. In effect, the outline summarizes Goethe's earlier ideas on the primacy of human organs in music. The ear is not just passive, we must assign reactive powers to its refined organism; the voice possesses natural qualities which the purely mathematical sound of instruments cannot match (Zelter, II, 427), and this primacy of the voice informs Goethe's reservations about pure instrumental music. Finally, Goethe reaffirms the equality of the minor and major modes as poles of a fundamental duality, defining the minor as the human and the major as the "natural" pole: "[der Mollton] entspringt nicht durch das erste Mitklingen. Er manifestiert sich in weniger faßlichen Zahl—und Maassverhältnissen, und ist doch ganz der menschlichen Natur gemäß, ja gemäßer als jene erste faßlichee Tonart" (Zelter, II, 427).

But what makes the minor mode more human than the major? The question came to haunt Goethe when, in 1816, Christian Heinrich Schlosser elaborated on Goethe's color theory and the human quality of the minor mode, albeit with arguments that displeased Goethe. Schlosser held that only the major mode was rooted in nature, and the duality of major and minor was therefore not fundamental (*WA*, Ser. 4, XXV, 303). Goethe disapproved of this belittling of duality, but he was delighted with Schlosser's idea that a *Tonmonade* generated both the major and the minor thirds: "Hier treffen wir nun völlig zusammen, indem Sie aussprechen, der Grund des sogenannten Moll liegt innerhalb der Tonmonade selbst. Diess ist mir aus der Seele gesprochen. . . . Dehnt sich die Tonmonade aus, so entspringt das Dur, zieht sie sich zusammen, so entsteht das Moll" (*WA*, Ser. 4, XXV, 305). Such a *Tonmonade*, though purely speculative, was for Goethe an *Urphänomen*, which verbal or mathematical analyses could grasp only very inadequately. But the correspondents differed fundamentally when comparing the major and minor modes. For Schlosser's romantic sensibility, music was a medium of inwardness and a yearning for the infinite, and the minor, in particular, expressed the uniquely human capacity for melancholy and morality:

Daß die Molltöne [der menschlichen Natur] gemäser seyen, als die Durtöne, ist in einem grosen Sinne wahr; . . . Sein Grund ist ein metaphysischer. Nemlich: so wie die Lichtwelt zu dem Sinne des Verstandes, dem Auge, spricht, und ein heiteres Verhältniß nach aussen gründet; so spricht die Tonwelt zu dem Sinne des Gemüthes . . . dem Ohre, und zerstört das Verhältniß nach aussen. Das Gemüth wird daher durch die Musik bewegt, wie durch keine andere Kunst, selbst die Poesie nicht ausgenommen. Der Hang des Unendlichen, Fernen, Ungetrennten in uns schwillt kraft ihrer über die Dämme von heute und gestern, erhebt sich zu Höhen und senkt sich in Tiefen, wo er nicht verweilen kann, weil ihm dazu der allein Würklichkeit gebende Sinn fehlt. . . . Ist daher der menschlichen Natur der Mollton gemäser als der Durton, so will das eigentlich sagen, die Befestigung des Menschen in der Natur ist eine gewaltsame, gezwungene, auch die heiterste; die Musik, und in ihr der Mollton, also das der Natur fernste, sie in ihren Fugen erschütternde, macht die Wehmuth in uns anklingen, gegen die wir alle zu kämpfen haben, die wir uns, wir mögen es gestehen oder nicht, alle verbergen möchten, und nicht los werden können.

Eben darum aber, weil er das Gemüth am entschiedensten gegen die Natur kehrt, oder aus ihr entwendet, liegt er selbst nicht in der Natur, wenigstens nicht auf eine ursprüngliche Weise. Sein Gefallen ist im Sittlichen zu suchen. [*WA*, Ser. 4, XXV, 308-09]

There are several issues in this passage that surely disturbed Goethe. Approaching music from its receptive rather than creative angle, Schlosser believes that music engenders in the listener a spirit of antagonism against nature, and he attributes to this spirit an intent of self-destruction. Goethe was, of course, well aware both of the affect-theories and of music's power to release violent, irrational, and potentially destructive forces. But neither in theater nor in music did he advocate a catharsis that would purge by arousing violent passions. His fear of the demonic underlies his inability to fully appreciate the talents of a Kleist or a Beethoven. As his own *Novelle* shows, he preferred music where its magic is used to neutralize, calm, harmonize, and harness rather than agitate the passions. And yet, the irrational powers dormant in music preoccupied him to the very end of his life, particularly while finishing *Faust II*. Thus, on March 2, 1831, he remarked to Eckermann that musicians had a stronger streak of the demonic than painters, and six days later he expanded on this, anticipating thereby Thomas Mann's faustian musician: [die Musik enthält etwas Dämonisches], "denn sie steht so hoch, daß kein Verstand ihr beikommen kann, und es geht von ihr eine Wirkung aus, die alles beherrscht und von der niemand imstande ist, sich Rechenschaft zu geben. Der religiöse Kultus kann sie daher auch nicht entbehren; sie ist eins der ersten Mittel um auf den Menschen wunderbar zu wirken." That music in the minor mode should dispose the listener against nature had little appeal to Goethe. But Schlosser's passionate words must have reminded him of Schiller's ethos, for he softened his polemical answer with the highly flattering proposal that Goethe and

Schlosser engage in a cooperation that Goethe had once developed with Schiller, namely, "bey völlig auseinanderstrebenden Richtungen ununterbrochen eine gemeinsame Bildung fortzusetzen" (*WA*, Ser. 4, XXV, 313). Like Schiller, Schlosser saw a confrontation rather than a harmony between man and nature: music was the medium of inwardness, and the minor mode expressed an ethical will to emancipate man from nature. Such an idealist and romantic interpretation of music could not satisfy Goethe, and he ingeniously reinterpreted Schlosser's notion of a *Tonmonade* to suit his theory of polarities. As an expansion of the monade, the major mode represented man's drive to reach out actively into the world of external objects. In turn, the minor represented a withdrawal of the subject into melancholy. While Goethe admits thereby the melancholic temper of the minor mode, he minimizes its romantic, self-destructive potential by stressing its positive force. The minor of a Polonaise, for instance, expresses no suffering or bereavement, but rather the social urge "sich concentriren, sich gern in einander verschlingen, bey und durcheinander verweilen."[16]

Here, as elsewhere, the instinct that leads Goethe from naturalism towards abstraction is countered by an equally powerful aversion to subjectivity. All appearances to the contrary, the sweeping and pulsating passion of romantic music was for him fundamentally akin to pure mathematics, for both of them were sheer inventions, human constructs without natural bases. His own metaphor for art was different:

> Alle Künste, indem sie sich nur durch Ausüben und Denken, durch Praxis und Theorie, heraufarbeiten konnten, kommen mir vor wie Städte, deren Grund und Boden worauf sie erbaut sind, man nicht mehr entziffern kann. Felsen wurden weggesprengt, eben diese Steine zugehauen und Häuser daraus gebaut. Höhlen fand man sehr gelegen und bearbeitete sie zu Kellern. Wo der feste Grund ausging, grub und mauerte man ihn; ja vielleicht traf man gleich neben dem Urfelsen ein grundloses Sumpffleck, wo man Pfähle einrammen und Rost schlagen mußte. Wenn das nun alles fertig und bewohnbar ist, was läßt sich nun als Natur und was als Kunst ansprechen? Wo ist das Fundament und wo die Nachhülfe? Wo der Stoff, wo die Form? Wie schwer ist es alsdann Gründe anzugeben, wenn man behaupten will, daß in den frühsten Zeiten, wenn man gleich das Ganze übersehen hätte, die sämmtlichen Anlagen, natur- kunst-, zweckmässiger hätten gemacht werden können. Betrachtet man das Clavier, die Orgel, so glaubt man die Stadt meines Gleichnisses zu sehen. [Zelter, I, 229]

Significantly, Goethe uses here the metaphor of the cityscape to characterize music, while in the *Wahlverwandtschaften*, written just a few years earlier, the relation between art and nature is represented through patterned and embellished organic forms. He obviously sensed that among all the arts music was the furthest removed from nature and most highly structured according to abstract principles.

From a historical perspective, the arguments made during Goethe's lifetime against musical imitation and "natural" harmony prepared the ground for symbolist, abstract, and formalist concepts in the arts. As we have seen, Goethe sensed the change, went along with it part of the way, but stopped in hesitancy. If Goethe's constructed city resembles neither Axel's symbolist castle, nor the elusive goal of Kafka's landsurveyor, if, in other words, Goethe felt an aversion to art as a purely human construction, a reification of thought or passion, this was not because of a deficiency in his imaginative powers. Here, as in the Philemon-and-Baucis scene of *Faust II*, he voices the paradoxical fear that the more our world will bear the stamp of our self the more dehumanized it may become.

University of Pittsburgh

Notes

*I gratefully acknowledge my debt to the commentators of this paper, and above all, to Luanne T. Frank, for her thoughtful reading of it.

1 *Vom Musikalisch-Schönen. Ein Beitrag zur Revision der Ästhetik der Tonkunst* (Leipzig: Weigel, 1854), pp. 32 and 35.

2 *Werke*, Berliner Ausgabe (Berlin: Aufbau, 1961-), XXI, 681. The following editions of Goethe's writings will also be used in the text: *Goethes Werke*, Weimarer-Ausgabe (Weimar: Böhlau, 1887-1919), and *Briefwechsel zwischen Goethe und Zelter in den Jahren 1799-1832* (Leipzig: Reclam, 1902). All further references to these works will be made in the text as follows: *BA, WA*, Zelter.

3 Goethe added that the two types of modern music ought to be reconciled; he also ventured the mistaken prophecy that the northern people will always prefer the second kind.

4 Diderot, *Oeuvres complètes*, ed. J. Assézat (Paris: Garnier, 1875-77), I, 407-08). Further references to this edition will be made in the text with the abbreviation *Oe*. Diderot was fond of comparing the rainbow to the harmonic "skeleton" of music; Goethe took issue with this analogy in his commentary on Diderot's *Essai sur la peinture* (*BA*, XXI, 771).

5 On the role of music in *Rameau's Nephew* see the following works: Jean-Michel Bardez, *Diderot et la musique: valeur de la contribution d'un mélomane* (Paris: Champion, 1971); Daniel Heartz, "Diderot et le Théâtre Lyrique: 'le nouveau stile' proposé par le Neveu de Rameau," *Revue de Musicologie*, 64 (1978), 229-52; Henry Lang "Diderot as Musician," *Diderot Studies*, 10 (1968), 95-107; Roland Mortier, *Diderot in Deutschland 1750-1850* (Stuttgart: Metzler, 1967).

Considering the enormous literature on Goethe and music, studies on his music theory are surprisingly rare. I found the following works most relevant or useful to my topic: Friedrich Blume, *Goethe und die Musik* (Kassel: Bärenreiter, 1948); Wilhelm Bode, *Die Tonkunst in Goethes Leben* (Berlin: Mittler, 1912); Ernst-Jürgen Dreyer, "Musikgeschichte in Nuce. Goethes dritte grundsätzliche Äußerung zur Natur der Musik," *Jahrbuch des freien deutschen Hochstifts* (1979), pp. 170-98; Hans Joachim Moser, "Goethe und die musikalische Akustik," *Festschrift Freiherr von Liliencron* (Leipzig: Breitkopf, 1910), pp. 145-72; Hans Joachim Moser, *Goethe und die Musik* (Leipzig: Peters, 1949); Rudolf Schlösser, *Rameaus Neffe* (Berlin: Duncker, 1900); Erich Schramm, "Goethe und Diderots Dialog 'Rameaus Neffe'," *Zeitschrift für Musikwissenschaft*, 16 (1934), 294-307; Frederick William Sternfeld, *Goethe and Music. A List of Parodies and Goethe's Relationship to Music. A List of References* (New York: New York Public Library, 1954); Dénes Zoltai, *Ethos und Affekt. Geschichte der philosophischen Musikästhetik von der Anfängen bis zu Hegel* (Budapest: Akadémiai Könyvkiado, 1970).

[6]D'Alembert's essay was actually a condensation, not a collection of excerpts.

[7]In order to demonstrate the universality of the exotic cabals of pre-revolutionary Paris, Goethe pointed out to the German readers the exemplary nature of various fortunes of mediocrity in a slightly sententious manner: Abbé Le Blanc illustrates that the luck of a mediocre talent will encourage other ungifted persons, Dorat that the theater irresistibly attracts mediocrity, Marivaux that "it is impossible to retain the favor of the masses," Poinsinet that minor talents may remain unperturbed even if they become ridiculous. Palissot, who ridiculed the encyclopedists, that if mediocrity strives for elevation it cannot escape vulgarity.

[8]Diderot called Batteux' book *acephal* (headless), because it never defined what "beautiful nature" was.

[9]Johann Christoph Gottsched, *Critische Dichtkunst*, 4th ed. (Leipzig: Breitkopf, 1751), p. 725.

[10]I have used Jacques Barzun's translation from *Rameau's Nephew and Other Words* (New York: Bobbs-Merrill, 1964), 66-68.

[11]Aspects of this Goethean notion of musical symbolism was anticipated by a number of eighteenth-century writers, including d'Alembert and Johann Jacob Engel. Beethoven's alleged remark that his Pastoral Symphony was *mehr Ausdruck der Empfindung als Malerei* (*Allgemeine Musikalische Zeitung*, January 25, 1809) seems to point towards a similar conception of musical symbolism.

[12]Zelter thought that in this sense every good artist was an imitator, and he singled out the works of Bach, Handel, Haydn, and Beethoven's *Charakter-Symphonien* (sic!) as examples (Zelter, II, 60).

[13]Goethe, *Werke*, Artemis-Ausgabe (Zürich: Artemis, 1948-63), XIII, 42-43.

[14]The passage yielded several epigrams in *Makariens Archiv*.

[15]Zelter, eager to mend his fences, agreed on April 14, 1831 with Goethe and called upon Rameau as his witness (Zelter, III, 393).

[16]Goethe adds that in more lively and agressive dances the major and minor modes may alternate like diastole and systole (one of Goethe's favorite metaphors for polarity), whereas marches should always be in the major mode.

Weimar's monument, dedicated to the memory of Schiller and Goethe. (Courtesy Walter Wadepuhl)

Goethe and the Novella

Henry H. H. Remak

Abstract

After passing in review the cardinal components of novellesque structure including Goethe's observations on the subject within his creative works as well as outside them, I test, one by one, due to limitations of space, only the three constituents of Goethe's deservedly famous definition of the novella, "eine Begebenheit / sich ereignete/unerhörte" against the first four inside stories of his *Unterhaltungen deutscher Ausgewanderten* (1794-95) as well as "Die wunderlichen Nachbarskinder" in *Wilhelm Meisters Wanderjahre* (1829). The congeniality or non-congeniality of classicism, in general, and of Goethe, in particular, with certain inherent and continuous features of the novellesque tradition of Romanic cultures (Italy, France, Spain) are delineated. On the basis of harmony or the lack of such between novellesque structure and the *Gestalt* of specific stories, value judgments are arrived at: of the novellesque stories transposed by Goethe from foreign models, the second ("Klopfgeschichte"), third, and fourth ("Bassompierregeschichten") of the *Unterhaltungen*, and "Die pilgernde Törin" in *Wilhelm Meisters Wanderjahre* are the best. The outstanding novellesque story written by Goethe without close adherence to foreign or domestic prototypes is not a novella as such but a protracted and occasionally interrupted episode in *Dichtung und Wahrheit* (1811), Part I, Book VI: the story of the "Frankfurter Gretchen." Embryonically but distinctly and exquisitely novellesque is, further, the story of the "schöne Mailänderin," also interrupted from time to time, in the *Italienische Reise* (second Roman sojourn, published 1829). The essay concludes with a succinct historical and critical assessment of Goethe's role in the evolution of the novella, or rather the novellesque, its continuity and change. (HHHR)

Goethe's adaptation—Germanization, if you wish—of a genre that had originated and flourished in Romanic territory for almost four hundred and fifty years constitutes a notable example of cross-cultural input into the evolution of European literature.[1] I hope to make a little contribution to several facets of this process: Romanic-

Germanic literary interaction; the definition of the novellesque; the symbiosis of content and form, type and text; and the analysis as well as the assessment of some of Goethe's novellesque works in the light of that definition.

There is an almost novellesque paradox about scholarship on the German novella. While the novella thrived throughout the nineteenth century and the early twentieth, research on the subject, while not negligible, was relatively modest in quantity. Ever since World War II writers have greatly slowed down in writing novellas, but novella scholarship has mushroomed. It is even more ironical that in the last fifteen to thirty years highly nominalistic views on the German novella have increasingly asserted themselves without in the least inhibiting research on a genre that is not supposed to exist. Finding the novella to be a nonphenomenon after well over six hundred years of apparently fooling smart people, including academics, is certain to send not only historical scholars into a state of deep melancholia but might, heaven forbid, even raise questions in the minds of the disinterested populace about the usefulness of literary scholarship as such. Fortunately, things may not be as bad as the dialectic of scholars eager to make their mark as iconoclasts may suggest. Ironically—once again—most of the nominalists themselves, after having launched their theoretical lightnings against the myth of the novella, merrily go on working with it in practice. There has also been, in the most recent past, an effort to rescue the term in some way or another. And most nonspecialists continue, of course, to operate with the term, unaware of how controversial it has become.

Much of the nominalistic argument, I submit, is flawed by a wrong premise. Stripped to its essence, the assumption seems to be that there is an absolute theoretical prototype, *the* novella, and if that exclusive model is not overwhelmingly realized in every specific novella then there is no such thing as the novella. We come much closer to reality, I suggest, by saying that there are existential options—Staiger called them the dramatic, the epical, the lyrical—which occur in literature as in life in all kinds of mixtures, but their prevalence or intensity in any particular work may justify calling it a drama, an epic, a lyric. The novellesque (and I propose this coinage because "novellistic" may too easily be taken as a reference to the novel, not the novella) is basically a synthesis of the dramatic and the epic in prose form. If that combination, moving within approximate confines and with some kind of balance, predominates in a story we can call it a novella—not *the* novella. (I admit that it is linguistically and stylistically awkward to use "novellesque" exclusively. Therefore I sometimes backslide into "novella." In such cases, unless I refer to a particular story, I mean the novellesque). This merger of the dramatic and epical in prose form has evolved certain specific characteristics, partly through logical consequence, partly through success, that give the novellesque a certain profile. For this profile to be verified it is normally necessary that a goodly number of these features be present, but there are probably few novellas—certainty few good ones—that contain all these traits. Furthermore, the absence of even major characteristics may be compensated for by the extraordinary intensity and effectiveness of others present. Most novellas, then, will have nonnovellesque components also: the didactic or the psychological or the lyrical, the moral tale or the ghost story or the fairy tale. But they are secondary. The novellesque represents the norm, a novella the relative particularization of the norm.

How about the objection: so what whether it is called a novella or a tale or a short story or a novel? What difference does it make? Three reasons why it does. 1) Any literary work of art will, through comparison with a norm, yield dimensions and fine points it is less likely to reveal when contemplated in isolation. Norm $<--->$ text comparison enriches textual analysis. 2) It also benefits norms. Norms must be constantly tested against texts and, if necessary, revised accordingly. One of the cardinal weaknesses of much contemporary German and French theory is precisely that it compares theory to theory, not theory to text, or that text is sporadically used to corroborate theory rather than shape it. 3) Genres, subgenres, or types are no longer, if they ever were, forms of artistic and scholarly repression. They are essentially natural, whatever their misapplications in practice. If a story tending in a novellesque direction mingles jarring elements in its composition, the mismatch may well affect is plausibility, effectiveness, its overall quality. But the novellesque may be found in other, especially related media. Certain portions or aspects of novels, autobiographical fiction, travel stories, ballads, anecdotes, even fairy tales may contain concentrations of the novellesque that may be "purer" than those encountered in some supposed "novellas."

Scholarship has let itself in for much grief by not adopting an analytical, critical stance toward novella nomenclature. Some German authors are knowledgeable about novellesque history and criteria: Goethe, Tieck, E.T.A. Hoffmann, Hebbel, Storm, Hofmannsthal, Musil, Bergengruen. What they say about their and others' stories must be taken seriously. But even in their cases what they say and what they do is often very different. Furthermore, the designation "novella" for prose of medium length has proved to be enormously prestigious and even remunerative ever since Boccaccio. The fact that an author or an editor calls a story a "novella" may mean something or next to nothing. It depends. Contrariwise, the greatest novellas of German literature, Kleist's, were not published as novellas but as tales—"Erzählungen." The decisive factor is not under what label a story has been launched but what it *is*.

It is therefore necessary, before discussing some of Goethe's novellesque works, to tell you what are, in my judgment, the constituents of the novellesque. I apologize for the apodictic impression that my list may make on you, but time is short.

The best definition of the core of the novellesque is still, after a century and a half, Goethe's "eine sich ereignete unerhörte Begebenheit" (the "one authentic unheard-of event"). The news item is reported because it happened; it requires no other justification except that it must be interesting. The happening is largely supposed to speak for itself. Didactic, moralizing interventions by the narrator are as out of place in the novellesque as they would be in a well-reported newspaper story. Such intrusions would only undermine the authenticity of the occurrence. Just as in a newspaper a novella does not require an omniscient narrator. Some of the very best novellas (Kleist!) report events certain facets of which do not seem to be known or clear to the narrator, surprise him as much as the reader (take, for example, the first four stories in Goethe's *Unterhaltungen*). Thus novellesque occurrences seem more determined by chance or destiny than by personal will.

The authenticity of the novellesque report is safeguarded by the matter-of-factness and objectivity of the narration and the distance kept by the narrator. In some novellas the frame enhances this distance. The frame also fits the socio-conversational origin of the novellesque situation: stories *told* (not *read*) to an audience, a feature of the *Decamerone* integrally maintained in the *Unterhaltungen*, still observed in the "Wunderlichen Nachbarskinder" (herafter cited as *WN*) of the *Wahlverwandtschaften*, becoming increasingly pro forma or unspecified in the stories inserted in *Wilhelm Meisters Wanderjahre* (hereafter cited as *WMW*), and abandoned in the *Novelle*. The audience, originally entirely aristocratic (*Decamerone*), still is predominately so in the *Unterhaltungen* and in *WN*, grows more and more bourgeois (*WMW*, E. T. A. Hoffmann's *Serapionsbrüder*) but retains its sophistication.

A novella must mediate an interesting action interestingly since it also has a social mission. Therefore tension is indispensable to the novellesque. The evolution of this tension in a novella may go through some or all of these stages: dilemma > crisis > catastrophe > or near-catastrophe > final effect (the nearest equivalent I can find to "Pointe") > release from tension > quiet stimulus for reflection. Dramatic peripeteias appear in the novella as turning points, especially the releasing and the resolving ones.

The literary novellesque, unlike the newspaper report, implies that the event reported be not only shocking but significant. While the nucleus of a novella often corresponds to an actual event and a number of excellent novellas keep some of the exact wording of the original document recording the event, the literary narrator furnishes most of the language for his report, he must select, omit, and complete. This is what might be called "the literary difference." The closer the narrator can integrate invention with the record, the more authentic his novella is likely to be. His manner of narrating will be economical, concentrated, taut. Objective length is far less important a factor in determining whether a story is a novella than the subjective brevity to the reader. One of the most difficult novellesque requirements for German scholarship to grasp is that a good novella does not say everything—on the contrary: the less it explains, the more it conveys. German lyrics are often exemplary by their sparing use of words, their suggestive power, but German prose, primary or secondary, tends to be prolix. Since a novella is condensed and disciplined, the linguistic and stylistic configuration of every sentence counts. Artistic expectations are all the higher just because the author must respect the autonomy of the events. The reluctance of German scholarship in the last sixty years or so to take the actual event seriously is, in part, due to its fear of being tagged as positivistic and, in part, to the romantic belief that the more the author invents, the greater the literary merit of his work. On the contrary, the best novellas are artistically preeminent through *how* they report or simulate to report, by what they do *not* explain, by what they leave to the reader to complete, to explain, to interpret. Nothing is more novellesque than the polarity between the lucidity, the soberness of its language and the impenetrability of the events. This makes a productive cocreator of the intelligent reader. The more charged the events, the more disciplined their representation (Goethe at his best, Kleist). This polarity is one of the principal causes of novellesque tension. Sophisticated formal restraint applied to explosive happenings, a device also related to the presence of women among the listeners and, later on, readers, makes of the novella, with few exceptions, a genre for gourmets. The gradual transition from an aristocratic to a bourgeois genre while keeping aristocratic expectations intact (a marked feature, by the way, of French literature) occurred during Goethe's lifetime, in and through his works.

The combustible material that nourishes the tension of the novellesque is fed by disharmony between human intelligence and human passion, between rationality and irrationality, sense and senselessness. The notion of fateful senselessness, or at least lack of explicability, getting the better of intelligence, courage, and justice foments irony and paradox in the novella.

The novellesque—again like a good newspaper report—prefers the visual, the concrete. Given the German penchant for abstractions, this will pose difficulties for German novellas. The picture, the image must speak for itself. It should not be dragged in allegorically but must be an organic part of the event. It gives the novellesque its object orientation, its profile. The well-known novellesque notions of silhouette, falcon, and object-symbol ("Ding-symbol") are different sides of the same coin. The acoustic-musical equivalent to the central object in a novella is the auditory leitmotif (see, for example, the first two stories in Goethe's *Unterhaltungen*).

At best the coherence of a novella bestows representativeness upon each of its parts. Like the overture to an opera the very beginning of a novella is said to be the microcosm reflecting the macrocosm of the total work.

This is the context in which I will examine Goethe's novellas or presumed novellas. Much of the grief of contemporary *Novellenfor-schung*, whether of Goethe or not, occurs because novellesque tales are looked at as just stories whose every ingredient is considered without a systematic probing of their genre-oriented structure.

*   *   *

Where did Goethe discover the novellesque? In Italy and France, principally; in Spain, secondarily: in Boccaccio's *Decamerone* (1348-1353), in the *Cent Nouvelles Nouvelles* (author uncertain, 1462-1486), in Bandello's *Novelle* (1554-1573), in Marguerite de Navarre's *Heptameron* (1559), in Cervantes' *Novelas ejemplares* (1613), to name only a few. These works do not only carry novellesque material but anecdotes, jests, fairy tales, legends, moral tales, adventure stories, character portraits, *etc.* The impurity of this mix will be inherited by Goethe. But it is the novellesque element among them that has had the greatest impact on the shaping of quality prose literature in Western and Central Europe.

Goethe found these congenial sources in the foreign civilizations to which he felt most attracted. The novellesque owes its origin to the enviable ability of Mediterranean cultures to join the release and entertainment functions of interesting occurrences deviating from official social and moral norms with the redeeming value of artistic discipline. The novellesque displays an irresistible combination of Italian and French *joie de vivre* tinged by determinism, unabashed realism about the facts of life balanced by economy and refinement of language. It takes an objective, somewhat detached view of actions judged by their interest rather than their morality. It displays sophistication of approach, and, when necessary, a thin veneer of morality not taken too seriously by either the author or the intelligent reader. Its realism in content and stylization in form, its urbanity, its visual orientation, its elegant vitality were bound to appeal to Goethe's keen sense of what German culture, tending toward the abstract, the ponderous, and the mediated required for equilibrium. With his profound empathy for the Italians and the French, Goethe must have found their distinctive combination of intelligence and passion particularly fetching, because they made up for the German tradition of dialectically separating rationality from irrationality. In the Romanic literary orbit, passion, particularly illicit one like adultery, is rewarded, provided it is genuine and generous, or punished, if it is mean and unsavory, depending on which side can muster more intelligence and skill. In Cervantes' *La Fuerza del sangre*, as in Kleist's related *Die Marquise von O . . .* , the raped and dishonored heroine finally manages—and deserves— to get the better of the transgressor and salt him away in matrimonial bliss not only because of the genuineness of their reciprocal attraction distorted by their first encounter and the woman's unblemished and steadfast character but because of the intelligence, even the craftiness of her and her family's strategy in righting a wrong. True love is not enough: it must be guided by brains and adroitness. The indirect manner which saves face and honor is, in true Romanic tradition, a better way of solving amorous problems than open confrontations. In the "Prokuratorge- schichte" of Goethe's *Unterhaltungen*, taken from *Cent Nouvelles Nouvelles*, you have a beautiful example for the workings of this devious process. Had the procurator rejected the advances of the young wife it would have been an insult to her and probably to her husband; had he taken advantage of the older husband's prolonged absence it would have been cheap; it is only via the round-about but delicate, psychologically superb strategy of the procurator that the desired aim, morally, psychologically, and narratively satisfying, is achieved. The covert passion of Honorio for the princess in Goethe's *Novelle* (1828) is not denounced or eradicated, but neither is it—can it be—satisfied. It is deftly acknowledged, she knows it, he knows it, but no word has been spoken, no deed has been done that would cause lasting embarrassment to the princess. In contrast, the lack of intelligence of the flirtatious wife in Goethe's "Nicht zu weit" in *WMW* (1829) has as much to do with the impending shipwreck of her marriage as the moral and social questionableness of her behavior. The impact of the Romantic novellesque is not exhausted by simply pointing to plots lifted from Romantic texts. As a cultural phenomenon, it had a penetrating impact on Goethe's thinking and may imbue stories in which direct links with Romantic models do not exist. German culture has shown, long before and ever since Goethe, a remarkable curiosity about foreign civilizations, but this exceptional passive receptivity has much more rarely resulted in significant departures in active German literary endea-vors, in primary texts. Goethe's writing was actively stimulated by Romantic classicism, including the novella, and through his works the influence continued in the nineteenth century German novella.

We cannot deal on this occasion with the considerable variations and the historical evolution of the Romantic novella, but need to mention at least that Goethe was receptive to the serious moral and ethical turn in Cervantes' novellas. This leads to the question: what did German classicism, principally Goethe, see in the Romantic novellesque that was particularly kindred to it? The need, I think, to circumscribe passion, a process indispensable to any dramatic genre or blend, to classicism, and to the existential accommodation deemed so vital to the continuity of Mediterranean culture. This balance is enforced not only by the counterweight of rationality and expediency but by linguistic discipline and tradition, by stylization. Human dignity against devastating odds is maintained by linguistic, by artistic dignity. Form compels distance, objectivity. Compact-ness, economy control southern expansiveness.

But German classicism is, on the other hand, less congenial to other features of the Romantic novellesque such as the higher social and individual worth attached to what is entertaining, interesting, amusing, to practical compromise, to hedonism, to vitality as an ultimate value. Goethe's novellesque writings reflect, on the one hand, this vitality most impressively (as, for example, in the two Bassompierre stories of the *Unterhaltungen* or in the "Pilgernde Törin" of *WMW*), but, on the other, do not escape the classicistic perils of blunting the profile of the novellesque through excessive stylization and didactic dilution of what are supposed to be uniquely silhouetted, "unheard-of," extraordinary events. The dramatic, unpredictable, lifelike occurrences and turning points of the novella are, not infrequently, screened, smoothed, slowed up, "epicized" and didacticized in Goethe's novellalike tales.

With these social, historical, cultural, structural, and artistic implications in mind, we will now analyze some aspects of Goethe's novellas. The texts examined included the frame and the "Binnenerzählungen" (except for the "Märchen") of Goethe's *Unterhaltungen deutscher Ausgewanderten* (1794-1795), "die wunderlichen Nachbarskinder" in the *Wahlverwandtschaften* (1808), the *Novelle* (1828), and "Die pilgernde Törin," "Der Mann von fünfzig Jahren," and "Nicht zu weit" in *Wilhelm Meisters Wanderjahren* (1821, 1829).

*   *   *

First, what does Goethe himself have to say about the novellesque either in his stories or in commenting about his work?

Neither in the frame nor in the six inside stories of the *Unterhaltungen* is there a single mention of the term "novella." But the presence of the phenomenon counts for more than the nomenclature, and the configuration of the novellesque has a rather distinctive place in the frame which, like Boccaccio's, assembles an aristocratic crowd fleeing from a catastrophe and trying to entertain itself, but is far more elaborate, differentiated, and interesting than Boccaccio's. There, Goethe dwells again and again on some key terms of the novellesque. There is reference to the therapeutic value of relating "überraschende Vorfälle" and "neue Verhältnisse." There is the clergyman's unconventional, realistic stress on the newness of a story: "Was gibt einer Begebenheit den Reiz? Nicht ihre Wichtigkeit, nicht der Einfluß, den sie hat, sondern die Neuheit." There is, twice, emphasis on the authenticity of a novellesque story as its prime and overriding asset: "Der Alte behauptete, (die Geschichte) müsse wahr sein, wenn sie interessant sein solle; denn für eine erfundene Geschichte habe sie wenig Verdienst," and, from Karl,

Jedes Phänomen, sowie jedes Faktum, an sich (ist) eigentlich das Interessante. Wer es erklärt oder mit anderen Begebenheiten zusammenhängt, macht sich gewöhnlich eigentlich nur einen Spaß und hat uns zum Besten, wie zum Beispiel der Naturforscher und Historienschreiber. Aber eine einzelne Handlung oder Begebenheit ist interessant, nicht weil sie erklärbar oder wahrscheinlich, sondern weil sie wahr ist.

Freedom of subject, including risqué ones, must, says the Baroness, be compensated for by socially acceptable form. The best combination is a story that is entertaining while we listen to it, but "sie hinterlasse uns einen stillen Reiz, weiter nachzudenken."

Goethe was, then, aware of the novellesque. How systematically is another question. And other theoretical statements in the frame fit other types of stories (moral tale, ghost story, "Familiengemälde"), and they, too are represented in the *Unterhaltungen.*

Even if we did not know from Goethe's diaries and other documents that this awareness of the novellesque was subsequently fortified by his explicit use of the term "Novelle," his creative work would furnish the evidence. *WN* in the *Wahlverwandtschaften* were not only subtitled "Novelle" by him when the novel was published but the novella is cited specifically by Goethe, two decades later, in his famous conversation with Eckermann of January 29, 1827; "In jenem ursprünglichen Sinne einer unerhörten Begebenheit kommt auch die Novelle in den *Wahlverwandtschaften* vor." To boot, in the novella itself and immediately after its conclusion the narrator describes what the novellesque is all about. The first formulation is almost an anticipation of the quasi unbearable novellesque tensions of the "Unerhörte" in Kleist's novellas:

Sich vom Wasser zur Erde, vom Tode zum Leben, aus dem Familienkreise in eine Wildnis, aus der Verzweiflung zum Entzücken, aus der Gleichgültigkeit zur Neigung, zur Leidenschaft gefunden zu haben, alles in einem Augenblick — der Kopf wäre nicht hinreichend, das zu fassen; er würde zerspringen oder sich verwirren.

And just three paragraphs thereafter the narrator gives one of the most sensitive analyses of the nuclear role of the "sich ereignete Begebenheit" known to me. As soon as the story of the *WN* has been related by the companion of the lord to the group assembled, Charlotte leaves the room "höchst bewegt,"

denn die Geschichte war ihr bekannt. Diese Begebenheit hatte sich mit dem Hauptmann und einer Nachbarin wirklich zugetragen, zwar nicht ganz wie sie der Engländer erzählte, doch war sie in den Hauptzügen nicht entstellt, nur im einzelnen mehr ausgebildet und ausgeschmückt, wie es dergleichen Geschichten zu gehen pflegt, wenn sie erst durch den Mund der Menge und sodann durch die Phantasie eines geist—und geschmackreichen Erzählers durchgehen. Es bleibt zuletzt meist alles und nichts, wie es war.

As to *WMW,* Goethe worked on the three inserts with the most marked novellesque features, "Die pilgernde Törin," "Der Mann

von fünfzig Jahren," and "Nicht zu weit," off and on, from 1807 to
1829, but I have not found more than occasional curt notations on
their novellesque characteristics such as, e.g., his conversation with
Sulpiz Boisereé of September 20, 1815: "Meisters Wanderungen.
Novellen. Bestimmte Zahl der verschiedenen möglichen Liebesverwicklungen. Pilgernde Schöne . . . "

And, finally, there is the famous definition of the novellesque in
the conversation with Eckermann already cited, "eine sich ereignete
unerhörte Begebenheit," repeated, without the "sich ereignete," for
emphasis, and the significant decision by Goethe to call a just
completed, major story by its generic name, *Novelle*, perhaps with
Wieland's *Novelle ohne Titel* (1804) in mind. His justification is
very revealing about his concept of the novella not only then but
previously, and about the evolution of the genre in Germany in the
thirty-odd years that had elapsed since the *Unterhaltungen:*

> "Wissen Sie was, sagte Goethe, wir wollen es die *Novelle* nennen; denn was ist
> eine Novelle anders als eine sich ereignete unerhörte Begebenheit. Dies ist der
> eigentliche Begriff, und so Vieles, was in Deutschland unter dem Titel Novelle
> geht, ist gar keine Novelle, sondern bloß Erzählung oder was Sie sonst wollen."

It is amazing and ironic that Goethe anticipated and refuted the
current nominalists who wish to depersonalize the novella and
make it an unprofiled ingredient of the vast and amorphous type
called "Erzählungen." It is also ironic, however, that Goethe's
practice contributed itself to the expansion and diffusiveness of the
"ursprüngliche Sinn" of the novellesque to which he refers in the
next sentence, cited earlier. His practice is sometimes consistent
with his theory, sometimes not, and it is more often than not
inconsistent even within the same story.

*   *   *

In the final portion of my essay I will try an approach not so far
attempted in Goethe or novella scholarship, and that is to take the
salient components of novella structure, of my empiric hypothesis,
and test each of them, one by one, against Goethe stories tending in
a novellesque direction. Time constraints force me to limit myself to
the "eine Begebenheit," the "sich ereignete," and the "unerhörte."

The "one event," the "eine Begebenheit" needs, for a change, to
be taken more literally: a real, compact, self-contained occurrence
which should have what Heyse called a silhouette. If there are a
series of events there must be a tight sequential unity to them, and
one must be the culminating or decisive one. In the first Bassom-

pierre story of the Unterhaltungen it is the *meteoric*, ephemeral but unforgettable affair of a subsequent Marshal of France with an enigmatic beautiful shopkeeper's wife, in the second one the regular adultery of another Bassompierre with a likewise mysterious beautiful woman. In the "Pilgernde Törin" it is the tramp-like arrival of a woman of high refinement in the von Revanne household, father and son fall in love with her, she disappears. An amusement—oriented wife and mother in "Nicht zu weit" leaves her family stranded and is then herself literally as well as figuratively ditched—for the coach in which she and her beau are riding ends up in a ditch, and he then ditches her in favor of another woman in the coach. When she finally gets home, her husband is no longer there. He has met an old flame of his. Here the story ends.

As Goethe himself has singled out the *WN* in the *Wahlverwandtschaften* as an exemplary novella by his standards, let us take a closer look at its silhouette. Two children of neighbors, a boy and a girl, of about the same age, destined by their parents for each other, fight in such a way that their parents are compelled to give up their matchmaking plans. The girl becomes engaged to another, worthy but less strongly profiled young man. The first young man, now a soldier, returns, the bride is seized by a strong passion for him of which he is not aware. Shortly before his planned departure he invites the bridal pair to a cruise, she jumps overboard, he saves her, swims with her to shore, not far from which they are sheltered by a young couple. They fall into each other's arms, swear eternal mutual faithfulness, receive wedding clothes from their just married hosts, put them on and thusly arrayed appear before the respective parents of bridegroom (one does not quite know which of the two bridegrooms!) and bride. The in-laws, it is intimated, will give their blessings to this fast switch.

The story, only six to eight printed pages long, turns, in a wider sense, on *one* event: the practical consequences of the love-hatred of girl and boy from childhood on. It culminates, more specifically, in the decisive water and land happenings. Clarity of the lines, tension, pace, absence of digressions, dilemma, turning point releasing the novellesque action (the girl jumps into the water to commit suicide—or to be saved by the man she wants desperately to capture? Who knows?? At any rate, a very novellesque ambiguity)[2], crises, threatening catastrophe (aquatic and social), resolving turning point (the inofficial couple requests and will probably receive parental blessings): all these are novellesque. But, as one looks more closely, the silhouette, especially towards the end, turns out to be conventional. It carries the marks of abstract invention, of melodrama. The youth who saves a recalcitrant but basically equi-attuned belle from great danger and thus wins her for himself is a very traditional theme. That he and the young woman are being sheltered, of all people, by a just-married couple whose wedding attire is still hanging around, that the clothes happen to fit the second couple to a *T*, that it then appears in these bridal garments before the parents, implores their blessings and most likely receives them all in a jiffy (what the lawful bridegroom has to say about it the narrator does not tell us)—all this would be judged, were it not written by Goethe, to be pure melodrama, not plausible as a "sich ereignete Begebenheit," non-authentic, a literary concoction. We further note that the time frame is very vague and that this novella manages not to mention a single solitary name of a person or a location: an extreme example of classicistic stylization and generalization that does not attain the minimum of selectively precise reporting demanded by the novellesque.

In the two paragraphs immediately preceding the *WN* the story is introduced as being told by the companion of the lord after he has, as the author puts it, stretched the attention of his audience to the highest degree by stories both strange and terrifying, whereas now, in the *WN*, he will relate a story strange, to be sure, but gentler than its predecessors ("eine zwar sonderbare aber sanftere Begebenheit"). That means, I think, an event with a happy ending. Even though the novellesque and a positive conclusion are not incompatible, it strikes us that the happy resolution of this novella is far less compelling than the preceding conflict. Goethe's novellesque stories, particularly those inserted into novels, tend to have taut, incisive novellesque beginnings followed by increasing diffuseness and a conventional resolution, or sometimes no resolution at all. Goethe may have recognized the problem himself in his conversation with Eckermann of January 29, 1827 when, referring to the story he finally entitled *Novelle*, he says:

> Es kam sodann zur Sprache, welchen Titel man der Novelle geben solle; wir taten manche Vorschläge, einige waren gut für den Anfang, andere gut für das Ende, doch fand sich keiner, der für das Ganze passend und also der rechte gewesen wäre.

Goethe's trouble is that he wants to report an extraordinary event as such but also wants to write a moral-psychological-classicistic 'exemplary' novella in the sense of Cervantes. He is cognizant of the principal structural conditions for such a novella but the artistic execution of the idea falters in the second, novellesque part of the story whereas the first, psychological part is far more persuasive. With the exception of the girl's jump into the water which is well motivated psychologically but equally effective as a novellesque action, the novellesque in this story is not good, and what is good in this story is not novellesque.

What is the "eine Begebenheit" in "Der Mann von funfzig Jahren"? Flavio is supposed to marry his cousin Hilarie. Hilarie is in love with Flavio's father, the major, Flavio with a beautiful young widow, who in turn loves the major. The major and Hilarie become engaged to each other even though not yet publicly. The widow rejects Flavio. Now Flavio and Hilarie fall in love, and finally the major and the widow join hands. This silhouette, which reminds one somewhat of *WN*, is too mathematically perfect to command authenticity. It raises the suspicion that the story is hyperstylized. And so it is. After the opening, which is brisk and novellesque, the author's creative discipline evaporates gradually: tying the knotty problem seems to interest him much more than untying it. Goethe's previously cited remark to Sulpiz Boisereé as he composed *WMW*: "Novellen. Bestimmte Zahl der möglichen Liebesverwicklungen" reflects this greater reliance on invented plots rather than fictional building on actual events.

The genesis of "Der Mann von funfzig Jahren" may provide a clue to the problem Goethe had with its structure and its integration into *WMW*. Off and on he worked on it for about twenty-two years, from 1807 to 1829. It was printed independently from *WMW* in 1818, as part of it in 1821 but only the initial chapter (less than one third of the story), finally published as such in the final version of *WMW* (1829) but in three very uneven parts: the first four-fifths together (Second Book, Chapters 3 to 5), then it skips a short chapter and the beginning of the following one and reappears in Chapter 7, then the reader hears nothing about it for over two hundred printed pages, until finally, toward the end of the novel, a few cursory bits of information provide a nonchalant anticlimax to a story that began so auspiciously, so firmly. We possess numerous schemata for this story. Goethe himself must have felt a bit uneasy about it even in the final text of the novel because, before relating it, he addresses the reader, admits that he had thought of publishing the story piecemeal but claims that its "internal consistency" argued for continued narration; he also asserts that while the "Begebenheit" it narrates appears to be separate from the mainstream of the novel, the reader will recognize at the end of the novel how close is the connection between the two. A good deal of German scholarship has performed veritable acrobatics in order to demonstrate that all these impediments notwithstanding both the internal consistency and the amalgamation with the larger work of these novellesque insertions have been little short of perfect. It is difficult to share that view. Thematic links do not, in themselves, signify artistic integration.

*   *   *

The impetus of the Romantic cult of originality, and scholarly reaction against positivism have stifled, especially in the last half century, a proper respect from researchers on the German novella, including Goethe's, for the seriousness with which the "sich ereignete" in Goethe's definition should be regarded. It would be well to keep in mind the observations of Aristotle which, though not referring to novellas, are eminently applicable to the novellesque:

> A poet who writes about something that has really happened is no less a poet for that reason. . . . It is probable that much that happens occurs against the odds of probability. . . . We must prefer the impossible that is credible to the possible that is incredible.[3]

The writer of novellas has a lot of room for maneuvering from close adherence to the nucleus of an event that has been recorded, via its artistic completion or truncation, to the periphery of imitation, that is, the invention of an improbable event that becomes probable through the strength of its artistic execution. But the risk of sliding into the non-novellesque is all the greater the farther the writer moves from what Wolfgang Kayser regards as the core of the novellesque,[4] "a real and unique occurrence defined locally and temporally."

In inverse proportion of credibility, the scope of the "sich ereignete" may range from a well-known, major historical event via public, scientific, or scholarly documents, a report of an event by a person directly affected or a witness, to literary sources and realistic inventions by the author. Does it need to be said that boundaries between these categories often are not sharp?

Take the "Beautiful Shopkeeper" novella in the *Unterhaltungen*. It closely follows, but with deftest nuances of translation, omission, and addition, the text of the published recollections (1666) of one of France's great military, diplomatic and court figures, the Marshal François de Bassompierre (1579-1646). Bassompierre's memoirs are written in a straightforward, unpretentious manner and thus invite credibility. From recollections—and novellas—one expects a fine mixture of precision and stylization in selected indications of time and place. This is what we get in Bassompierre and Goethe: "Marschall von Bassompierre — seit fünf oder sechs Monaten — die kleine Brücke [in Paris] — Laden an einem Schilde mit zwei Engeln — Fontainebleau — eine sehr schöne Frau von zwanzig Jahren — Nacht von Donnerstag auf den Freitag," *etc.* But as important is the mediation of the cultural and psychological prerequisites of a specific, past epoch whose *historical* uniqueness enhances the *particular* uniqueness of the episode reported by the Marshal and by Goethe. If you want to reward invention, then Hofmannsthal's neo-romantic adaptation is, of course, 'superior' to Bassompierre and to Goethe. But ignoring the difference in historical consciousness, as Hofmannsthal does, transferring the neoromantic complexes of fin-de-siècle nineteenth century to these two figures bursting with vitality, the Marshal and the shopkeeper, dissecting and subjectivizing the lapidary, honest, nonanalytic style of the late Renaissance which Goethe maintains with clean dignity—all this is such a violation of authenticity that as a total literary text Hofmannsthal's is vastly inferior to Goethe's.

When the author makes use of a source that itself is literary, his access to the "sich ereignete" is even more indirect. The original version of the story of the procurator in the *Unterhaltungen* is already a blend of the novellesque and the moral tale, communicated with remarkable concentration. Goethe used the first printed version from the fifteenth century ("Le sage Nicaise ou l'amant vertueux," last story in the *Cent Nouvelles nouvelles*, author unsure, written about 1462, printed about 1486), that is, the version coming closest to the original occurrence whatever it was. He quadrupled the story in length but preserved the basic structure. In "Die pilgernde Törin" Goethe likewise kept very close to the printed French version ("La Folle en pélerinage," 1789) whose technique, we are told, is looser, more psychological, more veiled than Bassompierre's stories but is still part of the older novellesque tradition. Goethe's translation is regarded as a very fine achievement: he has respected the novellesque integrity of the events with admirable "Fingerspitzengefühl" and has not succumbed to the temptation of interpreting explicitly. In his beautiful tribute to the story, Erich Trunz at the same time defines some of the subtle essence of the novellesque:

> Es ist wie im Leben selbst: man erfährt nur, was man selber sieht und hört. Es ist in diesem Falle zu wenig, um genau Bescheid zu wissen, aber genug, um den psychischen Verhalt zu erschließen. Mit feinem Takt verschleiert die Pilgernde

ihre Erlebnisse, und doch gibt sie aus innerer Not manches davon frei. In dieser
Verhaltenheit, diesem Schleier liegt der Reiz der Novelle . . . Der psychologische
Tiefblick ist auch in dieser Novelle. Aber er wird nicht vordergründig, er wird
nicht präsentiert . . . Der Leser muß vieles selbst erschließen.[5]

Farthest from the "sich ereignete" is a story invented by the author with the aim of verisimilitude. To this category belong, predominantly or wholly, the *WN*, "Der Mann von funfzig Jahren," "Nicht zu weit," and the *Novelle*. To the best of my knowledge, the overwhelmingly invented nature of these stories is, in my judgment, detrimental to the quality of the novellesque in these works. The *WN* and the *Novelle* are so stylized that hardly a reader could believe that they narrate an actual occurrence. "Der Mann von funfzig Jahren" and "Nicht zu weit" start in a most novellesque fashion and then slow down noticeably, the author seems to lose interest, the story oozes away and ceases, like the *WN*, abruptly. The lack of an authentic source seems to aggravate the author's task of untying the knot of the plot. A tendency toward melodramatizing could be the substitute for the lack of a genuine novellesque core.

*   *   *

The unheard-of, the unprecedented, the "Unerhörte" in Goethe's novella definition traverses a scale that extends from the unusual, for example, Bassompierre's silent encounters with the beautiful shopkeeper, to the totally unexpected rendez-vous with two cadavers in place of his mistress. Fabricated events, no matter how skilfully manipulated, seem unable to carry through the element of the unexpected, so crucial to the novellesque, with the same authenticity as a core of actual events. Whatever is calculated possesses a planned logic and is therefore typical rather than unique. A novella in which one can predict what this or that person will say or do is unlikely to be a good novella. But a novella author who tries to manufacture surprises by intricate contrivances is likely to achieve results as bad. Sooner or later he will get caught up in his web, like the cleverest but false testimony of a witness in a trial is bound to make a fatal mistake sooner or later.

How about the "Unerhörte" in Goethe's practice? In the first inside tale of the *Unterhaltungen*, the Antonelli story, the unheard-of is, as a matter of fact, very audible but scary and weird: the "fürchterliche Ton." But this phenomenon is blunted as the story moves on or rather declines. First because the horrible noises are attenuated from occurrence to occurrence: the frightful plaintive sounds become shots which become clapping which become heavenly sounds and then vanish completely. Second, because the consequences of these phenomena are too monotonous: three times, after such sounds, the singer faints and so do her companions. Since Goethe followed the original account of a personal experience related by the French actress Hippolyte Clairon, he cannot be blamed, in this case, for the progressive dilution of the "Unerhörte," but it *is* characteristic for some of his work, particularly the later one.

In the second, the "mysterious knocking" story, we experience on less than a page two "unerhörte Begebenheiten": the knocking sound without any ascertainable cause, pursuing a nice-looking, nubile orphan girl serving a noble family, and the outrageous but successful cure:

> Entrüstet über diese Begebenheit und Verwirrung, griff der Hausherr zu einem strengen Mittel, nahm seine größte Hetzpeitsche von der Wand und schwur, daß er das Mädchen bis auf den Tod prügeln wolle, wenn sich noch ein einzigmal das Pochen hören ließe.

The knocking ceases. Here the "Unerhörte" is undiluted and remains extremely effective. Goethe wisely refrains, in this as in the Antonelli and Bassompierre pieces, from offering any explanations in the story: he delegates that to the persons in the frame, and even there we are left with a choice of possible interpretations, and only samplings at that.

In the meetings between Bassompierre and the shopkeeper the "Unerhörte" builds up quietly but with pervasive effectiveness: first the almost speechless encounters, the restrained drama where the bending forward of the shopkeeper's wife tells more, and better, than wordy paragraphs; the abrupt alternation between aggression and restraint in an exquisite tradeswoman who immediately insists on spending a night under one cover with the subsequently celebrated Marshal of France, then rejects his caresses in the most self-possessed manner, demands to go to bed with him forthwith and confesses to having so insuperable a desire of joining him that she would have accepted any condition to achieve it. The same woman proclaims unapologetically a double faithfulness to her husband and to her lover. And then she disappears without a trace, leaving her lover two corpses to puzzle about.

The second Bassompierre story contains, on about half a page of print, half a dozen unheard-of features: it is not the adulterous husband who sneaks up to his mistress when he can but a beautiful woman who loves the husband so much that *she* visits *him* regularly; this adulterous relationship takes on the complexion of a second, parallel marriage in that they meet for two years every Monday. The legitimate wife finally discovers them sleeping together but refuses to create a scandal. Trusting her instinct she takes off her veil, covers the feet of the lovers, and leaves quietly. On waking up and seeing the veil, without requiring an explanation, the mistress immediately decides to break off the relationship and not to approach her lover again by a hundred miles. She leaves gifts for the three legitimate daughters which accentuate the fairy-tale potential of the story without jeopardizing, in this case, the novellesque.

After the first four stories of the *Unterhaltungen* the novellesque component, including the "Unerhörte," dwindles rapidly. As the baroness correctly states in the frame commentary, the procurator story is primarily a moral tale. The tale about the tribulations of Ferdinand, invented by Goethe, is also a "moralische Erzählung" of some psychological refinement. The *Märchen*, which concludes the Unterhaltungen, is *sui generis*.

We have already touched on the "unheard-of" in the *WN*: the story ends, conventionally enough, with a bride and a bridegroom, but the bridegroom is not the one to whom she had been engaged the morning of the same day. Perhaps it is this awkward combination of the conventional and unconventional that is the fatal flaw in the ending.

The "Pilgernde Törin" of *WMW* is chock-full of unheard-of events and turns. A beautiful, charming young woman tramps companionless along the way. Her clothing components clash (just like those of the beautiful shopkeeper in Bassompierre's story): dusty shoes and shining silken stockings. Her behavior is also strange: her manners are exquisite, she is tactful, intelligent, well read, sings, plays the piano, sews—but nobody knows where she comes from. She is alternately deeply mournful and frivolous, serious and derisive. The "fool" or "simpleton" designation in the title is alternately confirmed and questioned. When father and son compete for her she hints to the father that she expects a child from the son and to the son that she expects a child from the father, and then vanishes never to be seen again. The "Unerhörte" is precise in detail, enigmatic in origin, and perfectly authentic, classical in its objectivity and conciseness. Here the stylization fits the mysterious side of the femme fatale.

The "Unerhörte" in "Der Mann von funfzig Jahren" with its jigsaw pattern is, as mentioned before, too fabricated, too disjointed in treatment and too strung out to be effective.

The initial situation of "Nicht zu weit": a wife and mother failing to appear at her birthday celebration which has been meticulously prepared by her husband and children, because she is gallivanting around in the neighborhood constitutes, in design and execution, the novellesque "Unerhörte" at its best, as does her being ditched by her beau later on, but the narrator then melodramatizes the "Unerhörte" into a mushy encounter of the husband with an old flame, and the story breaks off there.

In the *Novelle*, the "Unerhörte" (the conflagration in town, the escape of a tiger and a lion and their threat to the princess) turns toward the end into the lyrical rendering of magical legend and presents, as a whole, an uneasy combination of the dramatic, epic, and lyrical, though individual parts are very beautiful.

What is "unerhört" is, be it noted, influenced by the cultural conditioning of the reader. When in the procurator story an elderly husband, during an extended absence, permits controlled infidelity to his beautiful young wife as long as she chooses a sedate, reliable, intelligent, and discreet partner, the Northern reader is likely to view this as "unerhört" whereas the Italian and French reader will find this arrangement historically anchored in the customs of a certain social class (the institution of a "cicisbeo," a "sigisbeé").

* * *

To sum up: Goethe has an extraordinary flair for the epic treatment of the "sich ereignete unerhöte Begebenheit," particularly at the beginning of his novellesque stories. Sometimes—and especially when he follows closely a foreign, usually French source—he implements his own definition of the novella successfully in much or all of the story and comes up with superb examples of the genre: in the story of the knocks and the two Bassompierre stories in the *Unterhaltungen*, and in the "Pilgernde Törin" of *WMW*. But in others novellesque discipline and intensity get sidetracked by excessive stylization (*WN, Novelle*) and formal fatigue (Antonelli story, "Der Mann von Funfzig Jahren," "Nicht zu weit"). The procurator story stands by itself: it is primarily a moral tale, but the novellesque potential, the humor, wit, and sophistication with which the impending adultery is turned into a moral lesson give it a novellesque spice which benefits the story.

Time and space do not permit us to pursue novellesque elements in all prose, let alone non-prose works of Goethe that clearly do *not* qualify as novellas. "Der Hausball" (1781), "Reise der Söhne

Megaprazons" (1792), and "Die guten Weiber" (1800-01) come to mind. The story of the beautiful young Milanese woman in the *Italienische Reise* (Second Roman sojourn, published 1829) is, in subject and narration, embryonically but distinctly and exquisitely novellesque. I hope to do it justice on another occasion. An early version, in some respects, of the "Schöne Mailänderin," is the fourteen-year-old Wolfgang's first love, the "Frankfurter Gretchen." It provides most of the substance for Book V and the beginning of Book VI, Part I of *Dichtung und Wahrheit* (1811). It comes in four installments, interrupted by the account of the crowning of the Archduke Joseph, but the two events are skillfully intertwined and the execution of the story so careful and elaborate that, with some excisions, it could well be published as a novella. Though we have little historical documentation about the events on which the Gretchen episode is based, it gives every indication of possessing just the right novellesque mixture of "Dichtung und Wahrheit."[6] The "Unerhörte" is represented by the totally unexpected criminal complications into which his association with the "Gretchenkreis" precipitate the adolescent. The coronation enhances the dramatic and epic texture of the story. The account conveys personal authenticity. It is chary of moralistic or didactic digressions, lets the events speak mostly for themselves, is fate oriented, objective and differentiated in approach, has the right blend of distance and empathy, humor and benevolent irony, is interesting and contains clear turning points. The tension proceeds from dilemma (the faked letters and the sweet uncertainties of love) via sudden crises, near-catastrophe (criminal, physiological, psychological), final effect ("Pointe": Gretchen's deposition that her affection for him was sisterly, which infuriates and disenchants the young lover), to the resolution of tension and the "stillen Reiz zum Nachdenken," since a number of points remain in the clair-obscur. Marked stylization, especially in the lack of identification by name of the protagonists and specific locations, is amply justifiable here by the author's understandable reluctance to embarrass his friends in view of the criminal turn of events. Artistic discipline is consistent and there are no signs of auctorial fatigue. The faked letters constitute the "Falke" of the story. While the Gretchen adventure has no novellesque frame, the coronation serves a frame-like function. To be sure, this is not a pure novella either: it has idyllic and fairy-tale elements, which here blend deftly with the novellesque. If you ask me which is the best novellesque story written by Goethe without close adherence to a model, my answer, "unerhört" as you may find it, is the "Gretchenepisode" in *Dichtung und Wahrheit*.

But that does not mean that we need to be apologetic about the high ranking we otherwise give to those novellesque stories by Goethe in which he has, if you want to put it that way, invented the least. Romantics among scholars may be disappointed by that, but, to me, that is a rather narrow view of the matter. In the first place, it is our job to evaluate the quality of literature. Who gets credit for it is a secondary question. Regardless who wrote it, a good story is a good story, a poor story is a poor story, and a so-so story is a so-so story. Secondly, just as style has been defined as what we omit, novellesque quality is likewise built as much on what you don't say as on what you say. Goethe's self-discipline in safeguarding the original source while translating it—and every translation is an adaptation, a rewriting—is worthy of admiration, not of condescension. Into this artistic self-denial was mixed Goethe's profound empathy and respect for the integrity of foreign cultures. Third, Goethe's weaknesses as a novellesque storyteller are related to his strengths, to his universality, to his existential deference to evolution, genesis, process, systole as well as diastole, which caused long pauses in his creative progress on numerous projects. Since the novellesque is based on a particularly demanding fusion of form and content, structural defects in this genre are more glaring than in others. Fourth, Goethe's historical merits in introducing the Romanic novella into Germany are of the highest order. The surge of the novella, along with the lyric, as the finest literary genre achievement of Germany in the nineteenth century bears witness to his seminal role, even though not all of his novellesque practices should have been followed.

A great deal of lip service is being paid by German literary scholarship to the "indissoluble unity " of form and content, of type and text. But I have not found a corresponding plethora of studies that really, systematically, patiently, textually verify this contention. In undertaking to illuminate the reciprocal relationships between type and text via text analyses viewed in the light of genre hypotheses I have hoped, primarily, to shed light on the nature of novellesque stories. I do not think it is entirely accidental that Goethe provided literary substance for this purpose, for one of his enduring existential concerns was with the polarity between the specific and the general.

Indiana University

Notes

[1]Now and then this essay parallels portions of a chapter, "Die Novelle in der Klassik und Romantik," which I am contributing to Volume XIV, "Europäische Romantik I," of the *Neues Handbuch der Literaturwissenschaft*, Wiesbaden: Athenaion, to be published in 1982. Limitations of space restrict me to the most indispensable references. In particular, a critical evaluation of the secondary literature has to be left for another occasion.

[2]The actual source of this "unerhörte Begebenheit" is to be found in the story from an English newspaper which Goethe utilizes, in October of 1787, to teach English to another of his novellesque heroines, the "schöne Mailänderin" with whom he is falling in love during his second sojourn in Rome: "Ich blickte schnell hinein und fand einen Artikel, daß ein Frauenzimmer ins Wasser gefallen, glücklich aber gerettet und den Ihrigen wiedergegeben worden. Es fanden sich Umstände bei dem Falle, die ihn verwickelt und interessant machten, es blieb zweifelhaft, ob sie sich ins Wasser gestürzt, um den Tod zu suchen, sowie auch, welcher von ihren Verehrern, der Begünstigte oder Verschmähte, sich zu ihrer Rettung gewagt" (*Italienische Reise, Zweiter Römischer Aufenthalt, Goethes Werke*, ed. Erich Trunz, (Hamburg: Christian Wegner, 1959), XI, 424.

[3]Transposed into English from the German translation of Aristotle's *Poetics* by Olof Gigon (*Poetik*, Stuttgart: Reclam, 1964, pp. 40, 67; see also p. 72).

[4]Translated from *Das sprachliche Kunstwerk*, 6th ed. (Berne and Munich: Francke, 1960), pp. 354-355.

[5]*Goethes Werke*, VIII, 619.

[6]I have dealt with this topic in an earlier publication: "Die novellistische Struktur des Gretchenabenteuers in *Dichtung und Wahrheit*," in *Stil-und Formprobleme der Literatur* (Heidelberg: Winter, 1959), pp. 303-308. My current accents are, however, not necessarily identical with those I chose at that time.

Symbolik des Glücks. Zu Wilhelm Meisters Bildergeschichte.*

Zum Andenken
an Paul Requadt

Hans-Jürgen Schings

Resümee

Vor dem Hintergrund des *Werther* und der Krisengeschichte des anthropologisch-psychologischen Romans der Spätaufklärung wird der Versuch gemacht, *Wilhelm Meisters Lehrjahre* als außerordentlichen Glücksfall vorzustellen — als Anti-Werther und symbolischen (nicht psychologischen) Roman des Glücks. Dabei verbindet sich die (alte) Frage nach dem Glück Wilhelm Meisters mit der (alten) Frage nach der symbolischen Struktur des Romans, in der Hoffnung, daß just diese gezielte Verbindung neues Licht auf die gattungsgeschichtliche Stellung des *Wilhelm Meister* wirft. Ausgangspunkt ist die Geschichte vom kranken Königssohn und seinen Amazonen, eine Bildgeschichte, die Wilhelm Meisters Ursprungsleidenschaft prägt und in ihren vielfältigen Verästelungen und Varianten seinen Weg bestimmt. Tatsächlich kann man die Geschichte des Helden als eine Geschichte seiner Prinzenrollen (David, Tankred, Prinz Harry, Hamlet, Hettore Gonzaga) lesen, in die sich natürlich auch die Reihe der Amazonen und Prinzessinnen einfügt (von Chlorinde bis zu Natalie). Im Gemälde vom kranken Königssohn (nach Plutarchs Geschichte von Antiochos und Stratonike), das Wilhelm im Haus Natalies wiederfinden wird, hält sich jene Geschichte auch in einem konkreten Motiv präsent.

Wilhelm rückt immer aufs neue in diese ursprüngliche Konstellation ein, auch und gerade in ihre tragischen Varianten. Doch handelt es sich dabei nicht um die leer in sich kreisende Wiederholung, die Goethe an Werther diagnostiziert, nicht um schwärmerische und pathologische Träume der puren Innerlichkeit, sondern um eine kontinuierliche Wiederkehr, die der Dialektik des Suchens und Findens gehorcht, den Antwortcharakter der Welt in einer Reihe "antwortender Gegenbilder" erfahrbar macht und so schließlich in die 'Wiederbringung aller Dinge' und den Gewinn Natalies, des Glücks, münden kann.

Goethes symbolische Poesie steht im Einklang mit diesem Antwortcharakter der Welt, da sie, ihrer Struktur nach, nicht Poesie der Entzweiung von Ideal und Wirklichkeit, von Allgemeinem und Besonderem, nicht sentimentalisch-transzendentalphilosophische Poesie der "Fremde des Lebens" ist, sondern Poesie der Versöhnung von Besonderem und Allgemeinem, von Erfahrung und Idee — und darin eine Poesie des Weltvertrauens von Gnaden der Natur. (HJS)

"Ich kann das Gefühl, das mich beim Lesen dieser Schrift, und zwar in zunehmendem Grade, je weiter ich darin komme, durchdringt und besitzt, nicht besser als durch eine süße und innige Behaglichkeit, durch ein Gefühl geistiger und leiblicher Gesundheit ausdrücken, und ich wollte dafür bürgen, daß es dasselbe bei allen Lesern im ganzen sein muß". Zu solchem "Wohlsein", das "ein fröhliches Leben in dem Menschen anzufachen und zu erhalten" vermag, bekennt sich, nach der Lektüre der beiden ersten Bücher, einer der ersten und kompetentesten, aber auch anspruchsvollsten Leser des *Wilhelm Meister*, Schiller — nicht ohne das "peinliche" Gefühl eines "melancholischen Augenblicks" und das Eingeständnis, daß ein solches Produkt der Heiterkeit, des Lebens und der Harmonie jäh die Kluft zwischen der Natur als "Synthesis" und der Philosophie als "Antithesis" aufreißt, "den unendlichen Abstand zwischen dem Leben und dem Räsonnement" erhellt.[1] Der Statthalter der Transzendentalphilosophie, der sentimentalische Geschichtsphilosoph der "Fremde des Lebens",[2] der Entzweiung von Wirklichkeit und Ideal macht die Erfahrung des ihm prinzipiell Verwehrten: die Erfahrung des Glücksfalles *Wilhelm Meister*.

In der Tat: ein Glücksfall ist Goethes Roman in mehr als einer Hinsicht. Als literaturgeschichtlicher Glücksfall macht er Epoche in der Formierung des 'modernen' deutschen Romans. Darüber hinaus aber ist er ein Glücksfall auch in der eminenten Bedeutung des Wortes — ein Roman des glückenden neuen Lebens, ein symbolischer Roman des Glücks. Denn Glück stand ja nun keineswegs auf der Tagesordnung des zeitgenössischen Romans. Wielands Agathon, Werther, Wezels Belphegor, Schillers Julius, Moritzens Anton Reiser — ein Blick auf diese paradigmatische Reihe zeigt deutlich genug, daß der neue Roman der "inneren Geschichte" durchweg einen Krisen- und Katastrophenkurs einzuschlagen genötigt ist. Alle jene Helden der "Poesie des Herzens"[3] werden mehr oder weniger rücksichtslos der Ort- und Weltlosigkeit überführt, der "transzendentalen Obdachlosigkeit" ausgesetzt.[4] Sie fallen, buchstäblich, aus der neuplatonisch-hermetischen "Chain of being" heraus — wie Agathon und Julius,[5] verzehren sich an ihrer Innerlichkeit, an der "tiefen reinen Empfindung", der "wahren Penetration", den "schwärmenden Träumen", der "Spekulation" — wie Werther,[6] werden in ihrem naiven Vertrauen auf die beste an der schlechtesten aller möglichen Welten zuschanden — wie der neue Candide Belphegor, drohen in der "Seelenlähmung", der acedia der Erniedrigten und Unterdrückten zu ersticken — wie Anton Reiser. In die Melancholie werden alle diese Schwärmer geführt, herabgestimmt, der Teleolo-

gie des Leibnizschen Universums entfremdet und auf eine Innerlichkeit zurückgeworfen, welche die äußere Wirklichkeit als disparates
Chaos erfährt. Die Hydra der Empirie überliefert die Welt schwarz-
galliger Metaphorik: eine von keinem Enthusiasmus zu erlösende
Zusammenballung egoismus- und interessegelenkter Leidenschaften
ist sie (Agathon), "nichts als ein ewig verschlingendes, ewig wieder-
käuendes Ungeheuer" (Werther),[7] ein "barbarisches Schlachthaus",
der Kampfplatz des "bellum omnium contra omnes" (Belphegor),[8]
"eine Welt von Würmern" (Julius),[9] ein Gewirr von "Zwecklosigkeit,
abgerissenen Fäden, Verwirrung, Nacht und Dunkelheit", das aller
Hoffnung auf Wohlklang und Harmonie spottet (Anton Reiser).[10]
Es ist namentlich und folgerichtig der psychologisch-anthropolo-
gische Roman, den sein Formgesetz dazu treibt, sich in die
Labyrinthe der inneren und äußeren Ursachenreihen zu verlaufen
und solchermaßen die Zerstörung der enthusiastischen Illusion mit
der stabilierten Disharmonie von Geisterwelt und Körperwelt, von
Kopf und Herz, von Ich und Welt zu bezahlen. Resignation,
Melancholie und Misanthropie heißt die Parole.

Erst vor diesem dunklen Hintergrund, den ich hier ohne weitere
Ursachenforschung lediglich skizzieren kann, hebt sich der wahrhaft
unerhörte Glücksfall ab, der im *Wilhelm Meister* zum Ereignis wird
— insonderheit natürlich vor dem pathologischen Kontrapunkt von
Werthers "Krankheit zum Tode". Kein Zweifel, der *Wilhelm Meister*
ist nicht zuletzt, und dies gezielt, ein Anti-Werther. Den hypochon-
drischen Trübseligkeiten der Selbstbeobachtung, wie sie der nachita-
lienische Goethe allenthalben entdeckte, nicht zuletzt in der neuen
Philosophie und Anthropologie, setzte der *Wilhelm Meister* eine
neue Form des reinen Anschauens entgegen — und damit eine neue
Form des Romans. Die realistischen Züge der *Theatralischen
Sendung* treten zurück; ebensowenig läßt sich Goethe auf die
Analytik des psychologischen Romans ein. Vielmehr entsteht jetzt
eine symbolische Organisation, die ihresgleichen in der Literatur der
Zeit nicht hat. Das Glück Wilhelm Meisters steht im Bündnis, in
Wechselbeziehung mit der neuen Verfahrensweise des symbolischen
Romans.

Damit habe ich zu meiner These gefunden. Ich stelle also noch
einmal die nicht eben neue Frage nach dem Glück Wilhelm
Meisters,[11] indem ich sie mit der ebenfalls nicht neuen Frage nach
der symbolischen Anschauungsform des Romans verbinde — dies
nun freilich in der Hoffnung, daß just diese gedoppelte Fragerich-
tung neues Licht auf den Roman wirft, auf den "ungeheuern
Aufwand"[12] der Konkretion, der in der anhaltenden, aber

abstrakten Diskussion über Sinn und Ziel des 'Bildungsromans' nur allzu leicht verschwindet. Ich versuche zunächst — Symbolik des Glücks —, den Bildungsroman als Bildergeschichte zu lesen, als die Geschichte einer Bildfiguration, die versteckt und doch offen den Weg des Romanhelden regiert, um sodann — Glück des Symbolischen — einige grundsätzlichere Folgerungen zu ziehen. Ich halte mich also vorerst ganz an Goethes "realistischen Tic",[13] an sein anschauendes, gegenständliches Denken, um dann, mit und gegen Schiller, Vorschläge zur "Pronunziation der Haupt-Idee"[14] zu machen.

Die Bildergeschichte, in die Wilhelm gerät und von der hier die Rede sein soll, ist die Geschichte vom kranken Königssohn auf der Suche nach den Amazonen. Man tut gut daran, dabei Friedrich Schlegels Einsicht zu folgen: "Der kleinste Zug ist bedeutsam, jeder Strich ist ein leiser Wink."[15] Und nicht weniger Goethes Maxime über die symbolische Poesie: "Wer nun dieses Besondere lebendig faßt, erhält zugleich das Allgemeine mit, ohne es gewahr zu werden, oder erst spät".[16] Erst spät ist denn auch die Forschung auf die Spur jener Geschichte geraten, ohne sich freilich über ihre Bedeutung einig zu sein.[17]

Sie setzt schon mit dem ersten Kapitel des Romans ein. Ist es Zufall, daß Mariane ausgerechnet "als junger Offizier gekleidet", als "das weibliche Offizierchen" (9)[18] die Szene betritt? Ist es zufällig, daß die alte Barbara sie vergeblich zum Umkleiden zu bewegen sucht: "es ist eine unbequeme Tracht, und für Euch gefährlich, wie ich merke" (10)? Und ist es von ungefähr, daß sich Wilhelms Interesse gerade auf eben diese Tracht richtet? " . . . mit welchem Entzücken umschlang er die rote Uniform! drückte er das weiße Atlaswestchen an seine Brust!" (11)

Der 'leise Wink' erschließt sich erst später. Im zweiten Kapitel hören wir dann vom Puppenspiel, jenem weihnachtlichen Ursprungserlebnis, der Initiation in ein magisches Geheimnis, das, "Wilhelms Lieblingsmaterie" (16), den Aufbruch des Bürgersohnes anzeigt und stiftet. Am Beginn steht, an jenem Weihnachtsabend, das Spiel von Saul, Goliath und David, dem "zwergmäßig gebildeten" "Glücksprinzen", der "die schöne Königstochter zur Gemahlin erhielt" (13). Die Phantasie des Kindes hat einen Gegenstand gefunden. Seinen Höhepunkt indes erreicht das kindliche Theaterspielen, als es sich an der Geschichte von Tankred und Chlorinde entzündet. Was den jungen Wilhelm an Tassos Epos besonders fesselt, ist die heroische Chlorinde, und was seinen sich entwickelnden Geist vorzüglich beeindruckt, ist ihre "Mannweiblichkeit" (26), ihr Amazonenwesen!

So prägt sich ihm "hundert und hundertmal" die Tankred-Chlo-
rinde-Tragödie mit ihrem tödlichen Ende ein, sagt er sich immer
und immer wieder "die Geschichte des traurigen Zweikampfs
zwischen Tankred und Chlorinde" vor, versenkt er sich in die Szene
im bezauberten Wald, als Tankreds Hieb Blut aus dem Baum
fließen läßt — "und eine Stimme ihm in die Ohren tönt, daß er
auch hier Chlorinden verwunde, daß er vom Schicksal bestimmt sei,
das, was er liebt, überall unwissend zu verletzen!" (27) Die
sentimentale Macht dieser Geschichte besetzt Wilhelms Einbildungskraft, dunkel bildet sie sich "zu einem Ganzen" in seiner Seele,
so daß er sie "auf irgendeine Weise vorzustellen gedachte" (27).
Ahnungslos erzählt Wilhelm von seiner Tankred-Rolle und von der
mißlungenen Aufführung, nicht ahnend, daß er sich gerade
anschickt, die Tragödie auf ganz andere Weise "vorzustellen", daß
die schlafende Mariane das erste Opfer der Tankred-Chlorinde-
Konstellation sein wird, in die Wilhelm selbst einrückt, Opfer
nämlich jener schicksalhaften Bestimmung, "das, was er liebt,
überall unwissend zu verletzen". Die Winke, die der Text gibt, sind
deutlich genug: hier bildet sich, in der überfließenden Fülle des
Herzens und der "herumschweifenden" Einbildungskraft, eine Ursprungsleidenschaft aus, eine "Urgeschichte",[19] die in der Sehnsucht
nach der Amazone das Aufbruchs- und Suchpotential Wilhelm
Meisters manifestiert. Kein erzähltechnisches Mittel der Vorausdeu-
tung ist das, sondern eine angeborene und deshalb zu neuer
Prägung befähigte Matrix,[20] die Wilhelms Wirklichkeitsapperzeption
bestimmt und nun auch in die Wirklichkeit hinübertritt — ob in der
tragischen oder in einer glücklichen Ausformung: das ist die Frage,
die Wilhelms Weg begleitet.

Kein Wunder, daß alle "Lieblingsgeschichten" des Helden die
Züge jener Urgeschichte annehmen. So natürlich auch die allegorische "Muse der tragischen Dichtkunst", die Wilhelm zum rhetori-
schen Kampf gegen das Gewerbe antreten läßt. "Kronen und
Dolche, Ketten und Masken" qualifizieren sie zur königlichen
Amazone, "die Königreiche verschenkt" (32 f.). Heroisch, "enterbt
und nackt", übergibt sich der junge Poet diesem Leitbild der
tragischen Muse, "die mir ihren goldnen Schleier zuwarf und meine
Blöße bedeckte" (33), — und nimmt damit die symbolische Handlung vorweg, die sich in der ersten Begegnung mit der "schönen
Amazone" aufs erstaunlichste wiederholen und erfüllen wird. Noch
aber vermischt Wilhelm, wiederum ahnungslos, das Bild der tragischen Musen-Amazone mit dem Marianes: "Hätte ich denken
können . . . , daß eine ganz andere, eine lieblichere Gottheit kom-

men, mich in meinem Vorsatz stärken, mich auf meinem Wege begleiten würde . . . " (33). Chlorinde—die tragische Muse—Mariane: von Wilhelms überquellender Phantasie gesteuert, überformt die Sehnsuchts-Geschichte seiner Innenwelt illusionär die Außenwelt, entwirft sie ein "Gemälde auf Nebelgrund, dessen Gestalten freilich sehr ineinanderflossen" (35).

Es sei zu wünschen, läßt der Erzähler angesichts der eingeschlafenen Mariane verlauten, "daß unser Held für seine Lieblingsgeschichten aufmerksamere Zuhörer künftig finden möge" (33). Gemeint sind natürlich auch aufmerksamere Leser. Besondere Aufmerksamkeit verdient deshalb schließlich das "Lieblingsbild", in dessen Beschreibung die Reihe der Lieblingsgeschichten des ersten Buches einmündet, jenes Gemälde aus der italienischen Sammlung des Großvaters, deren Verkauf für das Kind "die ersten traurigen Zeiten" seines Lebens (69) zur Folge hatte — das "Lieblingsbild" vom kranken Königssohn, der sich über die Braut seines Vaters in hoffnungsloser Liebe verzehrt. Ein Kasus aus der ägyptischen oder babylonischen Geschichte, wie der närrisch gelehrte Friedrich am Ende des Romans sagt (605). Es handelt sich um den Kasus von Antiochos und Stratonike, der zumal in der Überlieferung durch Plutarch eine folgenreiche Geschichte in Literatur und Malerei erlebt.[21] Seleukos I. von Syrien ist mit Stratonike verheiratet (spätere Varianten sprechen von dessen Braut); sein Sohn Antiochos siecht in heimlicher Liebe zur Gemahlin des Vaters dahin, bis der Arzt Erasistratos dem Geheimnis dieses Leidens auf die Spur kommt, Seleukos der Stratonike entsagt und sie mit Antiochos vermählt, nicht ohne dabei dem Sohn auch das Königreich zuzusprechen. Das Gemälde des Romans — Goethe dürfte zumindest Bearbeitungen des Motivs von Antonio Belucci in Kassel und von Januarius Zick in Ehrenbreitstein gekannt haben[22] — faßt jene Peripetie ins Auge, als der Arzt am Krankenbett des Antiochos in der hereintretenden Stratonike die Ursache der Krankheit entdeckt und damit den Weg zur glücklichen Lösung einschlagen kann.

"Unauslöschlich" sei der Eindruck, den das Gemälde auf ihn gemacht habe, erklärt Wilhelm dem Unbekannten, dem ersten Sendboten der Turmgesellschaft, der seinerzeit die Sammlung begutachtet und dem Oheim Natalies den Kauf empfohlen hatte. "Unauslöschlich" — das ist die Sprache Wilhelms für seine Ursprungssehnsucht, für seine Urgeschichten. Noch immer geht ihm das Herz über: "Wie jammerte mich, wie jammert mich noch ein Jüngling, der die süßen Triebe, das schönste Erbteil, das uns die Natur gab, in sich verschließen und das Feuer, das ihn und andere erwärmen und beleben sollte, in seinem Busen verbergen muß, so daß sein Innerstes unter ungeheuren Schmerzen verzehrt wird!" (70) Wilhelm ahnt auch diesmal nicht, wie sehr er in eigenem Namen und in eigener Sache spricht. Denn die Mariane-Katastrophe steht ja unmittelbar vor ihrem Ausbruch. Sie wird alle Schmerzen des kranken Königssohns, die Schmerzen Werthers, in ihm entfachen.

Lieblingsgeschichten, Lieblingsmaterie, Lieblingsbild — eine kontinuierliche Reihe ist im Verlauf des ersten Buches sichtbar geworden, eine weit in die Kindheit Wilhelms zurückreichende Folge von Identifikations-, Such- und Leitfiguren, in denen die ursprüngliche Mitgift Wilhelms ihren Ausdruck findet, in deren Zeichen Aufbruch und Weg Wilhelms stehen werden — mit der in diesen Urgeschichten angelegten Konkurrenz des tragischen (Tankred-Chlorinde) und des glücklichen Paares (Antiochos-Stratonike). — Indes, mit dem Verlust Marianes, "die anstatt einer Gottheit mich zu meinen Wünschen hinüber führen sollte" (85), scheint diese Reihe auch schon abzubrechen, scheinen die Ursprungsleidenschaften Wilhelms zerstört. "Wie wenn von ungefähr unter der Zurüstung ein Feuerwerk in Brand gerät" (76), so wird in Wilhelms Innerem das ungeheure Feuer des Antiochos verzehrend entzündet, bis der "ausgebrannte hohle Becher eines Vulkans" (78) zurückbleibt. Und das Autodafé, dem die eigenen poetischen Versuche zum Opfer fallen, übersetzt die Metapher in die Realität, läßt "jede Hoffnung der Liebe, des poetischen Hervorbringens und der persönlichen Darstellung" (80) in Flammen aufgehen. Zerrissenheit, Abgründe, Wiederholungen des Schmerzes, Grausamkeit gegen sich selbst — Wilhelm gerät in die Sphäre und auf den Kurs Werthers. Der Griff "ins Unendliche" (84) ist ins Leere gegangen, die Arme seines Geistes sind "zerschmettert" (84).

Aber nicht Werther ersteht wieder, sondern ein Gegen-Werther. Wilhelm bleibt nicht sich selbst überlassen. Die Natur hält in der Krise die Hand über ihren Liebling (77). Die frühen Wünsche erlöschen keineswegs, haften immer noch im Herzen. So kann der Beginn der Reise Verjüngung und Erneuerung bringen, weckt sie jene ursprüngliche, belebende, produktive Kraft, die Wilhelm auszeichnet: "Er belebte die Welt, die vor ihm lag, mit allen Gestalten der Vergangenheit (!), und jeder Schritt in die Zukunft war ihm voll Ahnung wichtiger Handlungen und merkwürdiger Begebenheiten." (87) Und wie sich Vergangenheit und Zukunft wieder belebend zusammenknüpfen, so knüpft sich auch die in der Krise abgerissene Reihe unserer Geschichte wieder an. Denn alsbald bildet sich jener "Kometenschweif" von Figuren,[23] den Wilhelm hinter sich herzuziehen pflegt, und sogleich belebt sich auch seine Lieblingsmaterie, seine Lieblingsgeschichte, sein Lieblingsbild — in der Rätselfigur Mignons, des 'Lieblings', wie der Name sagt.[24]

Wilhelm ist auf Anhieb gefesselt, und diese Faszination hat ihre Gründe. "Seine Augen und sein Herz wurden unwiderstehlich von dem geheimnisvollen Zustande dieses Wesens angezogen". (98) "Diese Gestalt prägte sich Wilhelmen sehr tief ein; er sah sie noch immer an, schwieg und vergaß der Gegenwärtigen über seinen Betrachtungen". (99) In solchem dämmernden, wirklichkeitsvergessenen "Halbtraum" (99) richtet sich Wilhelms Blick nach innen, kehrt die verdrängte Vergangenheit zurück, erneuert sich die Urgeschichte und ihre Prägung. Die Grenzen von innen und außen verfließen. Mignon wird solchermaßen zur Figur der Selbstbegegnung und Selbstauslegung Wilhelms, in der ihm seine Innenwelt, sein innerster Trieb als gegenständliches, "wunderbares" "Rätsel" (98) gegenübertritt. Das Bekenntnis zu Mignon ist deshalb das Bekenntnis zum eigenen Dämon, gipfelnd in jener emphatischen Szene der Adoption, in der Wilhelm den symbolischen Vorgang der Verinnerung nachvollzieht und "dieses verlassene Wesen an Kindesstatt seinem Herzen [einverleibt]" (116).

Kein Wunder also, daß Wilhelm auf den ersten Blick nicht weiß, "ob er sie für einen Knaben oder für ein Mädchen erklären sollte" (91) — ein Schwanken, das in der *Theatralischen Sendung* noch einen raschen Wechsel von maskulinen und femininen Anredeformen gezeitigt hatte. Kein Wunder, denn das "zwitterhafte Geschöpf" (193), der "artige Hermaphrodit" (439) — so, mißbilligend, Jarno — antwortet in einer neuen Metamorphose auf das Idol der "Mannweiblichkeit", das Wilhelm seit dem initiierenden Chlorinde-Erlebnis befeuert — und ihn schließlich zu Natalie führen wird. Zweifellos gehört es zu den heikelsten und umstrittensten Kunstleistungen des Romans, den Übergang von Mignon zu Natalie ins Werk zu setzen, den Genius der unbedingten poetischen Sehnsucht durch den Schutzgeist der Harmonie abzulösen, das Adoptivkind Mignon gegen den natürlichen Sohn Felix auszuwechseln. Denn Mignon muß sterben — wie Chlorinde, wie Mariane —, damit der kranke Königssohn geheilt werden kann. Erst das Absterben der dunklen und pathologischen Mignon-Potenzen öffnet den Weg in die Welt des Lichts, der Tätigkeit, der unsentimentalen Selbstbeschränkung. Mignon stirbt ihren symbolischen Tod zu Füßen Natalies und Thereses, weil ihr Hermaphroditentum, ihre Androgynie zwar, im Gefolge des platonischen Mythos und der hermetischen Tradition,[25] paradiesische Identität und Sehnsuchtserfüllung verheißt, dies aber um den Preis unbedingter Heterogenität auf dieser Welt. "Wahnsinn des Mißverhältnisses" notiert Goethe 1793 zu Mignon.[26] Und er meint damit auch die Krankheit Wilhelms, die Disproportion des Talents mit dem Leben, die Werther-Gefahr der modernen, sich verzehrenden Subjektivität mit ihrer verzweifelten Sehnsucht, "ins Unendliche" zu greifen.

Die nächste Station der Geschichte vom kranken Königssohn entsteht vor unseren Augen geradezu als perfektes Tableau, als lebendes Bild, in dem die Motive des Antiochos-Stratonike-Gemäldes wie von selbst zusammenschießen, um in der bedeutenden Konstellation des Bildes auch, wie sich versteht, dessen Pointe vorwegzunehmen. Dies alles geschieht in der Szene nach dem Räuberüberfall. Als shakespearisierender Prinz Harry hat Wilhelm die republikanisch-romantische Schauspielergesellschaft sorglos in einen Hinterhalt geführt. Jetzt liegt er, der auch noch just zuvor mit seinem Helden Hamlet "zu einer Person" zu werden glaubte (217), der gerade noch mit Laertes den Zweikampf darstellte, "in welchem Hamlet und sein Gegner ein so tragisches Ende nehmen" (223), verwundet, buchstäblich, theatralisch und symbolisch ein kranker Königssohn, "in der wunderbarsten Lage" (224). Und es erscheint das Frauenzimmer auf dem Schimmel, im "weiten Mannsüberrock", die "schöne Amazone" (226). Wie Chlorinde und Minerva[27] betritt sie die Szene. Wie Stratonike nähert sie sich, mit dem "heilsamen Blick ihrer Augen", dem Liegenden. Wie einst die Muse der tragischen Dichtkunst ihren Schleier, so legt die Unbekannte jetzt den Überrock über den "Verwundeten und Unbekleideten" (228). Für einen Augenblick scheint sogar der Oheim die Stelle des Seleukos einzunehmen. Und selbst der Arzt des Gemäldes ist zur Stelle, in Gestalt des Chirurgus mit der Instrumententasche. Gerade als dieser den Verletzten berührt, um die Kugel zu entfernen, gerinnt die Szene in Wilhelms "angegriffenen Sinnen" zur Epiphanie,[28] so "daß es ihm auf einmal vorkam, als sei ihr Haupt mit Strahlen umgeben, und über ihr ganzes Bild verbreite sich nach und nach ein glänzendes Licht" (228). Die Amazone wird zur "Heiligen". Kein romantisch-triviales Wunder wird hier dem Leser zugemutet, auch nicht etwa eine schlichte Augentäuschung Wilhelms. Immerhin hat die Lichterscheinung Wilhelms ihre Äquivalente in der *Farbenlehre*.[29] Wilhelm ist für dieses Glanz- und Strahlen-Bild disponiert. Ohne die produktive Kraft der Urbilder wäre die Erleuchtung nicht möglich. Die Epiphanie antwortet nun auch von außen auf Wilhelms Urgeschichte. "Unauslöschlich" (235), natürlich, ist dieser Eindruck auf Wilhelms Gemüt; "tausendmal" läßt er das Bild an sich vorüberziehen, erneuert er dessen "Nachbilder". Wie ein Traum, beinahe wie ein Märchen kommt ihm die Erscheinung seiner Innenbilder vor (236). Wilhelm selbst beginnt zu ahnen, daß diese Epiphanie mit seiner ursprünglichsten Sehnsucht zu tun hat: "Alle seine Jugendträume knüpften sich an dieses Bild. Er glaubte nunmehr die edle, heldenmütige Chlorinde mit eignen Augen gesehen zu haben: ihm fiel der kranke Königssohn wieder ein, an dessen Lager die schöne, teilnehmende Prinzessin mit stiller Bescheidenheit herantritt" (235).

Es kann mit Wilhelm nicht schlecht ausgehen — so viel ist nach dieser Szene gewiß, in der ihm seine frühesten Wünsche entgegenkommen, seine ersten Sehnsuchtsbilder Gestalt annehmen, auch wenn sich hier noch die Konkurrenz zwischen Chlorinde und Stratonike abzeichnet. Jäh durchschießt Wilhelm deshalb die glücksverheißende Ahnung, daß "uns in der Jugend wie im Schlafe die Bilder zukünftiger Schicksale umschweben und unserm unbefangenen Auge ahnungsvoll sichtbar werden", daß "die Keime dessen, was uns begegnen wird", schon ausgestreut seien, daß "ein Vorgenuß der Früchte, die wir einst zu brechen hoffen", möglich sei (235).

Wohl gerät der kranke Königssohn auf seiner Suche nach der "heilsamen" Amazone noch auf manche Irrwege, die seine Krankheit, seine "falsche Tendenz"[30] erneuern, wohl gibt es 'falsche' Wiederholungen des Bildes, 'falsche' Prinzenrollen und 'falsche' oder doch vorläufige Amazonen — und die Angst, die einzig ihm bestimmte zu verfehlen, wie Hamlet "fremd" zu bleiben "in dem, was er von Jugend auf als sein Eigentum betrachten konnte" (224). Beklemmend häufen sich die tragischen, ja tödlichen Verläufe der Tankred-Geschichte. Die schöne Gräfin glaubt einen Krebsschaden davongetragen zu haben; die unglückliche Amazone Aurelie wird an der Seite Wilhelm-Hamlets zu einer wahren zweiten Ophelia und richtet sich in der Rolle der Orsina — wieder ist Wilhelm als Prinz Hettore Gonzaga ihr Partner — zugrunde; die Nachricht vom Schicksal Marianes und der Tod Mignons beschließen diese düstere Serie. Ich muß über Wilhelms Identifikation mit dem kranken Königssohn Hamlet ebenso hinweggehen wie über seinen letzten großen Irrtum, der das Pendel in die entgegengesetzte Richtung ausschlagen läßt, die Werbung um die prosaische Ökonomie-Amazone Therese — die, eine "wahre Amazone" (439), sich keineswegs dem sentimental-melancholischen Amazonen-Idol Wilhelms fügt und deshalb dem Schicksal Chlorindes entgeht.

Ich wende mich stattdessen gleich jener außerordentlichen und bewundernswerten Szene zu, in der Wilhelm der schönen Amazone endlich wiederbegegnet. Was Wilhelm hier widerfährt, und was mit einer sicheren Kunst der lakonischen Andeutung und Summation ins Bild gesetzt wird, legt einen (Goethe gut bekannten) theologischen Begriff nahe: was hier geschieht, kommt geradezu einer 'Wiederbringung aller Dinge' gleich.

Wilhelm findet sich an dem "heiligsten Orte, den er je betreten hatte". Mit dem Signalsatz "Jugendeindrücke verlöschen nicht, auch in ihren kleinsten Teilen", erkennt er Stücke aus der Sammlung des Großvaters wieder, zuvörderst, ausdrücklich, eine Muse. Wieder glaubt er ein Märchen zu erleben. Kommt er doch in einem genauen (und noch zu erläuternden) Sinne nach Hause. So fällt sein Blick denn auch sogleich auf das "wohlbekannte Bild vom kranken Königssohn", das im Vorsaal hängt. Ins Kabinett geführt, sieht er dann, "hinter einem Lichtschirme, der sie beschattete", ein lesendes Frauenzimmer. " 'O daß sie es wäre!' sagte er zu sich selbst in diesem entscheidenden Augenblick". Und sie ist's. "Die Amazone war's!" Sie nähert sich, Wilhelm sinkt ein zweites Mal in die Knie, legt den eingeschlafenen Felix nieder, küßt ihre Hand. "Das Kind lag zwischen ihnen beiden auf dem Teppich und schlief sanft" (512 f.).

In knappen Andeutungen durchlaufen der Aufbau dieser Szene und Wilhelms Assoziationen alle Stadien seiner Sehnsucht, alle Nachbilder seiner Urgeschichte: die Heilige (an dem "heiligsten Orte"), die Muse, die Stratonike des Gemäldes, die Lichterscheinung, die Amazone. Alle diese Bilder erfüllen sich in Natalie. Und doch ist Natalie, deren Namen der Erzähler an dieser Stelle zum erstenmal in Zusammenhang mit Wilhelm nennt, noch mehr, überbietet sie die früheren Bilder. Nicht von ungefähr bleibt das Lieblingsbild im Vorsaal zurück. Auch der überwältigende Glanz der Lichterscheinung wiederholt sich nicht, weicht vielmehr dem temperierten Licht des reinen Anschauens. Aber was sich da für einen Augenblick wie von selbst und doch bedeutend gruppiert, Natalie, der knieende Wilhelm, das schlafende Kind Felix zwischen ihnen — erinnert das nicht auch an ein Gemälde, ist das nicht ein neues lebendes Bild, das Bild des neuen Lebens, das Bild einer neuen heiligen Familie? Erfahren wir deshalb in diesem Augenblick den Weihnachtsnamen 'Natalie'? Hatte nicht Wilhelms Aufbruch mit einem Weihnachtsabend, einem "Christgeschenk" begonnen? Darf man sich vielleicht auch daran erinnern, daß der 25. Dezember der

Geburtstag sowohl Charlotte von Steins wie von Goethes Sohn August war? Und wird nicht der Wilhelm der *Wanderjahre* ausgerechnet in der "halb wunderbaren" Geschichte von Sankt Joseph dem Zweiten sich wiedererkennen — auch dies eine Geschichte von Bildern, "die sich . . . in eine schöne Wirklichkeit auflösten"?[31]

" . . . ich war meiner Sache, ich war meines Glücks gewiß", erklärt der Joseph der *Wanderjahre*, als sich ihm die Bild-Präfigurationen erfüllen.[32] Bis es für den Wilhelm der *Lehrjahre* endgültig dazu kommt, muß er freilich noch das schwierige achte Buch hinter sich bringen, mit seinen Irritationen, Demütigungen, Verstimmungen, mit seinen Reduktionen und Rektifikationen, die Wilhelm umschaffen, die tragischen Möglichkeiten eliminieren, die märchenhaften Wünsche auf die (gesellschaftliche) Wirklichkeit zurückführen, die pathetische Sentimentalität durchkreuzen, kurzum das "unbedingte Streben" (553) in einer Serie von "Aufopferungen" begrenzen und den Helden 'gesellschaftsfähig' machen. Die Vermutung, daß es nicht ohne Korrektive abgehen wird, befällt Wilhelm nicht umsonst, als er, gleich nach der entscheidenden Begegnung, sein Urbild der Amazone, angefüllt mit dem grenzenlos sentimentalen und melancholischen Pathos des kranken Königssohns, mit der neuen, gegenwärtigen Freundin vergleicht: "Sie wollten noch nicht miteinander zusammenfließen; jenes hatte er sich gleichsam geschaffen, und dieses schien fast i h n umschaffen zu wollen." (516) Natalie ist keine heroisch-sentimentale Amazone — und Wilhelm muß deshalb nicht länger den Tankred oder den Hamlet spielen, kann deshalb die Pointe der Antiochos-Stratonike-Geschichte erfahren, die seine Empfindsamkeit so völlig verkannt hatte. Die Rektifizierungen der Turmgesellschaft führen Wilhelm zwischen Tragödie und Märchen hindurch, bis zu der letzten Deutung des Gemäldes, seiner glückbringenden Entzifferung. Nach den Ereignissen um den Selbstmord Augustins sehen wir die Gesellschaft in einem einigermaßen desolaten Zustand, aus dem Gleis geraten, Zuflucht zu geistigen Getränken nehmend, Wilhelm vom Arzt für krank erklärt und mit Arznei versorgt. Ein letztes Mal: der kranke Königssohn. Da bricht der tolle Friedrich den Bann, mit einer indiskret schwadronierenden und jedenfalls ganz und gar unsentimentalen Dechiffrierung des Lieblingsbildes: "Wie hieß der König? . . . Wie heißt der Ziegenbart mit der Krone dort . . . ? Wie heißt die Schöne, die hereintritt und in ihren sittsamen Schelmenaugen Gift und Gegengift zugleich führt? Wie heißt der Pfuscher von Arzt . . . ?" (606) Jetzt braucht Wilhelm, trotz neuerlicher Verzweiflung, nur noch drei Romanseiten bis zu seinen Schlußworten, die sich in ihrer verhaltenen Prägnanz sehr von seiner früheren Rhetorik unterscheiden: "Ich kenne den Wert eines Königreichs nicht . . . , aber ich weiß, daß ich ein Glück erlangt habe, das ich nicht verdiene, und das ich mit nichts in der Welt vertauschen möchte" (610).

Symbolik des Glücks: die Bildergeschichte vom kranken Königssohn hat zu ihrer Pointe, zum Glück gefunden. Es war, so hoffe ich, zu beobachten, wie sich diese Geschichte und ihre präfigurative Kraft gebildet haben, als zweisträngige Urgeschichte der Paare Tankred-Chlorinde einerseits und Antiochos-Stratonike andererseits — Erscheinungsformen von Wilhelms Ursprungsleidenschaft und Ursprungshoffnung, die seinen angeborenen Trieb zugleich sichtbar machen und wecken. Und das Erstaunliche ist geschehen: die Bilder der Innenwelt treten nach außen, stiften Konstellationen, in die Wilhelm immer erneut einrückt, kehren in Metamorphosen wieder, gerinnen zu lebenden Bildern — bis Stratonike den Sieg über Chlorinde davonträgt, das Gemälde des Großvaters sich gegen die tragische Tasso-Episode und ihre gefährlichen Potenzen behauptet.

Symbolik des Glücks: die Bildergeschichte, die zu Natalie führt, verkörpert das Glück der 'Wiederbringung aller Dinge', das Wilhelm zuteil wird, das Glück des Zusammenhangs, das Glück eines Suchens, das nicht ins Leere geht, das vielmehr das Finden zum Wiederfinden macht. " . . .ich werde mich des Eindrucks von gestern abend zeitlebens erinnern, als ich hereintrat und die alten Kunstbilder der frühsten Jugend wieder vor mir standen" (519), bekennt Wilhelm Natalie; sie schließen seine frühesten Erinnerungen unmittelbar an den gegenwärtigen Augenblick, so daß sich Wilhelm in seinem "Erbteile" wiederfindet: "und mich . . . , mich Unwürdigen, finde ich nun auch hier, o Gott! in welchen Verbindungen, in welcher Gesellschaft!" (519) Glück — das bedeutet ein solches Zusammenschließen von frühester Zeit und Gegenwart, ein Zusammenschießen aller Fäden, das bedeutet Wiederfinden, Heimkehr, Heimat, das bedeutet, in Natalie Gestalt annehmend, die Erfahrung vom Antwortcharakter der Welt. Denn dies war ja die entscheidende Hoffnung, die ihm das hochbedeutsame Symbol des Regenbogens zu Beginn des siebenten Buches zugespielt hat, "die stille Hoffnung, daß die angeborne Neigung unsers Herzens nicht ohne Gegenstand bleiben werde", das Gefühl, "daß wir nicht ganz in der Fremde sind", daß wir einer "Heimat" näher sind, "nach der unser Bestes, Innerstes ungeduldig hinstrebt" (421). *Wilhelm Meisters Lehrjahre* sind der symbolische Roman dieser Hoffnung. Einer Hoffnung, hinter der sich freilich auch Angst verbirgt — die Angst

Wilhelms vor der "Fremde des Lebens", vor der unheilbaren Entfremdung, vor der "Lücke" (569) zwischen der angeborenen Neigung und ihrem Gegenstand, vor der Hypochondrie der sich selbst untergrabenden Subjektivität. Goethes Roman ist ein Roman gegen diese Angst und ihre Melancholien.

Allerdings wäre es völlig verfehlt, Wilhelm Meister nun einfach-hin als einen "Hans im Glück" zu betrachten.[33] Dem Glück Wilhelms entspricht eine produktive Kraft in ihm. Eine "Vorempfin-dung der ganzen Welt" nennt sie Aurelie (257). Ihr entspringen die Wünsche und Sehnsüchte, die Wilhelms Urgeschichten hervor-treiben, ihr verdankt sich die besondere Auszeichnung von Wilhelms Suchen. Die klarsichtige Therese weiß darüber Bescheid: "aber nicht das leere Suchen, sondern das wunderbare gutmütige Suchen begabt ihn, er wähnt, man könne ihm das geben, was nur von ihm kommen kann." (532) Ein "edles Suchen" ist das, "wodurch wir das Gute, das wir zu finden glauben, selbst hervorbringen" (531). Und noch mehr sieht Therese: dieses Suchen macht Wilhelm Natalie ähnlich. Über das von Therese Gemeinte hinaus ist damit ein Schlüssel für das produktive Suchen und Finden Natalies gegeben. Wilhelm kann Natalie nur deshalb finden, weil er ihr ähnlich ist, weil zwischen dem Suchenden und seinem Gegenstand ein Verhält-nis der Gleichheit herrscht, weil sein Suchen deshalb in gewissem Sinne das Gesuchte "hervorbringt".

Wilhelm verfügt mithin über ein Vermögen, das Goethe auch "Antizipation" nennt und am eigenen Beispiel erläutert. So heißt es im Gespräch mit Eckermann vom 26. Februar 1824: " . . . hätte ich nicht die Welt durch Antizipation bereits in mir getragen, ich wäre mit sehenden Augen blind geblieben, und alle Erforschung und Erfahrung wäre nichts gewesen als ein ganz totes vergebliches Bemühen. Das Licht ist da, und die Farben umgeben uns; allein trügen wir kein Licht und keine Farben im eigenen Auge, so würden wir auch außer uns dergleichen nicht wahrnehmen."[34] Im Blick auf den Roman dürfte man übersetzen: Natalie ist da — allein trüge Wilhelm nicht ursprünglich ihr Bild, ihre Vorempfindung in sich, so würde er sie nicht wahrnehmen, so gäbe es weder jene Epiphanie noch das Wiederfinden, so würde sein Suchen tatsächlich leer bleiben, ein totes vergebliches Bemühen.

"Erfreulich" nennt die *Farbenlehre* den Vorgang, wenn dem Auge von außen die Farbentotalität als Objekt gebracht wird, "weil ihm die Summe seiner eignen Tätigkeit als Realität entgegen kommt".[35] Ein analoger Vorgang liegt Wilhelms Bildergeschichte zugrunde. Er macht das Glück Wilhelm Meisters aus. Denn seine produktive

Antizipation findet und stiftet, aller Irrwege, Ängste und Rektifizierungen ungeachtet, ihren Gegenstand, die "antwortenden Gegenbilder".

Der Ausdruck stammt aus dem Essay *Winckelmann und sein
Jahrhundert* und gehört in den Rahmen einer Typologie der
Bildung, die Goethe eingangs entwirft. Von drei Menschenarten ist
dort die Rede: von "gewöhnlichen Menschen" und der "köstlichen
Mitgift" der Natur, dem "lebhaften Trieb, von Kindheit an die
äußere Welt mit Lust zu ergreifen, sie kennen zu lernen, sich mit ihr
in Verhältnis zu setzen, mit ihr verbunden ein Ganzes zu bilden";
von "vorzüglichen Geistern", die öfters, aus Scheu vor dem wirkli-
chen Leben, "sich in sich selbst (zurückziehen), in sich selbst eine
eigene Welt . . . erschaffen und auf diese Weise das Vortrefflichste
nach innen bezüglich . . . leisten"; und schließlich von "besonders
begabten Menschen": "Findet sich hingegen in besonders begabten
Menschen jenes gemeinsame Bedürfnis, eifrig zu allem, was die
Natur in sie gelegt hat, auch in der äußeren Welt die antwortenden
Gegenbilder zu suchen und dadurch das Innere völlig zum Ganzen
und Gewissen zu steigern, so kann man versichert sein, daß auch so
ein für Welt und Nachwelt höchst erfreuliches Dasein sich ausbilden
werde".[36] Unschwer läßt sich in dieser Typologie auch Wilhelm
Meister wiedererkennen: er verfügt über jene "köstliche Mitgift" der
Natur, er durchläuft, der kranke Königssohn, aber auch die
pathologischen Zonen der modernen Innenbezüglichkeit, doch sein
"gutmütiges Suchen" führt ihn endlich zu den "antwortenden
Gegenbildern". Es ist dieses Zusammenspiel der "köstlichen Mitgift"
und der "antwortenden Gegenbilder", das in der Bildergeschichte
vom kranken Königssohn zu Gesicht kommt.

Der Winckelmann-Essay holt wenig später zu dem berühmten
Hymnus auf den glücklichen Menschen aus: "Wenn die gesunde
Natur des Menschen als ein Ganzes wirkt, wenn er sich in der Welt
als in einem großen, schönen, würdigen und werten Ganzen fühlt,
wenn das harmonische Behagen ihm ein reines, freies Entzücken
gewährt — dann würde das Weltall, wenn es sich selbst empfinden
könnte, als an sein Ziel gelangt aufjauchzen und den Gipfel des
eigenen Werdens und Wesens bewundern. Denn wozu dient alle der
Aufwand von Sonnen und Planeten und Monden, von Sternen und
Milchstraßen, von Kometen und Nebelflecken, von gewordenen und
werdenden Welten, wenn sich nicht zuletzt ein glücklicher Mensch
unbewußt seines Daseins erfreut?"[37] Freilich, das Glück der Alten ist
das, antike Existenz, die hier aus der Sicht der Neueren beschworen
wird, wiederholbar allenfalls für antike Naturen wie Winckelmann.

Wilhelm hat den Weg der "Neueren" zu gehen, flankiert von
Aufopferungen, Entsagungen, Reduktionen. Und doch fällt zumindest ein Abglanz jenes Glücks auf ihn, weil er, ihr ähnlich, Natalie
gewinnt. Denn Natalie, die "der Anbetung einer ganzen Welt
würdig" ist (459), die man "bei Leibesleben selig preisen" kann
(539), eine "Erscheinung", deren sich "die Menschheit freut", die
wahre "schöne Seele" (608) — ist sie nicht, unter manchem anderen,
zuerst und zuletzt ein Symbol des glücklichen Daseins, der in
Wirkung und Tätigkeit erfahrenen Angemessenheit von Ich und
Welt?

Glück des Symbolischen: die Bildergeschichte des Bildungsromans
steht symbolisch Modell für den Antwortcharakter der Welt, und
das heißt: für die "Vereinigung von Objekt und Subjekt".[38] Die
Symbolik des Glücks ist, mit anderen Worten, fundiert im Glück
eines symbolischen Verhältnisses zur Welt. Vor dem Hintergrund
der "neueren Philosophie", wie sie nicht zuletzt der *Wilhelm
Meister*-Leser und -Kritiker Schiller repräsentiert, nimmt Goethes
Roman Züge einer konkreten Epistemologie an.

Denn auf seine Weise, mit dem beharrlichen "realistischen Tic",
hat auch er teil an dem "größten, vielleicht nie ganz zu schlich-
tenden Wettkampf zwischen Objekt and Subjekt", der, wie Goethe
rückblickend erklärt, den Bund mit Schiller besiegelte.[39] Den Sinn
dieses Wettkampfs, Gewinne und Defizite der "neueren Philosophie"
resümiert vielleicht am prägnantesten der Brief an Schultz vom 18.
September 1831: "Ich danke der kritischen und idealistischen
Philosophie, daß sie mich auf mich selbst aufmerksam gemacht hat,
das ist ein ungeheurer Gewinn; sie kommt aber nie zum Objekt,
dieses müssen wir so gut wie der gemeine Menschenverstand
zugeben, um am unwandelbaren Verhältnis zu ihm die Freude des
Lebens zu genießen."[40] In diesen Zusammenhang gehören nun aber
auch die bekannten Maximen und Reflexionen, die den Unterschied
zwischen Symbolik und Allegorie darlegen.

Ausdrücklich macht Goethe bei dieser Gelegenheit sein durch
Einheit des Zwecks, aber Verschiedenheit der Mittel bestimmtes
Verhältnis zu Schiller namhaft sowie die "zarte Differenz", "die einst
zwischen uns zur Sprache kam".[41] Gemeint ist doch wohl das
Gespräch über die Urpflanze, über Erfahrung und Idee, das
"Glückliche Ereignis" nach der Sitzung der naturforschenden Gesellschaft im Juli 1794. Die Pointen des Duells sind bekannt. Goethe
zeichnet eine "symbolische Pflanze". Schiller dazu: "Das ist keine
Erfahrung, das ist eine Idee". Goethes Entgegnung: "Das kann mir
sehr lieb sein, daß ich Ideen habe ohne es zu wissen, und sie sogar
mit Augen sehe".[42]

Erfahrung und Idee, so muß Goethe hören, sind für den "gebildeten Kantianer" schlechterdings inkongruent, sofern keine Erfahrung der Idee angemessen sein kann. Damit kommt nicht nur das Problem der bloß komparativen Allgemeinheit ins Spiel. Zur Debatte steht vielmehr, sehr viel grundsätzlicher, jene Inkongruenz, die das Schicksal des sentimentalischen Dichters ausmacht. Sentimentalische Poesie heißt deshalb: Poesie der Entzweiung — von Idee und Erfahrung, von Ideal und Wirklichkeit, von Zeichen und Bezeichnetem, von Allgemeinem und Besonderem —, Poesie der Entzweiung, die nie zum Objekt kommt. Damit aber wird sie in Goethes Augen auf den Weg der Allegorie gewiesen, ist sie nichts anderes als allegorische Poesie, die das Allgemeinere nurmehr "als Traum und Schatten" zu repräsentieren vermag.[43] Als allegorisch, gekennzeichnet durch den allegorischen Abgrund zwischen bildlichem Sein und Bedeuten, hat denn auch Walter Benjamin, Goethes Wertung umkehrend, die Signatur der Moderne beschrieben, in einer Rehabilitation der Allegorie, die zwar am barocken Trauerspiel entfaltet wird, aber doch weit darüber hinauszielt.[44]

Ideen sogar mit Augen sehen: das ist das Wagestück und das Glück des "hartnäckigen Realismus",[45] der zum Objekt kommt, das Glück der symbolischen Poesie auch, "wo das Besondere das Allgemeinere repräsentiert, nicht als Traum und Schatten, sondern als lebendig-augenblickliche Offenbarung des Unerforschlichen",[46] das Glück der "Vereinigung von Objekt und Subjekt", also auch der Vereinigung von Ich und Welt. Das klassische Zeugnis dafür stellen *Wilhelm Meisters Lehrjahre* dar — ein Roman gegen die sentimentalische Entzweiung, ein Roman der Glücksfindung, ein symbolischer Roman des Glücks.

Ein Glücksfall also. Niemand hat das früher gespürt als Schiller, dem natürlich nicht entging, wie heiter und sicher dieser Roman sich seiner Denkform widersetzte. Seine Reaktion zeigt souveräne Noblesse. Mit einem Schillerschen Leseeindruck habe ich begonnen, und so schließe ich auch. Nach der Lektüre aller acht Bücher, am 2. Juli 1796, bekennt Schiller: "Ohnehin gehört es zu dem schönsten Glück meines Daseins, daß ich die Vollendung dieses Produkts erlebte, daß sie noch in die Periode meiner strebenden Kräfte fällt, daß ich aus dieser reinen Quelle noch schöpfen kann . . . Wie lebhaft habe ich bei dieser Gelegenheit erfahren, daß das Vortreffliche eine Macht ist, daß es auf selbstsüchtige Gemüter auch nur als eine Macht wirken kann, daß es dem Vortrefflichen gegenüber keine Freiheit gibt als die Liebe".[47]

Universität Heidelberg

Anmerkungen

*Der hier vorgelegte Text ist die leicht überarbeitete Fassung des Vortrags, der im Rahmen des Goethe-Symposiums der Texas Tech University in Lubbock, Texas sowie am 5. Februar 1982 anläßlich der Feier des 80. Geburtstages von Paul Requadt in Mainz gehalten wurde. Der kritische Apparat beschränkt sich auf das Notwendige. Eine ausführlichere Behandlung des Themas behalte ich mir vor.

[1]An Goethe, 7. Jenner 1795. Der Briefwechsel zwischen Schiller und Goethe, hrsg. v. Hans Gerhard Gräf und Albert Leitzmann, Frankfurt a.M. 1964, S. 49.

[2]Zur grundsätzlichen Bedeutung dieses Wallensteinschen Kennwortes vgl. Emil Staiger, Friedrich Schiller, Zürich 1967, S. 13 ff.

[3]Georg Wilhelm Friedrich Hegel, Ästhetik, hrsg. v. Friedrich Bassenge, Berlin 1955, S. 983.

[4]Georg Lukács, Die Theorie des Romans, 3. Aufl., Neuwied 1965, S. 35.

[5]Vgl. dazu Hans-Jürgen Schings, Der anthropologische Roman. Seine Entstehung und Krise im Zeitalter der Spätaufklärung, in: Studien zum achtzehnten Jahrhundert, hrsg. von der Deutschen Gesellschaft für die Erforschung des 18. Jahrhunderts, Bd. 2/3, München 1980, S. 247-275.

[6]Goethe an Gottlob Friedrich Ernst Schönborn, 1. Juni — 4. Juli 1774. Goethes Briefe. Hamburger Ausgabe, hrsg. v. Karl Robert Mandelkow und Bodo Morawe, 4 Bde., Hamburg 1962-1966, Bd. I, S. 161. Künftig zitiert als HA Br.

[7]Goethe, Die Leiden des jungen Werther, Erstes Buch. Am 18. August. Goethes Werke. Hamburger Ausgabe, hrsg. v. Erich Trunz, 14 Bde., München 1981, Bd. VI, S. 53. Künftig zitiert als HA.

[8]Johann Carl Wezel, Belphegor oder die wahrscheinlichste Geschichte unter der Sonne, hrsg. v. Hubert Gersch, Frankfurt a. M. 1965, S. 104.

[9]Friedrich Schiller, Philosophische Briefe. Schillers Werke, Nationalausgabe, Bd. XX, S. 112.

[10]Karl Philipp Moritz, Anton Reiser. Ein psychologischer Roman, hrsg. v. Wolfgang Martens, Stuttgart 1972, S. 122.

[11]Vgl. Gerda Röder, Glück und glückliches Ende im deutschen Bildungsroman. Eine Studie zu Goethes *Wilhelm Meister*, München 1968.

[12]Goethe an Schiller, 9. Juli 1796. Gräf-Leitzmann, S. 180.

[13]Goethe an Schiller, 9. Juli 1796. Gräf-Leitzmann, S. 179.

[14]Dahin zielte Schillers Drängen. An Goethe, 19. Oktober 1796. Gräf-Leitzmann, S. 222.

[15]Friedrich Schlegel, Über Goethes Meister, in: F. Schlegel, Kritische Schriften, hrsg. v. Wolfdietrich Rasch, Darmstadt 1964, S. 452.

[16]Maximen und Reflexionen 751. HA XII, 471.

[17]Dabei lassen sich vor allem eine psychoanalytisch inspirierte und eine symbolistische Forschungsrichtung unterscheiden. Anregungen für die erstere gehen neuerdings aus von K. R. Eissler, Goethe. A Psychoanalytic Study 1775-1786, 2 Bde., Detroit 1963. Vgl. jetzt Per Ohrgaard, Die Genesung des Narcissus. Eine Studie zu Goethe: *Wilhelm Meisters Lehrjahre*, Kopenhagen 1978; David Roberts, The Indirections of Desire. Hamlet in Goethes *Wilhelm Meister*, Heidelberg 1980. Zur Symbolinterpretation: Christoph E. Schweitzer, Wilhelm Meister und das Bild vom kranken Königssohn, in: PMLA 72, 1957, S. 419-432; Ronald D. Gray, Goethe the Alchemist. A study of alchemical symbolism in Goethe's literary and scientific works, Cambridge 1952, S. 223 ff.; William Larrett, Wilhelm Meister and the Amazons. The Quest for Wholeness, in: PEGS 39, 1969, S. 31-56; Erika Nolan, Wilhelm Meisters Lieblingsbild: Der kranke Königssohn. Quelle und Funktion, in: Jb. d. Freien

Deutschen Hochstifts 1979, S. 132-152; Hellmut Ammerlahn, Goethe und Wilhelm Meister, Shakespeare und Natalie: Die klassische Heilung des kranken Königssohns, in: Jb. d. Freien Deutschen Hochstifts 1978, S. 47-84.

[18]Eingeklammerte Ziffern im laufenden Text beziehen sich auf die Ausgabe von *Wilhelm Meisters Lehrjahren* von Erich Trunz: HA VII (10., neubearbeitete Aufl., München 1981).

[19]Den Ausdruck verwende ich hier anders als Wilhelm Emrich, Die Symbolik von Faust II. Sinn und Vorformen, 3. Aufl., Frankfurt a. M. 1964.

[20]Von einer "generating matrix of the structure of relations" spricht im Hinblick auf das Bild vom kranken Königssohn auch D. Roberts, The Indirections of Desire, S. 11.

[21]Dazu Wolfgang Stechow, The Love of Antiochus with Faire Stratonica in Art, in: The Art Bulletin 27, 1945, S. 221-237.

[22]Zur Suche nach dem möglichen Vorbild des Gemäldes: Georg Gronau, Das "Bild vom kranken Königssohn" im Wilhelm Meister, in: Zs. f. bildende Kunst 50, 1915, S. 157-162; Erika Nolan, Wilhelm Meisters Lieblingsbild, S. 132 ff.

[23]Emil Staiger, Goethe, Bd. I, Zürich 1952, S. 450.

[24]Dazu die ungemein erhellende Abhandlung von Hellmut Ammerlahn, Wilhelm Meisters Mignon — ein offenbares Rätsel. Name, Gestalt, Symbol, Wesen und Werden, in: DVJS 42, 1968, S. 89-116. Dort S. 103 f. auch der Hinweis auf die Komposita auf "Liebling".

[25]Vgl. Emil Staiger, Goethe, Bd. I, S. 454 ff.

[26]Zitiert nach HA VII, 616.

[27]Vorweggenommen wird die Rolle der Minerva im Vorspiel zu Ehren des Prinzen, das Wilhelm als Anführer der Landleute sieht, die nach einem Überfall durch das Eingreifen Minervas gerettet werden (169 f.). Handelt es sich zunächst noch um "eine Person, über deren Bestimmung der Dichter [Wilhelm] noch ungewiß war" (169), so greift Wilhelm das Minerva-Motiv sogleich auf, erlaubt es ihm doch, sein Amazonen-Bild erneut auszuprägen. Deshalb auch sein Votum dafür, daß man sie, "eben weil sie in der Mythologie eine doppelte Person spielt, auch hier in doppelter Qualität erscheinen ließe" (171).

[28]So Emil Staiger, Goethe, Bd. II, Zürich 1956, S. 166; David Roberts, The Indirections of Desire, S. 207; Hellmut Ammerlahn, Goethe und Wilhelm Meister, S. 55 f. Vgl. auch Hellmut Hermann Ammerlahn, Natalie und Goethes urbildliche Gestalt: Untersuchungen zur Morphologie und Symbolik von Wilhelm Meisters Lehrjahren, Diss. Austin, Texas (Masch.), 1965, S. 56 ff.

[29]Zur Farbenlehre. Didaktischer Teil, § 30: "Die Gelehrten, welche auf den Cordilleras ihre Beobachtungen anstellten, sahen um den Schatten ihrer Köpfe, der auf Wolken fiel, einen hellen Schein. Dieser Fall gehört wohl hieher; denn indem sie das dunkle Bild des Schattens fixierten und sich zugleich von der Stelle bewegten, so schien ihnen das geforderte helle Bild um das dunkle zu schweben . . . Auch mir ist ein Ähnliches begegnet. Indem ich nämlich auf dem Felde sitzend mit einem Manne sprach, der, in einiger Entfernung vor mir stehend, einen grauen Himmel zum Hintergrund hatte, so erschien mir, nachdem ich ihn lange scharf und unverwandt angesehen, als ich den Blick ein wenig gewendet, sein Kopf von einem blendenden Schein umgeben". (HA XIII, 334 f.)—So weit ich sehen kann, hat die Forschung die Beziehungen, die sich nicht nur an dieser Stelle zwischen der *Farbenlehre* und dem *Wilhelm Meister* knüpfen lassen, fast völlig vernachlässigt. Vgl. jetzt aber Ilse Graham, Portrait of the Artist, Berlin-New York 1977, S. 182 ff. Ich werde diesem Zusammenhang in der angekündigten Abhandlung weiter nachgehen.

[30]Tag-und Jahreshefte. Bis 1786. HA X, 432.

[31]Wilhelm Meisters Wanderjahre I, 2. HA VIII, 23. Zum Rückbezug auf die *Lehrjahre* vgl. Wolfgang Staroste, Raum und Realität in dichterischer Gestaltung. Studien zu Goethe und Kafka, Heidelberg 1971, S. 60 ff.; Hannelore Schlaffer, Wilhelm Meister. Das Ende der Kunst und die Wiederkehr des Mythos, Stuttgart 1980, S. 26 ff. (mit einer ganz schiefen Beurteilung der Josephs-Geschichte).

[32]Wilhelm Meisters Wanderjahre I, 2. HA VIII, S. 26.

[33]So Hans Eichner, Zur Deutung von *Wilhelm Meisters Lehrjahren*, in: Jb. d. Freien Deutschen Hochstifts 1966, S. 165-196, hier S. 195. Vom märchenhaften Gang der Dinge, den "wunderbaren Fügungen eines Märchens" spricht auch Karl Viëtor, Goethe. Dichtung, Wissenschaft, Weltbild, Bern 1949, S. 142.

[34]Johann Peter Eckermann, Gespräche mit Goethe, hrsg. v. Fritz Bergemann, Wiesbaden 1955, S. 88. Vgl. auch Tag- und Jahreshefte. Bis 1780. HA X, 430 f.

[35]Zur Farbenlehre. Didaktischer Teil, § 808. HA XIII, 502.

[36]Winckelmann, Eintritt. HA XII, 97.

[37]Winckelmann, Antikes. HA XII, 98.

[38]Goethe an Schultz, 18. September 1831. HA Br IV, 450.

[39]Glückliches Ereignis. HA X, 541.

[40]An Schultz, 18. September 1831. HA Br IV, 450. Damit faßt Goethe die Stellungnahme zum Einwirken Schillers und seine Kritik am "transzendentellen Idealisten" noch einmal zúsammen, wie er sie bereits im Brief an Schiller vom 6. Januar 1798 gegeben hatte: "Wenn ich Ihnen zum Repräsentanten mancher Objekte diente, so haben Sie mich von der allzu strengen Beobachtung der äußern Dinge und ihrer Verhältnisse auf mich selbst zurückgeführt . . . Der transzendentelle Idealist glaubt nun freilich ganz oben zu stehen; eins will mir aber nicht an ihm gefallen, daß er mit den andern Vorstellungsarten streitet, denn man kann eigentlich mit keiner Vorstellungsart streiten . . . Ebenso mag sich der Idealist gegen die Dinge an sich wehren, wie er will, er stößt doch, ehe er sichs versieht, an die Dinge außer ihm . . . Mir will immer dünken, daß, wenn die eine Partei von außen hinein den Geist niemals erreichen kann, die andere von innen heraus wohl schwerlich zu den Körpern gelangen wird, und daß man also immer wohl tut in dem philosophischen Naturstande . . . zu bleiben und von seiner ungetrennten Existenz den besten möglichen Gebrauch zu machen, bis die Philosophen einmal übereinkommen, wie das, was sie nun einmal getrennt haben, wieder zu vereinigen sein möchte". (Gräf-Leitzmann, S. 417-419) Zur "erkenntnistheoretischen Unruhe", die Kant und die kritische Philosophie hinterlassen hatten — und auf die nicht zuletzt die Bilderge-schichte des *Wilhelm Meister* mit ihrer symbolischen Epistemologie antwortet —, vgl. die treffenden Bemerkungen bei Andreas Wachsmuth, Geeinte Zwienatur. Aufsätze zu Goethes naturwissenschaftlichem Denken, Berlin-Weimar 1966, S. 86 ff. Allzu harmonisierend behandelt demgegenüber das Verhältnis Goethes zu Kant Ernst Cassirer, Goethe and the Kantian Philosophy, in: E. Cassirer, Rousseau, Kant, Goethe, New York 1963, S. 61-98.

[41]Maximen und Reflexionen 751. HA XII, 471.

[42]Glückliches Ereignis. HA X, 540 f.

[43]Maximen und Reflexionen 752. HA XII, 471. Die Differenzen von Goethes, Kants und Schillers Symbolbegriffen erläutert scharfsinnig Bengt Algot Sørensen, Symbol und Symbolismus in den ästhetischen Theorien des 18. Jahrhunderts und der deutschen Romantik, Kopenhagen 1963, S. 91 ff. und 96 ff. Vgl. neuerdings auch Bengt Algot Sørensen, Altersstil und Symboltheorie. Zum Problem des Symbols und der Allegorie bei Goethe, in: Goethe-Jb. 94, 1977, S. 69-85.

[44]Walter Benjamin, Ursprung des deutschen Trauerspiels, hrsg. v. Rolf Tiedemann, Frankfurt a. M. 1963, S. 174 ff.

[45]Glückliches Ereignis. HA X, 541.

[46]Maximen und Reflexionen 752. HA XII, 471.

[47]Gräf-Leitzmann, S. 160 f.

Goethe's study in Weimar. (Courtesy Walter Wadepuhl)

Ivan Franko:
Goethe's Translator
and Interpreter

Wolodymyr T. Zyla

Abstract

Ivan Franko (1856-1916) was the writer who truly put Goethe in the forefront of the Ukrainian conscience. Goethe's image gains in immortality from Franko's works. Franko loved the great poet from his youthful years and lived with this love until his death. He studied Goethe's works carefully, translated them, and searched in them for consonance, simplicity, wisdom, emotion, and artistic peculiarity. Goethe attracted Franko with his optimism, with his humanism, and with his ability to portray reality philosophically.

Franko dedicated most of his attention to *Faust*. For him *Faust* was a unique work of great artistic value, one filled with a philosophical background. It was a work of great faith in man's creative powers. It offered a glimpse of a better future. Franko appreciated it as a revolutionary work, one which caused profound spiritual changes in Germany in the fields of philosphy and art. It was a universal work in which true human situations are portrayed. In his translation Franko carefully considered the original by preserving its tone and meter as well as the main ideas of individual fragments. His rendition of the First Part of *Faust* has shortcomings, but it is of great historical value for anyone who attempts a translation into Ukrainian. The translation of the Third Act of the Second Part of *Faust*—"Helena i Favst" (Helen and Faust)—is of great quality in its imagery and in its music. The rare imperfections that do occur are almost insignificant in the total picture.

Through his contributions to the Ukrainian art of translation, Franko enlarged and perfected his own masterful creative abilities. The lyrical poem *Ziv'jale lystja* (Withered Leaves), for example, gives an excellent portrayal of love that is not mutually shared. Such a love ends with a tragedy that has its roots in the structure of society. We have tried to indicate, at least in the most important features, that Franko drew from his understanding of Goethe, underlining at the same time his own native genius. Our purpose in doing so is to single out *Ziv'jale lystja* as an original creative Ukrainian variant of *The Sorrows of Young Werther*. (WTZ)

The perception, study, and development of Goethe's themes by Ukrainian writers have had a conspicuous place in the history of

179

Ukrainian-German literary relations of the nineteenth and twentieth centuries. Johann Wolfgang von Goethe, the great German poet, thinker, and scholar, was already widely known in the Ukraine in the early 1800s. His works were highly valued there, his opinions were carefully considered, and, most important, the specific peculiarities of his poetical individuality were understood by Ukrainians.

In 1827 Goethe was elected an honorary member of the Kharkiv University Council.[1] In that same year the journal *Vestnik Evropy* published his ballad "Der Fischer," the first Ukrainian recast from his works. This recast was done by Petro Hulak-Artemovs'kyj. In it, he made use of folk creativity and the style of folk songs. This version reflects the stylistic variegation that appears in song forms and is combined with typical burlesque expressions. It is masterfully versified: four-foot iambic forms are combined with five- and six-foot iambic forms. The literary scholar Mykola Petrov believed that this work manifested "the clearest sounds of Romantic poetry,"[2] and Pavlo Fylypovych, the neoclassical poet and literary scholar, considered that "this first attempt of Hulak-Artemovs'kyj to transplant the Romantic into Ukrainian poetry was successful because good soil was found for the transplantation." Furthermore, according to Fylypovych, in the Ukrainian soil of folk poetry and folk creativity, the ballad "'Der Fischer' grew into a flower different from the German, more simple, more vivid, more tender."[3]

The second Ukrainian version of one of Goethe's works appeared in 1838 in Galicia. A true translation, it was prepared by the Rev. Josyf Levyc'kyj. It is the ballad "Erlkönig," which appeared under the title "Goddess" in the supplement "Rozmaitości" to the Polish newspaper *L'viv Gazette*. The poet Kostjantyn Dumytrashko, whose poetical ability was positively evaluated by Taras Shevchenko, translated in the 1850s some fragments from *Faust* ("Gretchen's Prayer," which was published first in 1884). Before Ivan Franko, recasts and translations into Ukrainian were made by numerous writers (e.g. Bohdan Didyc'kyj, Marija S., Ksenofont Klymkovych, Antin Kobyljans'kyj, Osyp Jurij Fed'kovych, Omeljan Horoc'kyj, Volodymyr Sashkevych, Mychajlo Staryc'kyj, Mykola Ustjanovych, Jevhen Zhars'kyj, Ivan Verchrats'kyj, Pavlo Bilec'kyj-Nosenko, Oleksander Navroc'kyj, Vasyl' Lymans'kyj, and others). Not all translations are worthy of notice. The early ones in the Western Ukraine were largely weak linguistically. While in those by Levyc'kyj the language is rather pure, the translations by Didyc'kyj, Marija S., and some by Ustjanovych are full of slang. Simultaneously, the translators from the Eastern Ukraine were freely Ukrainianizing the

German poet and even making travesties out of his works by badly neglecting the original as far as the number of strophes and meter were concerned.[4]

Ivan Franko (1856-1916) was the one who truly brought Goethe to the Ukrainian conscience. Numerous research works of Franko's heritage quite clearly show his role and place in history of Ukrainian literary translation. Because of his untiring and many-sided activity, translation became an active factor of perception and assimilation of artistic values of the works of many great poets and writers and became an integral part of the Ukrainian national culture.

For his work, Franko possessed exceptional ability and concentration; his hunger for knowledge became apparent during his study in gymnasium (1867-1875). He avidly read books that were available in the gymnasium library; among them were works by Goethe, Schiller, Lessing, Wieland, Molière, Racine, Corneille and others. Franko read German and French writers in the original. Even during gymnasium years he conceived the idea of translating masterpieces of the world literature into Ukrainian. He was translating then the works of Homer, Sophocles, Anacreaon, Horace, Goethe, Heine, and others. The writer paid great attention to translations, which in his opinion, widely served for the dissemination of world literature and contributed much to the development of culture and the strengthening of friendship among peoples. According to Franko, "The translation of foreign poetry of various centuries and of different people into the native tongue enriches the spirit of the whole nation and appropriates for it such forms and expressions of feelings that it did not have. It builds a golden bridge of understanding and of sympathy with distant people and ancient generations."[5]

Franko never believed in completely literal translations, especially "when the translation has to transmit not only the words but the thought of the original."[6] However, he thought that the translator had to adopt the style of the author, his genre, composition, the pictorial side of the work, its syntactic structure, its rhythm, etc.

Thus Franko's translation of "Der Fischer" is free of the old tradition of previous translators, Hulak-Artemovs'kyj and others. It is more masterful and original in transmitting Goethe's images. It is somewhat shorter than the original—Goethe has 32 lines, Franko only 20—undoubtedly its most serious defect, since the exact translation should have the same number of lines as the original.[7] This omission destroys the imagery of the ballad and its creative structure. On the whole, however, the translation is coherent lexically, and Franko accurately reproduces the atmosphere of the original and correctly transmits its mood. He also preserves its stylistic and ideological qualities.

In Franko's version of Goethe's "Prometheus" the language of the translation is elevated; individual phrases are strong in their intonation and contribute to a unity of thought and content. Franko's lines are somewhat elongated, and the imagery is widened, but their reinterpretation is identical to the original. The translator preserves Goethe's poetical power of the "Sturm und Drang" period. By introducing rhyme into the translation, Franko does deviate from the original and somewhat weakens its poetical tone. In the original there is no rhyme, and the lines in general have three rhythmical stresses. There are also lines that show variations, where the stress falls on different syllables and may even increase to five stresses. Franko's translation does not always account for these variations, and therefore some of the lines are lacking strengthened emphasis of language and emotional intensity. However, the translation preserves such romantic features of the original as the heroism of the titanic fight for the mastery of a better life and the passion for Prometheus' courage. These features are transmitted figuratively and masterfully.

From Goethe's smaller poetic works, Franko translated the ballads "Der Gott und die Bajadere" and "Die Braut von Korinth." Unfortunately I have been unable to obtain them.

In translating *Faust* Franko performed a great work. In 1882 he published the translation of the First Part and, in 1899 there appeared his translation of the Third Act of the Second Part, entitled "Helena i Favst" (Helen and Faust). According to Oleksandr Bilec'kyj, a well-known Ukrainian literary scholar, "this translation is a result of scrupulous and assiduous work."[8] Franko started translating the First Part of *Faust* as early as the 1870s while attending gymnasium. For the young Franko, *Faust* was a work of high artistic quality, filled with profound philosophical ideas and great faith in the creative forces of the man who strives for a better future. Most likely, at that time, *Faust* was one of the works Franko loved most. He had just become acquainted with Olha Roshkevych

and together with her he read Goethe's *Faust* from a small illustrated edition with which, at that time, he almost never parted. Through this close connection with that happy event of Franko's young life, *Faust* became for him more than the brilliant artistic work of the German genius; it became for him a symbol of a love drama between him and Olha, "a drama that was full of the most profound experience."[9]

Franko translated the First Part of *Faust* for six years on and off. He added notes to his translation, using *Goethes Faust*, the edition with comments by Heinrich Düntzer.[10] He also added an introduction in which he wrote:

Faust was a declaration of a revolution similar to that which flared up with menacing fire in Paris, destroyed the autocratic kingdom, the domination of the nobility and pronounced "the rights of man." But in France this revolution started in the social and political fields, whereas in Germany it embraced the spiritual field: philosophy and art. But the difference was only formal; the content of the revolution was the same: to destroy the medieval limits that were fettering man's *freedom*, to destroy these limitations in the name of the *inborn natural rights of man*.[11]

In the introduction Franko also discusses Goethe's universal ideas and provides a thoughtful analysis of his work. He writes:

The historical significance of Faust is linked directly to his universal meaning and importance. Neither science itself, nor happy-go-lucky free life, nor distinctions, nor fame, nothing can make man happy, as long as he is always and forever dedicated only to himself. Only when man, in all of his achievements, in all of his power will turn his work to making other people happy even if the provision of a secure life and development are at stake in his great struggle, only then can man be happy. This great truth, with which *Faust* culminates, gives this work even today, a living revolutionary force. *Faust* does not age for us in its ideas; on the contrary, because of its great poetical beauty, it will long serve as a model and as a leading work. This is how I understand *Faust* and such understanding caused me to translate it into the Ukrainian language. [XVIII, 406]

Franko ends his introduction with an analysis of the metrical forms of his translation:

I tried to translate *Faust* as accurately as I could, to transmit every thought of the author in the same way that he presented it as far as it was in agreement with the requirements of the Ukrainian language. I preserved the same meter as is used in the original, taking liberties only with some lines where I used the five-foot instead of the four-foot iamb, or the six-foot iamb in place of the five-foot one, or the other way around. But I made this change only where in the original the lines were different in size or appeared mixed. When in the original the author uses artificial complexes of verses (octaves, as occurs in the refrain in the first prologue, terza rima, and others), I tried to render them in exactly the same form. Freer translation and further diversification, as far as rhythmic forms are concerned, I tolerated only where, in the original, the verses are of diversified rhythmic forms, of where such a treatment serves the clarity of the translation. [XV, 588]

The literary scholars Leonid Rudnytzky[12] and Jakym Ja. Jarema[13] confirm that Franko's translation is accurate. The translator fully preserves the ideas and the form of the original; he does not try to enhance it with his own imagery, etc. However, this restraint was not easy for Franko. He achieved such accuracy by the loss of purity of language and thus lowered the literary value of his work. At the first glance, the verses of the original look simple, but they hide great difficulties for the translator. In order to preserve the rhymes of the original, Franko often used dialectal expressions, words with the wrong stresses and even unnecessary words. It must be stressed that many of Franko's difficulties are inherent in the nature of the Ukrainian and German languages. As one scholar points out, "The German language has far more one-syllable and two-syllable words (especially in the field of concrete notions) than the Ukrainian language and therefore, in order to render into Ukrainian the German four-foot iambic verse, the necessary reductions had to be made which Franko was foreseeing by using short forms of the Galician dialect, archaic words or ordinary provincialisms."[14] Such an approach gave the translation a local Galician coloring.

The beauty of Goethe's original is in the full harmony between the contents and form. To illustrate this beauty let us cite Faust's address to Mephistopheles after the signing of a contract:

> Werd' ich zum Augenblicke sagen:
> Verweile doch! Du bist so schön!
> Dann magst du mich in Fesseln schlagen,
> Dann will ich gern zugrunde gehn!
> Dann mag die Totenglocke schallen,
> Dann bist du deines Dienstes frei,
> Die Uhr mag stehn, der Zeiger fallen,
> Es sei die Zeit für mich vorbei![15]

In Franko's translation:

> Koly ja skazhu do khvylyny:
> Tryvaj ishche! tak harna ty!
> Todi khoch u puta m"ja skrutyty,
> Todi nekhaj navik zahynu.
> Todi nekhaj vyb"je smerti chas,
> Todi ty volnyj sluzhby svoji,
> Hodynnyk stane, spade skaz,
> Ja v vichnosti potonu mori. [XV, 358]

In English translation:

> If to the movement I should say:
> Abide, you are so fair—
> Put me in fetters on that day,
> I *wish* to perish then, I swear.

> Then let the death bell ever toll,
> Your service done, you shall be free,
> The clock may stop, the hand may fall,
> As time comes to an end for me.[16]

The translation correctly conveys the original; in it the elevated tone of narration is preserved as is the evolvement of the plot. Both Rudnytzky and Jarema agree on this point. Moreover, the latter correctly notices that "every verse which forms a separate rhythmic unity also contains in itself a separate logical unity which by its size agrees with it and thus every new verse has a new idea or its component part."[17]

Therefore, Franko's translation of the First Part of *Faust* may not be perfect as far as the beauty of the language is concerned, but it has its historical value and is "worthy as a translation that must be taken into consideration by any modern or future Ukrainian translator of *Faust*."[18]

In 1899, in commemoration of the 150th anniversary of Goethe's birth, Franko translated and published, in *Literaturno-Naukovyj Vistnyk* (Book 10), the Third Act of the Second Part of *Faust* entitled "Helena i Favst." In the introduction to this publication, the translator calls Goethe "the greatest universal poet of all times." Franko writes: "Goethe knew how to perceive everywhere beauty and humanity wherever he could find them despite language, dress and national coloring." The translator tells us why he translated the Third Act: "Many times I tried to translate the Second Part of *Faust* but somehow my endeavours were unsuccessful. More often I tried to translate the Third Act, this highly original Classical-Romantic tragedy about Faust and Helen who is brought to life." In this same introduction Franko gives a good evaluation of the Second Part of *Faust*: "The Second Part is generally considered as a dark and obscure work. But this is a completely unjust evaluation. It is true that this is not a very popular work. . . . But in spite of this evaluation, when one takes into consideration its composition as a whole, it is a very clear and pellucid creation." For Franko the Second Part of *Faust* is a symbolic "artistic image of life and emulation of a highly educated man of his age," and the episode "Helena i Favst" "is at first a demonstration of contradictions, and then a blending of the classical world with the medieval, especially of classical poetry with romantic, and following from that, of European poetry . . . This new poetry should have been personified in the figure of Euphorion, 'whose songs' by their tone and powerful passion cause us to remember Byron's songs and give us at the same time an idea and impression of the impact those songs were making on significant people of Europe."

In the conclusion to his introduction, Franko gives a short but very interesting explanation of the main theme of the work and makes some valuable remarks about *Faust's* symbolism:

> It is clear that in addition to the symbolic meaning, the figures of the tragedy, especially of the tragedy about Helen, live their individual lives. It seems to us that this work should be considered foremost as a poetic work, and one should spontaneously feel in it significant human situations and conflicts. The symbolic meaning of these figures and conflicts should appear to us not as ribs and bones that are projecting from the lean body but rather as a golden gleam which throws light on the whole work and gives to it a broad perspective on all.[19]

The juxtaposition of Franko's expression from three introductions (two to the First Part of *Faust*[20] and one to the Second Part) shows that his understanding of Goethe, from the time that he translated the First Part and the Second Part, grew incomparably and came to include the problematics of the work and its artistic structure. His approach to the translation also changed, despite the fact that the imagery and the rhythm of the Second Part are more complex. The feelings of Goethe reach the highest intensity of his spirit: he perceives the world as he did in his youthful years, but, with the rising tide of his artistic forces as he reaches manhood, he also tends to share with his readers his rich experiences of the fruitful life that is also filled with the capacity for contemplation.

Franko follows exactly the original, preserves its tone and meter and faithfully transmits the main ideas of the individual fragments. The language of his translation is simple and almost perfect in expressing the imagery and the music of the text. If somewhere an imperfection occurs, which happens rarely, it appears not in the keynote sentences but in rather subordinate situations. Franko does not approach his work subjectively; he views it objectively, accounting for all peculiarities of the original. Here, he is the mature translator who has a profound knowledge of the German and Ukrainian literary languages, and he carefully views the metaphoric imagery of the original. Rarely does he deviate from that original; he knows how to detect sensual and aesthetic elements in it and how to reproduce them accurately.

His diligence in preserving the meter of Goethe's verses is not easy for him. Sometimes his translation has lines where a break occurs in the logical and metrical unity. Therefore Goethe's poetic power, in Franko's translation, sometimes is the same, sometimes is more condensed, and sometimes is weakened. As an example we will cite the words by Phorkyas in German, Ukrainian and English:

Buchstabiert in Liebesfibeln,
Tändelnd grübelt nur am Liebeln,
Müßig liebelt fort im Grübeln!
Doch dazu ist keine Zeit. [V, 439]

Slebezuj bukvar ljubovnyj,
Trat' v ljubovi chas koshtovnyj,
Char zmirkovuj nevymovnyj!
Ta na ce teper ne chas! [XIX, 150]

Spell in lovers' primers sweetly.
Probe and dally, cosset featly
Test your wanton sport completely.
But there is not time, nor place.[21]

As already noted by Rudnytzky, the English translation is closer to the original because of a very successful use of the soft syllable "ly" (sweetly, dally, featly, completely).[22]

Another fault in Franko's translation is the fact that he attempts to render the original with more comprehensible and common words; he slightly transforms individual verses by introducing new images through comparisons or through transplanting their interrelationship or replacing them with simpler words of more concrete connotation for a better understanding of the original. "All of these differences between the original and the translation," as already stated by Rudnytzky, "have no such negative impact on the quality of the translation as the ones mentioned in the analysis of the First Part of *Faust*. Here these deviations are rare and almost unnoticeable while reading."[23]

In 1913 Franko translated *Hermann und Dorothea*. This epic, according to the translator, is Goethe's first national and completely patriotic work. For Franko it is also "a very real work as far as its contents are concerned, a work that has a pure and moral atmosphere and is of great literary value." These features make *Hermann und Dorothea* "a costly pearl in the treasury of universal human literature" (XIX, 182). The translation has its positives, but it also has its negatives. In it, Franko did not contribute greatly to the art of translation and did not show the growth of his translating abilities,[24] despite the fact that he translated it quite masterfully, especially in showing its mood and its spiritual world.

Franko is also an author of a versed tale *Lys Mykyta* (1890) which occupies a very distinguished place among his tales and is one of the most popular works in Ukrainian literature.[25] The plot of the ambulatory theme about the fox, written by Goethe in his *Reinecke Fuchs*, gained the greatest dissemination of all similar works. There were other reworkings of this theme that were certainly familiar to Franko but, as a model for writing his poem about the fox, he mentioned Goethe's work on the title page of his *Lys Mykyta* "reworked from German."[26] In reality *Lys Mykyta* is an original work in Ukrainian and Franko's mention that it comes from German is highly conditional and apparently caused by censorship considerations.[27]

Up to this point we have considered Franko's artistic translations of Goethe's works. It is obvious that to make good translations of Goethe's works, Franko had to study as carefully as he could and to work as constantly as he had time. As a result of his doing so, these works took their place in his memory and conscience and formed for him a special world of poetical tradition that in time joined with a creative force of his own.

The juxtaposition of the works of two great original artists, Goethe and Franko, is highly complicated, especially when we have to talk about two men of different epochs and different "Weltanschauung." But no one will deny that such a juxtaposition has its benefits.

There is no doubt that Goethe and Franko were related in something essential. They both possessed an optimistic world outlook, a profound humanism and philosophical approach to reality. The great German poet attracted the Ukrainian with his organic merger of simplicity and sageness, with his sincere humane feelings, with romantic impetuosity, with stern pathos combined with striking emotionalism and soft lyricism—features which form the basic foundation of Franko's outstanding lyrical drama *Ziv"jale lystja* (Withered Leaves).

The influence of Goethe on Franko's poetry is only slightly researched. Jarema considers that the difference between Franko and Goethe is essential, but he only mentions Goethe's poetic impulses, which found place in the creative work of Franko.[28] Rudnytzky also handles this question. He searches for influences of Goethe's *Faust* in Franko's poetry, in particular in *Ziv"jale lystja*. He considers the motif of avidity (where man strives to achieve his desire even at the risk of losing his soul) which, in his opinion, appears in the tenth poem of the Third Fragment of the lyrical drama. This same motif Rudnytzky finds in the eleventh poem, where the hero is ready to give to the devil "the heavens, paradise, the whole world," in order to have his wish realized. In the twelfth poem of the Third Fragment, Franko portrays the devil very much as Goethe did.[29] There are many similar associative images from

Goethe's poetry in Franko's work, but they do not actually reveal the spiritual relationship of the two great poets who were ruled by emotional order and the profound flow of spiritual vitality.

As we know, Goethe is viewed by many critics as the poet who combines Romanticism and Classicism, the subjective and objective which are to a certain degree intermingled in him.[30] Furthermore, he himself insisted that all poetry should be of occasional origin and, however ethereal, it should be rooted in some kind of real events, portrayed in a beautiful poetic way.[31] Franko, on the other hand, believed that literature should be rich as life insofar as themes, contents and motifs were concerned. Every writer should have his own individual creative face, his own way of writing, because "poetic creativity is a free thing dependent upon the nature and ability of man; true great poets are never similar to each other, each has something of his own and something that the other does not have."[32] But Franko never denied that "the true poet can succeed without knowing how other poets are expressing themselves."[33]

In the introduction to the second edition of *Ziv'jale lystja*, Franko acknowledges that "the publication of this collection of lyrical songs, the most subjective of all . . . and at the same time the most objective in a way of depicting complex human feelings,"[34] are presentations of the typical subjective author's experiences and moods, described objectively. In other words, lyrical songs express "what we all feel, what produces pain for us or makes us joyful and what no one can clearly express."[35] And here is this essential relationship with Goethe, the base on which the author created his *Ziv'jale lystja*—a Ukrainian variant of *The Sorrows of Young Werther*. Both works are free of pessimism and hopelessness, but full of pain, grief, and disappointment, combined with a profound social tragedy that occurs for their generations of young people.

Concluding his introduction to the first edition of *Ziv'jale lystja*, Franko wrote:

Was it worthwhile to labor in order to let into the world this bunch of withered leaves, to put into the motion of our present lives a few gouts poisoned with pessimism, or rather hopelessness, dispair and sadness? We have already had enough of that! And who knows? I was thinking maybe this sorrow is a kind of smallpox which we heal with inoculation of smallpox? Perhaps the imagery of the suffering and sadness of the sick soul will heal some other sick soul in our society? I remember Goethe's Werther and especially the words that Goethe wrote on one of the books that he sent to one of his acquaintances. With these words I submit verses to our own young generation: "Sei ein Mann und folge mir nicht nach (Be a man and do not follow me).[36]

The Sorrows of Young Werther and *Ziv'jale lystja* are tragedies of unrequited love. The spiritual state of the lyrical heroes is portrayed as are the complex human feelings of love in space and time. The emotions of the heroes are given in numerous nuances in order to depict the complexity and inconsistency of their feelings. Both Goethe and Franko portray some special moment, ascertain a different facet of the spiritual state of their heroes in order to illustrate the imagery of their complex inward life.

It is important to emphasize that the plots of *The Sorrows of Young Werther* and *Ziv'jale lystja* are rooted in the real events from Goethe's and Franko's lives that correspond to the insistence of the great German poet that creativity must be eased upon the personal experience of the poet, and not upon abstract ideas, or, as Franko demanded, that the beauty of an artistic work must be in "its contents, in the true and profound portrayal of life."[37] It should be remembered that both poets were creating artistic works and not writing autobiographical sketches. The most diverse facts and events of their lives upon entering the creative forge were emerging as generalized typified artistic products. While portraying his Werther, Goethe depicted a generalized image of his contemporary in all the fullness and complexity of his inner world. Franko similarly depicted his hero of *Ziv'jale lystja.*

Franko's hero is nameless; he has fallen in love with a girl without any hope that she will respond. At times he curses her, at others he tries to forget her, and at still others he calls to her, remembering her image that is so dear to his heart. Then a despair and despondency seize him. However, in the First Fragment of the drama there is still a barely noticeable feeling of hope that is present in the mind of the hero. This glowing feeling turns into a new love in the Second Fragment. The concluding verse of this fragment "Scattering, scattering, scattering snow" indicates the dying love in the hero's heart. Instead sorrow appears, then indifference and finally deep weariness. In the Third Fragment Franko offers the solution to the drama: the young hero loses his beloved—she becomes the wife of another man. He becomes completely disappointed in his ideal; his love is disdained, trampled and lost forever. He has no purpose in his life; it has disappeared. Having reached extreme despair, he commits suicide. There is no single, concretely defined heroine in the drama. Now she appears as a lightminded beauty, now as an enigmatic unknown woman, now as an ordinary narrow-minded philistine, and very often as a simple, beautiful girl as if borrowed from folk song. Thus there is much in common with *The Sorrows of Young Werther*, but there are certain elements that are original and characteristic of Franko's period.

In the First Part of *The Sorrows of Young Werther* there is nothing tragic in Werther's love. He does not even try to gain Lotte for himself. She likes him and discloses that she is "as good as engaged" (ich so gut als verlobt bin)[38] and at the same time she especially stresses the words "as good as." It is possible to assume, as the Polish writer and translator Tadeusz Boy-Żeleński says, "Should Werther have declared his love clearly, he certainly would have gained Lotte's heart."[39] Here are noticeable differences between *Ziv"jale lystja* and *The Sorrows of Young Werther*, despite the fact that the state of the emotional tension in both of them is about the same. Goethe and Franko load us with meditations, reflections and many descriptions of social events. Werther behaves like Goethe himself did with respect to Charlotte Buff; he wants to love, to suffer, but not to marry. As Boy-Żeleński stresses, he needs suffering "for his own spiritual development" (p. 63). The First Part of *The Sorrows of Young Werther* ends with Werther's departure. Here comes a certain pause, a temporary state of balance and soothing for the hero. He begins to work at Court. Under new unusual circumstances, Werther feels quite well. He becomes acquainted with a girl, new relations start, and he finds enough force in himself to look quietly around and to live with new hope: "I rather begin to enjoy myself. The best feature is that there is enough work to do, and that the variety of people, the many new characters, form a colorful drama for my spirit" (pp. 78-79). One might assume that his relations with Lotte would have been soon forgotten, as occurred in Goethe's life. But it did not happen this way, despite the fact that news about Lotte's marriage to another man found him in a state of spiritual balance. There was a conflict with an envoy and then with the local aristocracy, provincial and absurd, and the Count had to ask him to leave his party and then this news spread in the city and caused some unpleasant comments. Werther, a son of the lower middle class who was capable and well educated, had no right to be the Count's guest during his social gathering with the aristocracy. This intrusion and the fact that everyone was already talking about it became very painful for him; his "blood was up." He writes:

> Everything is against me . . . I was completely crushed, and am still furious. I wish that someone would have the courage to blame me openly so that I could thrust my dagger through his body; if I saw blood, I should certainly feel better. Today I have taken up a knife a dozen times, intending to relieve with it my

suffocating heart . . . I often feel the same. I should like to open one of my veins
and gain eternal freedom for myself. [pp. 91-92]

This abrupt change has nothing to do with love; the change took
place because of social reasons and caused Werther's astringent
experiences. His incurable sorrow, nostalgia, and loneliness change
his inner world; he becomes aware that the new state of a miserable
social torment and the continuation of unbearable experiences
cannot persist forever. He resigns from the Court and his discharge
is signed; he returns to the place where Lotte lives with her
husband, but nothing can restore balance to his life and bring him
peace of mind: he is a marked man.

"But what is interesting," writes Boy-Żeleński,

is that Goethe himself, after having introduced this motif, does not draw
consequences from it and acts as if he did not pay much attention to it. And it
was so, Werther writes: "I know quite well that we are not and cannot ever be
equal." Goethe himself instinctively felt on the other side and soon he found
himself there.

But Goethe was never a revolutionary and therefore he did not
stress any social episode in order to create a reaction in the mind of
the reader, despite the fact that the episode made a serious impact
on Werther's fate. Boy-Żeleński proceeds with his comment that
Werther returns

with the feeling of disgust and injustice. He is completely humbled, without
work and future, with total emptiness in his soul. And then comes the
resurrection of his love to Lotte, and Werther concentrates all of his energies on
this love. He sublimates his whole dissatisfaction with himself and with the
world now into this love. He is not interested in the past; only Lotte is the
center of his attention. Everything turns into a mascarade of feelings that is so
well known in modern psychology. Werther suffers his *Weltschmerz*, which is
fully permeated with this unhappy love that could have been spared long ago
had the social event not occurred. In Werther's suicide, Lotte has only an
indirect role because the fate of the young man has been decided at the Count's
house during this unpleasant confrontation with the aristocracy. And now
nothing could have quieted him down except blood. [p. 65]

Thus this social episode has a great impact on Werther's life. He
dies not so much because of unhappy love but because of social
rejection, the pity, that he felt wherever he went.

Ivan Franko's profound social conflicts and serious personal
tragedy found a place in the lyrical drama *Ziv'jale lystja*. These
personal problems are significant features that point towards the
relationship with *The Sorrows of Young Werther* and fill the drama
with motifs from reality. From these problems comes the depressed
tonality of the work. Franko was involved in a constant mēlee with

the populists, clericals, and Polish chauvinists. He was dismissed from editorial work on the journal *Zorja* and the newspaper *Dilo*, was bullied before the elections to parliament and persecuted by both avowed foes and false friends, and finally tortured by severe illness.[40] These unconquerable obstacles in life are defined by the abstract word "destiny"; they are quite apparent when one reads Franko's drama. But Franko's hero constantly keeps contact with life, with people, and with the social struggle; personal grief cannot break him because his strong character gives him protection against life's calamities, social evil and injustices. Yet when the hero loses the contact with life, when he becomes indifferent to the lives of other people, to their fight for happiness, then in fact he suffers first a moral death and then a physical one:[41]

> All interest for me has fled
> In all your arrows and your slings,
> Your petty brawls and bickerings
> The fame of which my people sing—
> In these, my interest has fled:
> For I am dead.
>
> Though all the world should topple down,
> And brother were to murder brother,
> It would not cause me smile or frown
> Or any dolour for another,
> A sharp knife in my heart plays clown—
> So all my soul's last words are said,
> And I am dead![42]

These lines indicate the apparent relationship to Werther's destiny. Werther perished not because he did not secure Lotte for himself but because he suffered spiritual degradation and humilation and then moral death because he lost faith in the struggle of life, he lost faith in himself, and he lost faith in the surrounding world. At the same time he felt a great injustice when love turned to death. Thus the essential relationship between Goethe and Franko grows. It seems as if they exchange their artistic means in order better to portray love, to show the contrast between uncontrollable emotions and difficult and unpredictable life. They want to show life's complexity and contradiction, especially for a person who is hopelessly in love. Werther and Franko's hero, having lost faith in life and especially in its social justice, contemplate death. Franko presents an imaginary meeting of his hero with the devil; like Faust, Franko's hero would sell his soul:

> Devil, demon of separation,
> Of wild dreams, that would not be fulfilled,

Of the torment that remains wakeful,
Of unfulfilled hopes!

Listen to the voice of separation,
I will be your serf, your prisoner,
I will pass myself completely into your hands,
But try to silence this heart!

With you, I am ready to go
And to suffer for ever—
But I have only one wish,
Calm me now.

For only one of her kisses
Let me burn for one hundred thousand years!
For her love, for her endearment
I will give you the heavens, paradise, the whole world.
                                                        [XVI, 90][43]

The dramatic tension of this poem steadily increases and with it
the profundity of the experiences of Franko's hero, who is ready to
give up everything—the soul, "the heavens, paradise, the whole
world," in order to turn aside death at least temporarily. We find a
similar parallel in *The Sorrows of Young Werther*, when Werther
talks about sin and about Almighty God, in front of whom he plans
to place his sufferings and to receive the calming of the pain in his
heart:

And what does it mean that Albert is your husband? Husband! That may be for
this world—and in this world it is sin that I love you, that I should like to
snatch you from his arms into mine. Sin? Very well, and I am punishing myself
for it; for this sin, which I have tasted in all its rapture, which gave me life-
giving balm and strength. From now on you are mine! mine, Lotte! I go before
you. I go to my Father, to your Father. I shall put my sorrow before Him, and
He will comfort me until you come; and I shall fly to meet you and clasp you
and stay with you before the Infinite Being in an eternal embrace. [p. 157]

The above quotations illustrate two opposite parallels which serve
the same purpose: to move away from death, to curtail the
sorrowful state, the lack of firmness and the passivity.

It should be noticed that in *Ziv"jale lystja* and in *The Sorrows of
Young Werther*, the motif of the mother is strongly stressed, and its
importance increases as the heroes are approaching death. Franko
expresses his feelings in a separate poem where this motif appears
distinctly and saliently:

O my mother, my mother, most precious and dear,
Mourn not for your son when his deed you shall hear,
And curse not in grief his defeated career!

> Nay, grieve not at having to live on alone,
> To be borne to your grave without me to make moan
> Or comforting words at your death to intone!
> [p. 214]

Werther, on the other hand, mentions the mother in several letters. But the strongest feeling of love comes from his farewell lines: "Farewell, you too! Dear Mother, forgive me! Comfort her, Wilhelm! God bless you both! My affairs are all settled. Farewell! We shall meet again and with more joy" (pp. 162-163).

Ziv'jale lystja and *The Sorrows of Young Werther* are significant in that they demonstrate the maturity of their authors' creativity. They further demonstrate their loftiness and their immortality. Franko, a highly original writer, was drawing from the values and ideas of world literature and from the works of Goethe. But he was able to digest those values and ideas and, as in the case of *Ziv'jale lystja*, to present the human tragedy in his own individual way. He considered both the individual and society and explored the common motifs and imagery, but through his own vision, his own interpretation.

Goethe's image gains in immortality from Franko's works. Franko loved the great poet from his youthful years and lived with this love until his death. He studied Goethe's works carefully, translated them and searched in them for consonance, simplicity, wisdom, emotion, and artistic peculiarity. Goethe attracted Franko with his optimism, with his humanism, and with his ability to portray reality philosophically.

Franko dedicated most of his attention to *Faust*. For him *Faust* was a unique work of great artistic value, a work filled with a philosophical background. It was a work of great faith in man's creative powers. It offered a glimpse of a better future. For Franko *Faust* was a revolutionary work which caused a spiritual revolution in Germany in the fields of philosophy and art. It was a universal work in which true human situations are portrayed.

Through his contributions to the Ukrainian art of translation, Franko enlarged and perfected his own masterful creative abilities. The lyrical drama *Ziv'jale lystja* gives an excellent portrayal of love that is not mutually shared. Such a love ends with a tragedy that has its roots in the structure of society. We have tried to indicate, at least in the most important features, that Franko drew from his understanding of Goethe, underlining at the same time his own native genius. Our purpose in doing so is to single out *Ziv'jale lystja* as an original and creative Ukrainian variant of *The Sorrows of Young Werther.*

Texas Tech University

Notes

[1] *Ukrajins'ka radjans'ka encyklopedija*, ed. M. P. Bazhan et al. (Kyjiv: Akademija nauk Ukrajins'koji RSR, 1960), III, 224.

[2] Mykola I. Petrov, *Ocherki ukrainskoj literatury XIX stoletija* (Kyjiv: Drukarnja I. and A. Davydenka, 1884), p. 67. Unless otherwise indicated, all translations in this paper are mine.

[3] Pavlo Fylypovych, "Shevchenko i romantyzm," *Zapysky istorychno-filolohichnoho viddilu VUAN*, 4 (Kyjiv, 1924), 6-7.

[4] Volodymyr Doroshenko, "Gete v ukrajins'kykh perekladakh, perespivakh ta nasliduvannjakh, *Materjaly do ukrajins'koji bibliohrafiji* (L'viv: Naukove Tovarystvo im. Shevchenka, 1932), VI, v-viii.

[5] *Istorija ukrajins'koji literatury v vos'my tomakh*, ed. Je. P. Kyryljuk (Kyjiv: "Naukova dumka," 1969), IV, 334.

[6] B. M. Lesyn et al., *Slovnyk literaturoznavchykh terminiv* (Kyjiv: "Radjans'ka shkola," 1965), p. 272.

[7] Despite the fact that Leonid Rudnytzky in his *Ivan Franko i nimec'ka literatura* (Munich: Ukrainisches Technisch-Wirtschaftliches Institut, 1974), p. 116, states that Franko's translation of the ballad "Der Fischer," forms "a certain unity and shows completeness," I doubt that Franko knowingly omitted the whole strophe (from the words "Labt sich die liebe Sonne nicht . . . " to words "Nicht her in ew'gen Tau?" See Johann Wolfgang von Goethe, *Gedenkausgabe der Werke, Briefe und Gespräche* [Zürich: Artemis Verlag, 1950], I, 116, lines 17-24). Knowing how accurate Franko was in handling translations, I believe that this strophe has probably been lost and therefore I propose that scholars who have entrance to Franko's archives recheck this matter.

[8] Oleksandr Bilec'kyj, "*Faust*, trahedija Gete," *Oleksandr Bilec'kyj: Zibrannja prac' u p'jaty tomakh* (Kyjiv: "Naukova dumka," 1966), V, 441.

[9] Rudnytzky, p. 73.

[10] *Goethes Faust*, erläutert von Heinrich Düntzer (Leipzig: E. Wartigs Verlag, 1879).

[11] Ivan Franko ["*Favst* Gete"] published as an Introduction to *Favst*. Tragedy by Johann Wolfgang Goethe, Part I. Translated from German and explained by Ivan Franko. L'viv, 1882, *Tvory v dvadcjaty tomakh* (Kyjiv: Derzhlitvydav, 1955), XVIII, 402. Franko's italics. Unless otherwise indicated, the page numbers referring to the ["*Favst* Gete"] of Ivan Franko are those in this edition.

[12] Rudnytzky, pp. 77-96.

[13] Jakym Ja. Jarema, "Ivan Franko i *Faust* Gete," *Doslidzhennja tvorchosti Ivana Franka* (Kyjiv: Derzhlitvydav, 1956), pp. 69, 102.

[14] Rudnytzky, pp. 77-78.

[15] Goethe, *Gedenkausgabe der Werke, Briefe und Gespräche*, V, 194. Other references from this edition are indicated by page numbers cited parenthetically in text.

[16] *Goethe's Faust*, trans. Walter Kaufman (Garden City, New York: Doubleday & Company, 1961), p. 185. Translator's italics.

[17] Jarema, p. 103.

[18] Jarema, p. 107.

[19] Ivan Franko, "Peredmova," *Tvory* (New York: "Knyhospilka," 1960), XIX, 109-112. Other references from this edition are indicated by page numbers cited parenthetically in the text.

[20] Ivan Franko, "[Persha peredmova do perekladu *Faust* J. W. Gete]," *Zibrannja tvoriv u p'jatdesjaty tomakh* (Kyjiv: "Naukova dumka," 1980), XXVI, 155-160.

[21] Johann Wolfgang von Goethe, *Faust: A Tragedy in Two Parts*, trans. Bayard Taylor (London: Oxford University Press, 1963), p. 301.

[22] Rudnytzky, p. 106.

[23] Rudnytzky, p. 105.

[24] Rudnytzky writes: "It remains an open question as to whether the given translation should be considered as Franko's work, and if so to what degree, because Franko himself stated that while translating he freely used the manuscript by Jaroslav Hordyns'kyj who in 1903 translated this work by Goethe" (p. 119).

[25] Ja. V. Zakrevs'ka, *Kazky Ivana Franka: movno khudozhnij analiz* (Kyjiv: "Naukova dumka," 1966), p. 43.

[26] Ivan Franko, "Khto takyj'Lys Mykyta' i zvidky rodom?" *Tvory*, VII, 5.

[27] Zakrevs'ka, p. 43.

[28] Jarema, pp. 83-85.

[29] See this article, p. 193.

[30] Walter Pater, "Winckelmann," *The Renaissance: Studies in Art and Poetry* (London: MacMillan and Co., 1907), pp. 226-228; Marjorie Perloff, "Yeats and Goethe," *Comparative Literature*, 2 (1971), 126-127.

[31] Edward Engelberg, *The Vast Design: Patterns in W. B. Yeats's Aesthetic* (Toronto: University of Toronto Press, 1964), p. vi.

[32] Ivan Franko, "Z ostannikh desjatylit' 19 viku," *Literaturno-Naukovyj Vistnyk*, 15 (1901), 128.

[33] Franko, *Tvory v dvadcjaty tomakh*, XVI, 159.

[34] Ivan Franko, "Perednje slovo do druhoho vydannja [*Ziv'jaloho lystja*]," *Tvory*, 1958, XVI, Book II, 11.

[35] Franko, *Tvory v dvadcjaty tomakh*, XVI, 160.

[36] Franko, "[Peredmova do pershoho vydannja *Ziv'jaloho lystja*]," *Tvory*, XVI, Book II, 8-9.

[37] I. I. Sirak, "Pytannja majsternosti khudozhn'oho tvoru v literaturnokrytychnykh stattjakh I. Franka," *Pytannja khudozhn'oji majsternosti* (L'viv: Vydavnyctvo L'vivs'-koho universytetu, 1958), p. 5.

[38] Johann Wolfgang von Goethe, *The Sorrows of Young Werther*, trans. Elizabeth Mayer et al. (New York: Random House, 1971), p. 28. Other references from this edition are indicated by page numbers cited parenthetically in the text.

[39] Tadeusz Boy-Żeleński, "Czytalem 'Wertera,'" *Polska krytyka literacka (1919-1939): Materialy* (Warszawa: Państwowe Wydawnictwo Naukowe, 1966), p. 63. Other references from this edition are indicated by page numbers cited parenthetically in the text.

[40] Maksym Ryl's'kyj, "Franko-poet," *Slovo pro velykoho kamenjara*, ed. O. I. Bilec'kyj (Kyjiv: Derzhlitvydav, 1956), p. 16; Arsen Kaspruk, "Lirychna drama *Ziv'jale lystja* ta jiji vidhomin u poeziji," *Radjans'ke literaturoznavstvo* 7 (1966), 81.

[41] Kaspruk, p. 86.

[42] *The Ukrainian Poets: 1189-1962*, trans. C. H. Andrusyshen and Watson Kirkconnell (Toronto: University of Toronto Press, 1963), p. 213. Other references from this edition are indicated by page numbers cited parenthetically in the text.

[43] Translation mine.

Luncheon Address

Goethe and Music: "Nur wer die Sehnsucht kennt"*

Meredith McClain

Abstract

As part of the commemorative act of rethinking Goethe's life, it is meaningful to recall aspects of his history which illuminate and help reveal the musical dimension of his existence. Although Goethe was not a musician in the strict sense of the word, he dwelt musically on this earth and it is in honor of this mode of being that this presentation focuses on the inspiration which radiated from Goethe to some of the greatest musicians of his day. Seven different settings of one small poem by Goethe, "Nur wer die Sehnsucht kennt" from *Wilhelm Meisters Lehrjahre*, will be discussed in order to illuminate the vitality of Goethe's poetry as well as to review the important evolution of the German lied which took place during Goethe's life-time.(MMc)

In 1822 at the age of 73 Goethe wrote in a letter the following: "Wer Musik nicht liebt, verdient nicht Mensch zu heißen; wer sie liebt, ist erst ein halber Mensch. Wer sie treibt, der ist ein ganzer" ('He who does not love music, does not deserve to be called human; he who loves it is only half a person. He who produces it, he is whole')[1]. One hundred and fifty years after Goethe's death it is still important to investigate his pronouncements concerning music, but the investigator of 1982 may draw on vast scholarly materials which have been accumulating on the topic of "Goethe and Music" and he may heed a recurrent warning not to define music in only the limited, technical sense. A too narrow and too technical translation of Goethe's quotation, "Only a musician is a whole person," may thus be avoided. In general, the extreme viewpoints of the past— criticism of Goethe's limited musicianship, on the one hand, and praise of Goethe, the musician, on the other—may be carefully resolved if one follows the advice of Hans Joachim Moser.[2] At the beginning of his book, *Goethe und die Musik*, written for the Goethe jubilee in 1949, Moser stressed the meaning of "musical." The term derives from the word "muse" and, therefore, may connote "poetic" or "lyrical."[3] Given this context the quotation from Goethe above may be interpreted as pointing toward a similar idea expressed by Hölderlin who wrote that "poetically dwells man on this earth."[4]

Many general facts of Goethe's relationship to music are well documented. He played the piano, he had studied cello, and, once established in Weimar, he had constant contact with music teachers, performers, and theoreticians. Goethe even had his own private choir for some eight years (1807-15). During Goethe's directorship of the theater in Weimar, Mozart's operas alone were performed two hundred and eighty times.[5] Research into these kinds of facts was greatly facilitated in 1979 when Frederick Sternfeld published his *Goethe and Music: A List of References.*[6] Hundreds of entries are gathered here in one binding and a brief and knowledgable preface points out the most important works on the topic.

In summary, Goethe's life was filled with music, but he was not a person who instinctively understood music as a language or who used it as a medium of expression. Goethe was not a musician in the strict, technical sense, but he dwelt musically on this earth and the goal of this paper is to pay homage to that mode of being by recalling the tremendous influence which Goethe's poetry exerted on the important musicians of his time. Not just the sheer number of Goethe's poems which were set to music tell of his enormous inspiration, but also the numerous poems which have been set several times by the same musician. There are also valuable quotations from the musicians revealing their opinion of Goethe's poetry. Beethoven, for example, said to a friend the following:

> Since that summer at Karlsbad, I have been reading Goethe every day—that is, when I read at all. He has killed Klopstock for me . . . But as for Goethe, he is alive, and he wants all of us to be alive with him. That is why he can be set to music. No one is so suitable for composition. Only, I am not so keen on writing songs.[7]

Equally flattering although entirely different in direction is Brahms' estimation of Goethe's writing:

> Close to the end of his life, Brahms could only think of one instance where a poem of Goethe's had been truly improved, or "raised," as he put it, by the music to which it was set; otherwise, he thought, Goethe's lyrics are so "finished" that music can add nothing to them.[8]

In order to review and renew the topic "Goethe and Music," we shall look at one very small poem, "Nur wer die Sehnsucht kennt," and then trace the musical life of this work as it evolved through the settings of six musicians. Goethe's own preferences concerning the musical setting of his lieder are well known and can be clearly exemplified on this music tour through history. It will also be clear that the great poet's personal preferences had little to do with the new direction which was ultimately followed by the greatest German song writers.[9]

Nur wer die Sehnsucht kennt,	Only one who knows longing
Weiß, was ich leide!	Understands what I suffer!
Allein und abgetrennt	Alone and separated
Von aller Freude,	From all joy,
Seh' ich ans Firmament	I look at the firmament
Nach jener Seite.	Toward that other side.
Ach! der mich liebt und kennt,	Ah, he who loves and understands me
Ist in der Weite.	Is far away.
Es schwindelt mir, es brennt	I am fainting, fire burns
Mein Eingeweide.	within me.
Nur wer die Sehnsucht kennt,	Only one who knows longing
Weiß, was ich leide!	Understands what I suffer![10]

This poem is one of the four well known Mignon songs which appear in Goethe's major work *Wilhelm Meisters Lehrjahre*. Goethe worked on *Wilhelm Meister* for a very long time, just as he did on *Faust* and the two are often compared as containing the wisdom of the poet in his mature stage.[11] It is fortunate for any reader who wishes to understand the exact context of the Mignon songs that the episode of Mignon and the harper form a distinct entity within the larger work. It is interesting to note in this regard that a school edition of the Mignon story was issued separately in Germany in 1909.[12] In the preface to that edition the reader is told that one consideration in publishing such a work was to acquaint as many readers as possible with the context which had inspired the wonderful Mignon compositions by Schubert and others, as well as to warn the opera goers of the inferiority of the banal French opera by Thomas on the Mignon theme.

Other pertinent facts concerning the context of the Mignon songs and their first appearance have been gathered by Jack M. Stein, whom I quote at length here:

When Goethe's celebrated *Wilhelm Meisters Lehrjahre* first appeared in 1795, it contained melodies by Reichardt to eight of the lyrics embedded in the work. These were printed on special oversized paper, which was folded into the edition at the appropriate place in the text. Reichardt was thus the first of many musicians to try his hand at providing musical settings for these poems. Willi Schuh's *Goethe-Vertonungen: Ein Verzeichnis* lists no less than eighty-four settings of "Kennst du das Land"; fifty-six of "Nur wer die Sehnsucht kennt"; forty of "Wer nie sein Brot mit Tränen aß." All the other lyrics have fifteen settings or more. Together they present a challenge that has often been too much for even the best of composers.

The songs in *Wilhelm Meister* are an integral part of the novel. They are actually sung, not recited, by the chief characters, under circumstances and in situations that are precisely, sometimes elaborately, described. Author and composer were in complete agreement that the melodies provided were to be suited to the characters and the situations.[13]

In an article written in 1925, Th. W. Werner quotes a slightly higher number of settings composed for "Nur wer die Sehnsucht kennt": sixty-four. Werner however agrees with Stein (and Schuh) that of the four Mignon songs, "Kennst du dad land" has exerted the greatest attraction for musicians. Werner goes on to say that simply considering the form, it might seem that "Nur wer die Sehnsucht kennt" would be more appealing to a composer, but that the certain prosaic problem presented in the second half of the text ("es brennt mein Eingeweide," literally 'it burns my intestines') could be solved musically by only the best.[14]

The specific context into which Goethe wrote this poem is the following: Wilhelm Meister had just fallen into a mood of longing and introspection when Mignon, alert to her master's every cue, sings this simple, yet haunting lied as a duet with the harper. Goethe described the performance in the text as an "irregular duet sung with the most heartfelt expression." Perhaps it is this specifically musical context which has caused so many composers to be drawn to this small work which combines a deeply melancholy message with an apparently simple form. The majority of the settings are for female voice, but there are two duet settings, and a setting for a quintett of male voices. Some of these settings have been arranged for solo male voice and/or mixed choirs. Before turning to the analysis of seven specific settings, it is necessary to point out some of the important features of the text:

wer	Nur wer die Sehnsucht kennt,	A	/ u u / u /
	Weiß, was ich leide!	B	/ u u / u
ich	Allein und abgetrennt	A	u / u / u /
	Von aller Freude,	(B)	u / u / u
hin	Seh' ich ans Firmament	A	/ u u / u /
	Nach jener Seite.	C	u / u / u
er	Ach! der mich liebt und kennt,	A	/ u u / u /
	Ist in der Weite.	C	u / u / u

ich	Es schwindelt mir, es brennt	A	u / u / u /
	Mein Eingeweide.	B	u / u / u
wer	Nur wer die Sehnsucht kennt,	A	/ u u / u /
	Weiß, was ich leide!	B	/ u u / u

The basic rhythmic structure indicates two stanzas based on the same pattern of alternating three beat and two beat lines ending without exception with alternating masculine and feminine cadences. One way to describe the pattern of metric feet is to assume that the basic foot is iambic (u /), but that the rhythm is suspended or counterbalanced by word stress in the first foot of lines, 1, 2, and 5 in stanza one and of lines 1, 5, and 6 in stanza two, causing trochaic feet (/ u).

Rhyme, like rhythm, is not a pure pattern here, but is a mix of regularity and irregularity: AB, A(B), AC, AC, AB, AB. The most outstanding feature of regularity in this poem is the exact repetition of the first two lines to form the closing lines. Through the rhyme scheme the center four lines are joined together so that the whole poem can be viewed as one strophe of 12 lines. The meaning of the words also supports this particular division since the center four lines express a direction away from the speaker—the distance, the other side—and a person away from the speaker—the beloved, the other one. The identical lines 1 and 2, 11 and 12 form the frame, the lament, while lines 3-4 and corresponding 9-10 described the inner state of the speaker.

Syntactically analyzed, yet another division of the poem is revealed. Lines 1-2 and 11-12 are syntactically identical: a lament ending with an exclamation point. Enjambement, a comma, and enjambement again tie lines 3, 4, 5, and 6 together in a sentence of four lines. Lines 7-8 have the same basic structure as the lament: a two line sentence broken by a comma, but without an exclamation point. The remaining two lines, 9-10, also form a sentence, but one broken inside the first line by a comma and having enjambement tying the two lines closely together.

It should now be clear from Fig. 1 that there are several ways to divide the structure of "Nur wer die Sehnsucht kennt" and that no one division has more credit than the others. Basic structural divisions of the various musical settings are indicated in graphic forms. Just as the German quotes in this paper have been written into the text in English for interested music students who might not be able to read the original German, now the musical indications have been reduced to the most apparent and readily understandable sketches for students of German not familiar with musical notation.

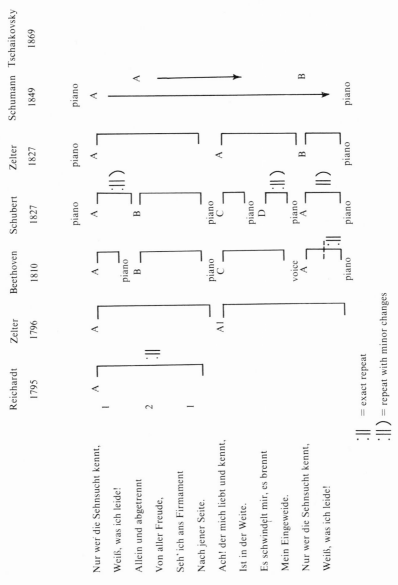

Fig. 1.—Structural Divisions of the Various Musical Settings.

It is extremely fortunate for our musical journey that Goethe commissioned the setting of the poem by Johann Friedrich Reichardt, his musical advisor from 1789 to 1800.[15] We know that Goethe approved of this setting and it is to be lamented that almost all other editions since the 1795 original did not include the music.[16] It is important to note that Reichardt was a founder of the Second Berlin Song School, a group of composers who believed strongly that musical accompaniment should be simple and should follow strictly the words of the poem. Only repetitions given in the original poem were allowed in the music. Given this philosophy it is easy to understand how Reichardt composed his setting. It is the only one on the chart which is entirely strophic; that is to say, the music for the first half of the poem is repeated exactly for the second. The entire text of two stanzas is printed on the one repeated stanza of music like a hymn. In order that the last two lines of the poem will have exactly the same melody as the identical first two, Reichardt simply repeated the first line of music again as the third line on the score with the single addition of one closing measure consisting of one single note: the unison tonic for both voices (c minor). This means that there are in reality only two different lines of music: line 1 and line 2. Within such a simple and repetitious structure it seems unlikely that Goethe's direction of "irregular" can be fulfilled by the slight rhythmic independence of the two voices at the beginning of the second line. Otherwise the singers move together rhythmically with each syllable receiving one note. Reichardt's absolute devotion to the correct expression of the meaning of the text through his settings is made clear in the following:

I have noticed that, no matter how attractively my songs were performed, the singer almost never quite sang them correctly. When I investigated I found that all those who failed to do so had first played the notes as a melodious instrumental piece and only later coupled the words to them. This is the exact reverse of the way I composed them! My melodies take shape automatically in every case from repeated reading of the poem without my having to search for them. And the only thing else that I do is this: I repeat them with slight changes, and do not write them down until I feel that the grammatical, logical, emotional, and musical accents are so closely interwoven that the melody speaks properly and sings pleasantly, and not just for one stanza, but for all of them. If the singer is to feel this when he performs them, he must first read the words in their entirety and keep reading thm until he feels that he can read them with the correct expression. Only then should he sing them.[17]

In 1796 a composer named Carl Friedrich Zelter sent a setting of one of the harper's songs, "Wer sich der Einsamkeit ergiebt" to a lady friend and requested that she send one of the two copies to the "excellent writer of *Wilhelm Meister*," who happened to be a friend of hers. The enthusiastic response from Goethe was in part the following:

> I am unable to judge music, for I lack knowledge of the means it employs to its ends; I can speak only of the impression it makes on me when I surrender myself to it wholly and repeatedly. Hence I can say of Herr Zelter's composition of my songs, that I had scarcely thought music capable of such heartfelt accents. Thank him sincerely, and tell him that I greatly desire to know him personally, so that I can converse about various matters with him.[18]

Amazingly enough it took Zelter four years to finally accept the invitation to meet Goethe, but when he did, the timing was fortuitous. Schiller and Goethe had cooled towards Reichardt because of his political views and thus Goethe was in need of another musical advisor. Zelter was not only to fill that role, but was to become one of Goethe's closest friends, one of the very few people after 1800 to whom Goethe offered the "du" form of address. During the years of their friendship Zelter set 73 of Goethe's texts to music and exchanged enough letters with the poet to fill five volumes. Like Reichardt, Zelter was a member of the Second Berlin Song School, so it is not surprising that his music supports and follows the poetic text. Once again we have a simple strophic setting of the text, but there are slight and pleasing variations in the melody in the second stanza, so that the music is written out without any repeat marks. Notice that the first line of poetry is composed to begin on the second half of the first measure. The equivalent line 7 (Ach!) starts with beat 1, so that the patterns, which are really quite similar, appear on the score to be different at first glance.

Each syntactical division of the text is made clear in the music with rests stopping both voice and piano after every period (except in the last line after "Eingeweide") and on the three occasions of enjambement, the music pushes the text over to the next word. Again, as with Reichardt, the setting is in a minor key (a minor).

In the spring of 1810 another musician was deeply involved with the reading of *Wilhelm Meister*. When the young Bettina Brentano paid Beethoven a visit in Vienna, she found him working at his piano. According to Bettina's report, even though she had entered unexpectedly, the great master was very friendly to her and asked her if she wanted to hear a song he had just composed. She reports: "Then he sang 'Kennst du das Land' in a sharp incisive tone, filling the hearer with the melancholy of the sentiment. 'It is beautiful, is it not?—wonderfully beautiful, I will sing it again,' he said enthusiastically."[19] On another afternoon Bettina and Beethoven went for a walk in the garden of Schönbrunn and her memory of his conversation brings up such interesting points that I quote it at some length here:

> Standing in the full glare of the burning sun, Beethoven said, "Goethe's poems have great power over me, not only by their matter, but by their rhythm; I am moved to composition by their language, and by the lofty spirit of harmony pervading them. Melodies radiate from the forms of inspiration, I pursue them, and passionately bring them back; I see them disappear in the varied mass of emotions, then I seize them in renewed ardor, and cannot let them go; hurriedly and with delight I develop them in all their modulations, and in the end I triumph in the production of a musical thought-a symphony; yes, music is the medium between the spiritual and sensuous life. I might say with Goethe, if he would understand me, melody is the sensuous life of poetry. Is not the intellectual meaning of a poem represented in sensuous feeling by melody—is not the sensuous element in the song of Mignon realized through the melody? and does not such emotion call forth new creations?"[20]

In September of 1810 Beethoven's setting of "Nur wer die Sehnsucht kennt" was published, the last and most successful of three attempted versions. It is clear from the outline chart that some innovations have appeared here since Zelter: the composer has maintained an identical beginning and ending, as we found in Reichardt's setting, but the center sections have their own character and the C section shows different rhythmic character for each of the two sentences contained there. Twice the piano punctuates the division in the text and once the voice is heard to carry over alone and it is stressing the rather "difficult" word "Eingeweide." One critic has said that in this setting we have what, for Beethoven, must be called one of his most singable, arching melodies.[21] Note that Beethoven takes a liberty at the last A section by adding the word "ja" and then repeating "weiß, was ich leide" as closing material.

Although we do not know Goethe's reaction to this piece, he did state his opinion of Beethoven's setting of "Kennst du das Land." The statement, made to another composer, J. W. Tomaschek in 1822, is very revealing of Goethe's main criteria of lieder settings. He said:

> You have understood the poem well. I cannot understand how Beethoven and Spohr could have so misunderstood the song when they wrote their music for it. Surely the punctuation and the stops coming at the same time in each stanza should be sufficient indication for the musician that all I expected him to do was to write a simple song. It is not in conformity with Mignon's temperament that she should intone a formal aria.[22]

Although there was at various times interest from both sides, there never came a collaboration between Goethe and Beethoven.

When, in 1812, the critic Rochlitz approached Beethoven for the publishers Breitkopf and Härtel about setting *Faust* to music, he replied: "Ha! that would be a fine piece of work. This is worth thinking about! But, for some time I have been thinking about three other great works. First of all I must get these off my chest."[23]

This next setting was published in 1827, the year of Beethoven's death. The master's funeral was a public event with his casket being carried by eight "Kapellmeister" and accompanied by thirty-six torchbearers "dressed and gloved in black, with black crepe flowing from their torches and sprays of white flowers fastened to the left sleeve. Among them walked Franz Schubert, torch in hand, carrying on his shoulders, unseen, the dead master's robes."[24] Schubert is acknowledged today as the greatest writer of German lieder. It is regretable that Goethe was not aware of the talent represented in a published book of *Goethe-Lieder*, which he received from Schubert in 1816 with this message: "This collection the artist desires in all humility to dedicate to your excellency, to whose glorious poems he owes not only the origination of a great part of it, but also virtually his own development as a German singer."[25] Goethe returned the gift without even an accompanying word. Among other things the volume contained settings of "Erlkönig," "Gretchen am Spinnrad," and "Heiden-Röslein." Again in 1825 Goethe, for various reasons, failed to respond to a second collection and letter from Schubert.

Even a brief glance at the chart of the settings allows us to see the evolving complexity and independence of the musical form in relation to the verbal structure. For the first time within this selection of examples the piano begins the piece alone. Notice too that, as Beethoven, Schubert uses the solo piano to define the various sections and allows the piano to conclude the piece without the voice. Although Schubert is concerned with musical articulation of the verbal syntax (each sentence represents one musical section), he does not hesitate to repeat the poet's words whenever it suits him. Sections A and D are both repeated segments of the text set in evolving, through-composed sections of music.

There is one report from a singer who visited Goethe in 1830 which gives some hope that even though Goethe had not been able to appreciate Schubert earlier, perhaps as an eighty year old he understood. After the singer's excellent performance of Schubert's "Erlkönig," Goethe said, "I have once before heard this composition and then it did not please me in the least—but as you sing it, it takes the shape of a realistic picture."[26]

In the same year that Schubert composed his setting (1827), Zelter created a second setting of "Nur wer die Sehnsucht kennt." The fact that Zelter composed in all four different settings of this text is especially interesting in view of his principle of composition which he explained to Eckermann thus: "If I am to compose music for a poem, I first try to bring before me a living picture of the situation. I then read it aloud till I know it by heart; and thus, when I again recite it, the melody comes of its own accord."[27] We can be sure that Goethe approved of this approach, but it raises a question about multiple settings. It is apparent from the sketch that Zelter in 1827 was certainly more cautious and conservative in his design than Schubert. But there are real points of interest in this second Zelter setting. Notice that Zelter has adopted the practice of constructing a piano frame around the whole which gives to the music the power to set the beginning mood and to close. For the first time we find in this Zelter setting a composition which offers entirely new material in the music where the opening lines of text are repeated exactly at the close (section B). As in all the other settings on the chart thus far, Zelter finds the minor key to evoke the proper lamenting mood. However, he uses the relative major (V) very effectively to punctuate the half way point between the two stanzas.

From this point on there is not much remaining to narrate. The changes underway in these settings all aim in the same direction of increasing expression in the musical accompaniment to the point where the music threatens to supplant the text. There are so many musical details and so much variety in the score that it is too difficult to make a meaningful simple graphic reduction. Independence of the composer from the poet is well exemplified by this Schumann setting. Robert Schumann, born in 1810 (the year Bettina visited Beethoven), has been called the founder of the Romantic Movement in music. The new direction in composition which he represents is clearly audible in the first two notes of this setting. On the chart a piano frame is indicated, but one must look at the score and hear the music to know what a departure from the other settings this really is. There are only two notes played by the piano before the voice begins, but which notes! The arrows on the chart indicate that the musical form is through-composed and that the music evolves without attention to syntactic breaks in the text. The musician expands the poet's text, almost repeating the entire poem twice. But no, a section is missing in the repetition, and another section is sung twice in a row. Individual words ("brennt,"

"Sehnsucht," "leide") are stressed musically by bold musical leaps. There is no question: the music is in control of the text.

Thirty-seven years after Goethe's death and twenty years after Schumann had composed his setting of "Nur wer die Sehnsucht kennt," Tschaikovsky set the poem to music. There is no attempt made to graphically analyze the music on the chart since that would be entirely too complicated and would not further the topic at hand. But there are, however, good reasons to end today's musical journey with reference to this work. Of all the settings presented it is the only one in which the music was such a successful entity that it lives on in performances of instrumentalists (piano, organ, orchestras) without the words and many people who today would recognize the melody would have no idea who Goethe was or that it was his poetry which had inspired the music. For this reason this setting completes the evolution we have been following since the discussion of the original Reichardt setting.

This piece is also particularly appropriate for a comparative literature symposium since it represents the transformation of German poetry through Russian music and language and further translation into an English version made popular in America by Frank Sinatra.

As we hear this last piece there are modulations of themes presented in other session of the conference which come to mind: the central theme of self-education (*Wilhelm Meisters Lehrjahre*) and the attendant isolation and longing ("Sehnsucht") of the demonic or angelic hero who concerns himself with such a goal. We are reminded of the concept of "false friends" and of other problems of translation ("Eingeweide" = intestines?). We may recall Goethe's "logo-centricity" and better understand his debt to Klopstock (his loyalty to Zelter, his problems with Beethoven). Turning back to a key word used in the opening address of this symposium, I believe it is correct to say in closing that the event which has brought Goethe scholars long distances to hear an English performance of Tschaikovsky's setting of Goethe's poem in Lubbock, Texas, is nothing less than "ein Glücksfall."

Texas Tech University

Notes

*I wish to acknowledge the excellent performance of the selected settings of Goethe's poem by my colleagues William Hartwell, Bassbaritone, and Lora Deahl,

Piano. My thanks go also to Michael Stoune of the Department of Music, Texas Tech University for the use of his unpublished Masters Thesis "Some Musical Settings of Goethe's Mignon Songs in View of his Remarks on Music," (The Univ. of Texas, 1965).

[1]The original German was quoted in Edgar Istel, "Goethe and Music," *Musical Quarterly*, XIV (1928), 216-254. The translation is mine.

[2]See, for example, Hans John, *Goethe und die Musik* (Langenzalza: Beyer und Söhne, 1928), which is discussed by Frederick Sternfeld in *Goethe and Music*: A List of References (New York: Da Capa Press, 1979), p. 133. See also Romain Rolland, "Goethe the Musician," in *Goethe Symposium*, ed. Dagobert D. Runes (New York: Roerich Museum Press, 1932) pp. 3-17.

[3]Hans Joachim Mose, "Vorwort," *Goethe und die Musik* (Leipzig: C. F. Peters, 1949), n. p.

[4]*Friedrich Hölderlin: Sämtliche Werke*, ed. Paul Stapf (Berlin and Darmstadt: Tempel-Verlag, 1960), p. 416.

[5]See Rolland, "Goethe the Musician," pp. 3-17.

[6]See note 3.

[7]Michael Hamburger (ed. and trans.), *Beethoven—Letters, Journals, and Conversations* (New York: Pantheon Books, Inc., 1952), pp. 185-186.

[8]Wolfgang Leppman, *The German Image of Goethe* (Oxford: Clarendon Press, 1961), p. 93.

[9]See Jack M. Stein, "Was Goethe Wrong about the Nineteenth-Century Lied? An Examination of the Relation of Poem and Music," PMLA, 77 (1962), 232-239.

[10]*Goethes Werke*, ed. Erich Trunz (Hamburg: Christian Wegner, 1962), VII, 240-241. The translation is mine.

[11]Fritz Martini, *Die Goethezeit* (Stuttgart: Crut E. Schwab, 1949), pp. 142-172.

[12]Goethe: Mignon. *Auszug aus Wilhelm Meisters Lehrjahren*, ed. Löcher (Bielefeld and Leipzig: Velhagen and Klafing, 1979).

[13]Jack M. Stein, *Poem and Music in the German Lied from Glück to Hugo Wolf* (Cambridge: Harvard Univ. Press, 1971), p. 35.

[14]Th. W. Werner, "Beethovens Kompositionen von Goethes 'Nur wer die Sehnsucht kennt,'" *Neues Beethoven-Jahrbuch*, Zweiter Jahrgang (Augsburg: Benno Filser, 1925), p. 67.

[15]The musical settings referred to in this article appear in order of their presentation in the attached appendix.

[16]Stein, *Poem and Music*, p. 35, f.n. 8.

[17]Ibid., pp. 34-35.

[18]Istel, "Goethe and Music," p. 229.

[19]Bettina von Arnim, "A Letter to Goethe," in *Great Composers Through the Eyes of their Contemporaries*, ed. Otti Zoff (New York: Dutton, 1951), pp. 145-146.

[20]Ibid., pp. 146-147.

[21]*Gedichte von Goethe in Kompositionen* seiner Zeitgenossen, ed. Max Friedlaender (Weimer: Verlag der Goethe-Gesellschaft, 1916), II, 233.

[22]Paul Nettl, "Schubert's Czech Predecessors," *Music & Letters*, XXIII, (1942), 61.

[23]Hamburger, *Beethoven—Letters, Journals, and Conversation*, p. 186.

[24]Carl Engel, "Schubert's Fame," *Musical Quarterly*, XIV (1928), p. 457.

[25]Otto Erich Deutsch, *Schubert: A Documentary Biography*, trans. Eric Blom (London: Dent, 1946), p. 57.

[26]Istel, "Goethe and Music," p. 221.

[27]Johann Peter Eckermann, *Conversations with Goethe*, trans. by John Oxenford (New York: E. P. Dutton, 1930), p. 28.

Appendix. Musical settings of Goethe's poem "Nur wer die Sehn-sucht kennt"

I. Reichardt, 1795.

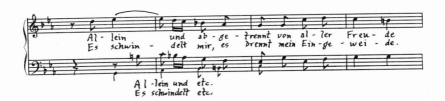

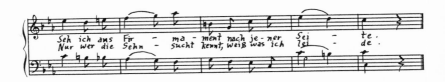

II. Zelter, 1796.

II. Zelter, 1796, continued.

te.   Ach, der mich liebt __ und kennt, ist   in der Wei - te.   Es schwindelt

mir, es brennt mein Ein-ge-wei-de.   Nur wer die   Sehn - sucht kennt, weiß, was ich lei - -

de.

III. Beethoven, 1810.

Nur wer die Sehnsucht kennt

1785

Assai Adagio

Ludwig van Beethoven, um 1810

Nur wer die Sehn-sucht kennt, weiß, was ich lei - de! Al -
lein und ab - ge-trennt von al - ler Freu -de, seh' ich ans Fir-ma - ment__ nach je-ner Sei -
te. Ach! der mich liebt und kennt, ist in der Wei - - te. Es schwindelt
mir, es brennt mein Ein - ge-wei - - - de. Nur wer die Sehn-sucht kennt,
weiß, was ich lei - de, ja weiß, was ich lei - - - de!

IV. Schubert, 1827.

Lied der Mignon.

Aus Wilhelm Meister, ged. 1788.

Franz Schubert, veröffentlicht 1827. (1797-1828). Op. 62 N°. 4.

Nur wer die Sehn - sucht kennt, weiss, was ich lei - de,

nur wer die Sehn - sucht kennt, weiss, was ich lei - - de! Al -

lein und ab - ge - trennt von al - ler Freu - de, seh' ich an's Fir - ma - ment nach je - - ner

Sei - te. Ach! der mich liebt und kennt, ist in der Wei - te.

IV. Schubert, 1827, continued.

V. Zelter, 1827.

Sehnsucht

C.F. Zelter, 1827

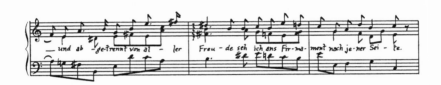

VI. Schumann, 1849.

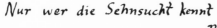

VI. Schumann, 1849, continued.

VI. Schumann, 1849, continued.

VII. Tschaikovsky, 1869.

VII. Tschaikovsky, 1869, continued.

Seh' ich ans Fir - ma - ment   nach je - ner Sei - te.

Ach! der mich liebt und kennt, ist in   der Wei - te.

Nur wer die Sehn-sucht kennt,   weiß, was ich

VII. Tschaikovsky, 1869, continued.

VII. Tschaikovsky, 1869, continued.

Notes on the Authors

STUART ATKINS, Professor of German, University of California, Santa Barbara, received his A.B. and Ph.D. degrees at Yale University. He has taught at Dartmouth College and Harvard University and has served as Department Chairman at Harvard University for almost ten years. In 1972 he was President of the Modern Language Association of America. Professor Atkins holds the gold medal of the Goethe-Institut, Munich. He is the author of *The Testament of Werther in Poetry and Drama* (1949) and *Goethe's Faust: A Literary Analysis* (1958; 3rd printing 1969), and author-editor of *The Age of Goethe: An Anthology of German Literature* (1969), *Heinrich Heine: Werke* (2 vols., 1973-79), *Goethe's Faust: The Bayard Taylor Translation Revised* (2 vols., 1962—vol. 1 also bilingual; various reprintings), and *Torquato Tasso* in the Hamburg edition of Goethe's works (1977). He was also editor of *The German Quarterly* for five years, and has published numerous essays, chiefly dealing with eighteenth and earlier nineteenth century literature.

DAVID J. DELAURA is Avalon Foundation Professor in the Humanities and Professor of English at the University of Pennsylvania. A native of Worcester, Massachusetts, he earned the A.B. and A.M. at Boston College and the Ph.D. from the University of Wisconsin. He taught for fourteen years at the University of Texas at Austin. He has held Guggenheim and NEH fellowships. In 1977-78 he conducted a year-long NEH seminar for college teachers on the image of the artist from Goethe to Joyce. He has served on the Executive Council of the Modern Language Association (1976-79). His article, "Arnold and Carlyle" (*PMLA*, 1964), won the first William Riley Parker Prize of the MLA. He is the author of *Hebrew and Hellene in Victorian England: Newman, Arnold, and Pater* and general editor of *Victorian Prose: A Guide to Research*. He has published many other studies on nineteenth and twentieth-century literary figures, including John Ruskin, Gerard Manley Hopkins, Thomas Hardy, and T. S. Eliot. His recent essay, "A Contest for Browning's Painter Poems: Aesthetics, Polemics, Historics" (*PMLA*, 1980), reflects his interest in the influence of Continental critical theory and of the fine arts on English Literature.

ALEXANDER GELLEY is Associate Professor in the Department of English and Comparative Literature at the University of California, Irvine. He earned the B.A. at Harvard University and the Ph.D. at the Yale University, and also studied at the universities of Tübingen and Zürich. He has held a Fulbright lectureship at the University of Tel Aviv, a Fulbright research fellowship at the University of Mainz, and has been a Fellow at the Society for the Humanities, Cornell University. He has taught at the University of Wisconsin, The City College of New York, The Hebrew University, and Cornell University. He is the translator of *Mythology and Humanism, The Correspondence of Thomas Mann and Karl Kerényi*. His publications have been on European fiction from the eighteenth century (notably, on Rousseau, Goethe, Stifter, Stendhal, Grass) and on contemporary literary theorists (Staiger, Heidegger, Curtius, Derrida, Gadamer, Merleau-Ponty). He is presently at work on a book dealing with issues related to the aesthetics of the nineteenth century novel from a present-day theoretical perspective. He has published articles in this area on a phenomenological approach to description, metonymy and space in literature, and character and person in the novel.

ULRICH GOEBEL is Professor of German and Chairman of the Department of Germanic and Slavic Languages at Texas Tech University. A native of Bremen, Germany, he earned his B.A. and M.A. at the University of Oregon and the Ph.D. at The Ohio State University. While at Virginia Polytechnic Institute and State University he was the recipient of a research grant from the NEH Research Division to investigate the application of computers to the humanities. His chief areas of research interest are Middle High German and Early New High German. He is one of the founding authors and coeditor of the series *Indices Verborum zum altdeutschen Schrifttum* and, at present, an author-editor of the new multi-volume *Frühneuhochdeutsches Handwörterbuch*.

VICTOR LANGE is John N. Woodhull Professor of Modern Languages, Emeritus, at Princeton University where, beginning in 1957, he taught German and Comparative Literature. Born in Leipzig (Germany) and educated at Oxford, Toronto, Munich, and Leipzig (Ph.D. 1934), he was subsequently a member of the German departments at Toronto and Cornell. He is Honorary Professor at the Free University in Berlin, has been Visiting Professor at numerous American and European universities and Fulbright Lecturer in Australia. He has been a Phi Beta Kappa Visiting Scholar and twice a Guggenheim Fellow. In 1966 he was awarded the Prize for German scholarship by the German Academy and in 1967 the Goethe Medal of the Munich Goethe Institute. From 1970-1975 he served as President of the International Association of Professors of German and, since 1979, as President of the Goethe Society of North America. His numerous publications from *Modern German Literature* (1945) to *The Classical Period of German Literature* (1982) have dealt with German letters from the eighteenth through the twentieth centuries and have been especially devoted to Goethe and his contemporaries.

MEREDITH LEE is Associate Professor of German at the University of California, Irvine, and Associate Dean of Humanities, Undergraduate Studies. She earned the B.A. from St. Olaf College and the Ph.D. from Yale University. She is founder of the Goethe Society of North America and serves as the Secretary-Treasurer of the organization. She has published a book entitled *Studies in Goethe's Lyric Cycles* and is currently writing on Klopstock and Goethe, and the development of the lyric in the latter decades of the eighteenth century. Her articles have appeared in *Seminar, The Lessing Yearbook*, and the *German Quarterly*.

MEREDITH MCCLAIN, Associate Professor of German at Texas Tech University, received her musical training at Oberlin College Conservatory, Oberlin, Ohio (B.Mus.) and at the Mozarteum in Salzburg, Austria. Her graduate degrees in German were earned at The University of Texas, Austin (M.A. and Ph.D.) where she also taught flute and was a member of the Austin Symphony. A Fulbright recipient and a Danforth Associate, her publications in the area of German poetry are concerned with the Dada writer, Kurt Schwitters. As Director of the Southwest Center for German Studies she has delivered numerous research papers documenting the German heritage of the Texas Panhandle-Plains.

JOHN NEUBAUER is Professor and former Chairman of the Department of Germanic Languages and Literature at the University of Pittsburgh. He earned the M.S. (in physics) at Amherst College and Ph.D. (in German) at Northwestern University. He has taught at Princeton University, and Case Western Reserve

University, has had appointments at the Universidad del Valle (Cali, Colombia), the University of British Columbia, and Harvard University. His publications include *Bifocal Vision: Novalis' Theory of Nature and Disease, Symbolismus und symbolische Logik*, and *Novalis*, as well as numerous articles mostly on eighteenth and early nineteenth-century European literature and intellectual history. At present he is doing research on "The Sound that Broke the Mirror? Music Theory and the Departure from Mimesis."

HENRY H. H. REMAK is Professor of German, Comparative Literature, and West European Studies at Indiana University. He was educated in the Collège Francais in Berlin; he earned the M.A. from Indiana University, and the Ph.D. from the University of Chicago. He holds an honorary degree from the Université de Lille. He has taught at the University of Wisconsin in Madison and at Middlebury College. In 1962-63 he was a Visiting Professor under Fulbright auspices at the Université de Lille; in 1967, under the same program at the Universität Hamburg. From 1969 to 1974 he served as Vice Chancellor and Dean of the Faculties at Indiana University. He has been a Fellow of the John Simon Guggenheim Foundation and of the National Endowment for the Humanities. His chief fields of research interest are the modern German novella and novel (Goethe, Keller, Fontane, Thomas Mann), Franco-German Literary and Cultural Relations, European Romanticism and Realism, and Principles and History of Comparative Literature.

HANS-JÜRGEN SCHINGS, Professor at the University of Heidelberg, was born in Königsberg, Prussia. He has studied Germanistic and History of Philosophy at the universities of Münster, Würzburg, and Köln. He holds the Ph.D. from the University of Köln. He has taught at the universities of Mainz and Würzburg and served as Dean of the Philosophical Fachbereich II at the University of Würzburg (1977-78). Since the winter semester of 1981-82, he occupies a chair at the University of Heidelberg (as a successor of Professor Arthur Henkel). He has been a Visiting Professor at the University of Kansas at Lawrence. Since 1957 he has held stipend of the Educational Foundation of the German People. He has lectured extensively in Germany and the United States. His publications include *Die patristische und stoische Tradition bei Andreas Gryphius* (1966), *Melancholie und Aufklärung. Melancholiker und ihre Kritiker in Erfahrungsseelenkunde und Literatur des 18. Jahrhunderts* (1977), *Der mitleidigste Mensch ist der beste Mensch. Poetik des Mitleids von Lessings his Büchner* (1980) and numerous articles published in German scholarly journals.

WOLODYMYR T. ZYLA is Professor of Germanic and Slavic Languages at Texas Tech University. He is a native of Ukraine, and he earned the B.Sc. and M.A. degrees from the University of Manitoba and the Ph.D. from the Ukrainian Free University in Munich. He was chairman of the Interdepartmental Committee on Comparative Literature (1969-1976) and chairman of the Symposium Committee (1968-1977). He edited ten volumes of the Proceedings of the Comparative Literature Symposium (beginning with Volume 5 as coeditor along with Wendell M. Aycock). He has received a grant from the National Endowment for the Humanities, and is a Vice President of the American Association of Teachers of Slavic and East European Languages and the Chairman of the Permanent Conference on Ukrainian Studies at the Ukrainian Research Institute of Harvard University. In January 1981, he presented "Goethes Lyrik in ukrainischen Übersetzungen" at the Deutsch-Ukrainisches Symposium "Goethe und die ukrainische Literatur" in Munich. He is the author of two books and many articles concerning Slavic literature and the study of names, the translator (along with Wendell M. Aycock) of Ivan Zilyns'kyj's *A Phonetic Description of the Ukrainian Language* (1979) and the editor of *Tvorchist' Jara Slavutycha* (1978), *Portrayal of America in Various Literatures* (1978) and *Zbarazhchyna* (1980). The Proceedings of the Comparative Literature Symposium, vol. XI (1980) were dedicated to W. T. Zyla in recognition of his efforts in creating and promoting the Comparative Literature Symposia for ten years at Texas Tech University.